印誠

功法

THE ART OF CHINESE SWORDSMANSHIP

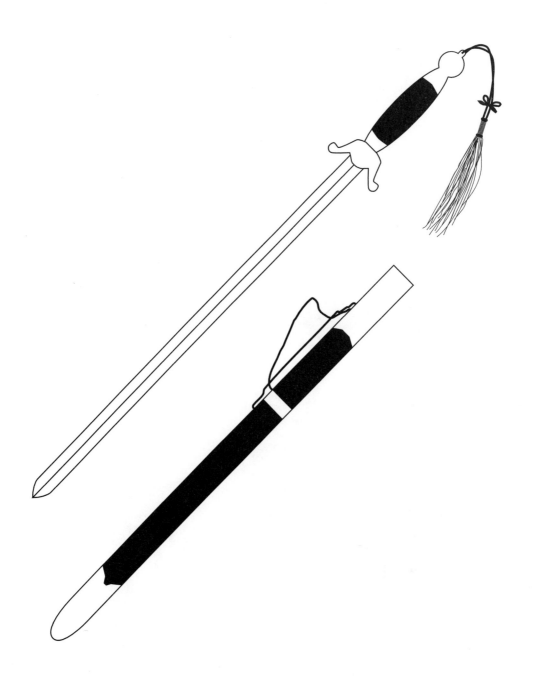

THE ART OF CHINESE SWORDSMANSHIP

A Manual of Taiji Jian

by Zhang Yun

WEATHERHILL
Boston · London

僅 以 此 書 獻 給 我 的 恩 師 駱 舒 煥 先 生

This book is dedicated to the memory of
my revered and beloved master
MR. LUO SHUHUAN

WEATHERHILL
an imprint of Shambhala Publications, Inc.
Horticultural Hall
300 Massachusetts Avenue
Boston, Massachusetts 02115
www.shambhala.com

First edition, 1998
Second printing, 2005

Printed in U.S.A.
⊛This edition is printed on acid-free paper that meets the American National Standards Institute z39.48 Standard.
Distributed in the United States by Random House, Inc., and in Canada by Random House of Canada Ltd

Library of Congress Cataloging-in-Publication Data
The art of Chinese swordsmanship: a manual of taiji jian / by Zhang Yun.—1st ed.
p.   cm.
ISBN 0-8348-0412-3
1. Martial arts—China. 2. Swordplay—China. I. Title.
GV1100.7.A2Z53 1998   97-47624
796.86'0951—dc21   CIP

CONTENTS

FOREWORD

I felt truly honored when Shifu Zhang Yun (*shi* meaning "master" or "teacher," and *fu* meaning "father") asked me to write a foreword for his book. The sword technique described here is a valuable part of Chinese martial art history, and even more, it represents part of an amazing man's life and reflects the fascinating story of how Yin Cheng Gong Fa came to be.

I began to learn about Yin Cheng Gong Fa after I had been studying martial arts for about five years. That summer I turned eighteen and a chance encounter changed my life forever: I was fortunate enough to meet Shifu Zhang Yun. My grandmother told me that a friend of hers had introduced her to a man from Beijing. She went on to say that he knew Taiji Quan and was very skilled and graceful. Taiji Quan (which many know by an alternate spelling, T'ai Chi Ch'uan) is a slow and dancelike martial art form in which I had little interest. After all, I was already almost a black belt in a "real" martial art. Why did I need to study a bunch of slow geriatric-looking moves? My grandmother insisted, however, that I meet this man and at least talk to him. I hesitantly agreed and the day I met him turned out to be a day I will never forget.

Thinking back to that day brings up a lot of memories. I am almost embarrassed at how arrogant I was when, thinking there would be nothing in it for me because I liked only fighting skill, I walked reluctantly into his house. At that time, Shifu Zhang Yun had just recently arrived from Beijing. He spoke maybe five words of English and had to have his friend translate. He asked me what I studied and I confidently recited my rank and proudly reported the number of trophies and medals I had won. He very humbly stated that he did Taiji Quan. "Oh yeah, I've seen that. It's the slow moving stuff that old people do," I said with a smile. "Taiji can be used for real fighting and can be very effective," he calmly returned.

With that, he and his friend began to move the furniture to clear a space, while he politely asked me if I wanted to try some fighting. As I attacked, the most bizarre thing happened to me. I ended up on the floor with absolutely no clue how I got there. Every time I came at him with a punch or a kick, I met emptiness. There he was, or at least there I thought he was but I repeatedly found myself on the floor with no recollection of how I had gotten there.

Needless to say, after that experience, I became Shifu Zhang Yun's biggest fan and his first student in the United States. I studied with him one year before he decided he wanted to teach more students. The group of students drawn to his classes grew quickly to about ten people, all of whom were intensely dedicated to training with a teacher of such astonishing skill.

After about three years of study, an unbelievable opportunity presented itself, when Shifu Zhang Yun suggested that I go to China to study with his Kungfu family. At first, the idea seemed like only a wonderful dream, but soon I was working hard to save money for the journey of a lifetime. Shifu Zhang Yun had constantly referred to his grandmaster Wang Peisheng and his legendary skill. I was very eager to meet this man whom my teacher so deeply admired. It was arranged that I would stay with Shifu Zhang Yun's Kungfu brother Lu Shengli. Before I knew it, I had the money, the visa and the plane ticket and it was time to leave.

Being in China was a breathtaking experience from beginning to end and would take a book's worth of words to describe. I stayed for four months, training six hours a day, six days a week. I lived with Lu Shengli, an incredible martial artist, who took care of me and trained me every day. As Shifu Zhang Yun's older Kungfu brother, Master Lu opened his home to me and treated me like a nephew. Master Lu, whom I called Shibo, meaning "teacher uncle," was kind, warm and generous and had a pleasant and chivalrous nature. Humble and always smiling at those he passed, he nevertheless possessed an intensity in fighting that was matched by very few. He seemed like a true warrior living in a modern day world. As you might expect, my training was hard and intense, bringing tears at times. Looking back, I wouldn't trade those moments for anything.

I will never forget my first meeting with the grandmaster Wang Peisheng. I was introduced as Zhang Yun's student who had traveled from the United States to train. Master Wang was very interested in what I had studied and asked several questions. He then began to talk about Taiji and internal force. Suddenly, he jumped up from his chair and began to demonstrate some Taiji and Bagua. I had never seen such movement or power from a person before, especially from a person of his age. He seemed to grow ten feet and moved with an astonishing grace and with fire in his eyes. I was in total awe of what was taking place.

Master Wang asked me to stand and, as he demonstrated the moves with me, I was astounded by his ability. At times he seemed to vanish as I pushed on him as precisely as I could. Yet if he wished, he could become like a mountain; hard as I might try, I could not move him. When he touched me, a wave of energy shot through me, yet his power was soft and undetectable until the last moment. He was relaxed and could guide his energy freely wherever and whenever he wished. From that day on, I knew that for me this Kungfu, called Yin Cheng Gong Fa, was going to be a way of life.

Yin Cheng means "to treat people always with heart-felt honesty." When Master Wang studied Buddhism, his master gave him this special name as a goal or aspiration to strive for. Gong Fa means "Kungfu (training) method." Yin Cheng Gong Fa, then, refers to the training method of the Kungfu of the man known as Yin Cheng. Having practiced for nine years with Shifu Zhang Yun and twice intensively with Master Wang and Master Lu in Beijing, I began to understand the real meaning of Yin Cheng Gong Fa. It is a highly developed martial arts training system that applies high level principles to the study of the martial arts and thereby makes it possible for students to understand more fully the meaning and fundamental tenets of martial arts practice. It offers not only clear explanations of basic principles but also many efficient techniques and training suggestions for people at all skill levels. Much more than a simple combination of facts and propositions, it is an integration of traditional wisdom and practice with more recent modifications that have been developed by Master Wang and others to facilitate training by practitioners all over the world and at all levels of expertise. It is a system imbued with centuries-old methods and values that transforms and condenses this knowledge so that students can incorporate it into any martial arts practice.

This system is not an exclusive one. Nor does it advance any system or style as superior to others. It encourages each practitioner to make individual choices about which forms to study and generally which path to take in the pursuit of high level mastery. It has been used by many practitioners to improve the performance of techniques and skills derived from the whole spectrum of traditional martial arts styles.

Master Wang, as one of the most outstanding martial arts masters in China today, has studied numerous martial arts styles with many of the most famous Chinese masters. His training has been rigorous, traditional, serious, and lifelong. His expertise extends to a detailed knowledge of traditional Chinese culture, including philosophy, history, and the arts. Throughout his life, he has prevailed in competitions with many famous masters and has justly earned a reputation as one of the great masters of martial arts fighting techniques. He has devoted his life to a thorough and deep exploration of the martial arts. During more than sixty-five years of studying, practicing, and teaching, he has gained superior skill in and knowledge of a great variety of styles. Because of this, he has been able to gain insight into the essential nature of the martial arts and to combine traditional knowledge with his own experience to devise this new martial arts training system.

The sword form taught in this book is part of the Yin Cheng Gong Fa system. With its publication, there is now a way for practitioners everywhere to learn the principles and methods of this system, which is at once innovative and tradition-based. Not only is the approach described in this book unique but also it is important for what it represents in the bigger picture. Master Wang's system provides a gateway to a world that has passed. There has been much lost over the years as China makes the transition into the twentieth century, including the fact that the martial way is no longer practiced by many martial artists. People today must work all day and keep pace with the modern world. Very few can train many hours a day for years on end as did the practitioners of the past, while guns and modern weaponry have replaced skill with swords and spears.

What used to be an integral part of Chinese culture and a vital part of everyday life is disappearing with the passage of time. Nevertheless, martial arts skills, traditions and principles are preserved by a dedicated few. Master Wang is one such man, working to pass this knowledge on to the willing. Shifu Zhang Yun is another and this book, one can hope, is just the beginning of many volumes aimed at preserving a part of classical martial arts history.

In this book, the reader will learn about one of the most refined and revered of Chinese weapons, the double-edged sword, or *jian*. The jian is a very special weapon with a long and significant history. It was carried by generals and noblemen and was considered a gentlemen's weapon. The skill required to wield it was regarded as refined and of a high level, attained by only accomplished practitioners. Mastering the elements that make the jian form beautiful and its applications effective is a challenging task. I feel that this book offers the most comprehensive and detailed method for learning the jian form and its applications. The details of where to direct the mind is especially characteristic of Master Wang's method. With careful training, one can feel changes and sensations while practicing the form. The insights passed down from master to student for generations give the modern student a clear path to mastery of the jian. Master Wang's method of study allows the student to perfect movements and to derive these movements from correct principles and feelings.

When studying the sword form by utilizing the points detailed by Master Wang, one feels instantly comfortable. The sword that initially felt like an unwieldy piece of metal, eventually comes to feel like a natural part of one's body. In my opinion, this book gives us a clear and safe way to master a very challenging and beautiful art, Taiji Jian. Even more, it gives us a way to understand Yin Cheng Gong Fa.

The day I became Shifu Zhang Yun's disciple and a member of his Kungfu family was one of the most exciting days of my life. At the initiation ceremony, Master Wang told me I was the first foreigner to join his martial arts family in the traditional way, having followed the same course of study and met all the same standards as the Chinese members. I could not believe my good fortune to be accepted as a full member of Yin Cheng Gong Fa

Looking out the window of the plane as I left Beijing, I knew that I would return to this age-old land again and again. I knew, too, that one day the Yin Cheng Gong Fa system would make its way into the mainstream of the martial arts community in the United States. After all, that was our goal so that all could benefit from this wonderful method of improving body and mind. This goal is served with the publication of Shifu Zhang Yun's book and the growing popularity of Master Wang's method here in the United States and abroad.

Strider Clark
Reno, Nevada

PREFACE

Throughout the world today, Taiji Quan (also spelled T'ai Chi Chu'an) is one of the most well known and popular of the traditional Chinese martial arts. As is commonly known, it promotes good health and can help people develop fighting skills. These, however, are not its only functions. It can also contribute to the development of personality and character.

Perhaps you have already practiced the empty-handed form of Taiji Quan for many years. What is next? You have many choices but I suggest you study the *jian*, a straight double-edged sword, of the Taiji school. Like Taiji Quan, it can help you in many ways. Jian training can increase your fighting skills by improving your footwork and the fluidity of movement in your body, especially in your waist. Jian practice promotes good health by strengthening your *qi* ("intrinsic energy") and allowing it to move more smoothly and with more vitality to every part of your body and even to the tip of the jian.

Most importantly, however, the principles underlying the practice of Taiji Jian can serve, like those of Taiji Quan, as a model for the development of personality and character. In traditional Chinese culture, the jian is regarded as much more than simply a martial arts weapon. It embodies the values and spirit of Chinese culture and has for centuries been celebrated in art, literature, and legend. Many people, from emperors to commoners and from generals to scholars, have practiced jian forms and have had their lives deeply shaped by the teachings and standards it represents. The symbolic significance of jian is expressed in many beautiful stories and myths passed down from generation to generation. To practice Taiji Jian is to enter into a highly developed and long-standing tradition that can deepen your understanding of many of life's important lessons.

In this book I introduce a short form of Wu style Taiji Jian. This form includes thirty-two postures and derives from the traditional sixty-four posture form. None of the original movements have been changed but some of the more difficult and complex movements from the long form have been omitted and some of the remaining movements have been rearranged. All of the important features of the traditional Taiji Jian long form have been retained, but this short form can be learned and mastered more quickly and easily and is, therefore, a good choice for people who live in our fast-paced contemporary culture and have only a limited time for practice.

The form presented here was developed at the Beijing Wu Style Taiji Quan Association under Master Wang Peisheng's direction and instruction. Master Wang Peisheng, whose special literary name is Yin Cheng, is President of the Beijing Wu Style Taiji Quan Association and one of the most outstanding martial arts masters in China. Master Wang began practicing martial arts at the age of twelve and studied with many renowned masters, including Ma Gui, Zhang Yulian, Yang Yuting, Gao Kexing, Liang Junbo, Zhao Runting, Han Muxia, Wu Xiufeng and others. He started studying Taiji Quan at the age of thirteen with Master Yang Yuting and then received special intensive training from his grandmaster Wang Maozhai, who was considered the best Taiji master in north China at that time. At eighteen, Master Wang became the youngest professional martial arts master in China and went on to acquire superior skills in Taiji Quan, Bagua Quan, Xingyi Quan, Tongbei Quan, Baji Quan, Tantui, Shuai Jiao (Chinese wrestling), Qigong, and Zhongyi (Chinese medicine). Master Wang has a special liking for jian and practices it with vigor and intensity. Besides Taiji Jian, he has also achieved high level skills in Bagua Chunyang Jian, Sancai Jian, Wudang Jian, Qingping Jian, Damo Jian, Panzixiangmo Jian, Qixing Jian and Kunwu Jian among other martial arts.

Over the years, Master Wang has traveled widely and brought an understanding of traditional Chinese philosophy, arts, and culture, to people from many countries. He has won many competitions with other famous masters and has continually improved his fighting techniques. These accomplishments have earned him an excellent reputation and he has become justly famous, especially for his weapons techniques. With more than sixty years' experience, his skill level is now so high that it cannot be adequately described in words. From principles to techniques, from history to lineage, from internal Kungfu to external Kungfu, his martial arts knowledge is broad and deep. He is a Grandmaster, respected not only for his fighting techniques, but also for his meditation skills, his character and his high level of spiritual attainment.

Having first studied Taiji Quan with Master Luo Shuhuan in 1975, I began training intensively with Master Wang in 1976 at the recommendation of Master Luo. Master Wang instructed me in Taiji, Bagua, Xingyi and a variety of other martial arts, with a special emphasis on weapons training. I do not know how to put into words my respect for Master Wang's skills and personality nor the gratitude I feel towards him. He has been my mentor and my ideal and has given me experiences and insights that will stay with me for a lifetime.

I remember when I studied Taiji Jian with him, he repeatedly told me that one must always pay attention to the intention of the jian. This has helped me to understand the jian. Later, I was lucky enough to have the opportunity of working with Master Wang to develop the thirty-two posture short form of Taiji Jian. With his instruction in this work, I was able to study jian form in great detail. When I came to the United States, he suggested that I teach the short form because people in this country are very busy and often do not have enough free time to undertake mastery of the jian long form. He gave me special instructions for teaching the short form, and his guidance has increased my understanding of the jian as a weapon that can express the intentions as well as the skills and techniques of the practitioner.

Everything in this book derives from the knowledge and wisdom of Master Wang. My contribution has been only to write down his teachings so that they are available to more people. I am very grateful to Master Wang for giving me permission to write this book. It is designed for people of all levels of experience and in it I describe not only the techniques Taiji Jian but also its underlying principles. I believe that only with an understanding of these principles can one truly excel at jian. I hope readers will enjoy this book and will gain the many benefits that mastery of jian can bring into their lives.

All Chinese words are spelled using the Pinyin system, the national standard for transliteration of Mandarin Chinese, and are italicized, except proper names, on the first usage. Thereafter they are spelled in Roman type. Some Chinese words, especially those referring to jian techniques, are difficult to translate directly into English. On the assumption that dedicated practitioners of Taiji Jian would want to learn these terms, I have used them in the text after providing brief definitions of their meanings. As an aid to learning, these definitions are frequently repeated.

I appreciate the help of Ms. Susan Darley, Mr. Jimmy Lee, and Mr. Dave McFarland in writing this book. Ms. Darley edited the book and Mr. Lee translated many special words and made numerous good suggestions. Mr. McFarland is shown with me in many of the "Application" photographs and was very helpful in this phase of the project. I also appreciate the assistance of Ms. Uma Bhagtnagar, Mr. Keith Endo, Ms. Aline Johnson, Ms. Juli Kinchla, Mr. Peter Kindfield, Mr. Won Park, Mr. David Rosner, and Dr. Mal Zarnfaller. Their many helpful comments contributed greatly to the final work presented here. I am also grateful to Mr. Edward Tenner who provided generous and sage advice about the ways of the world and its commerce.

Although I owe my knowledge of Taiji to my masters, it is my wife, Zhang Haihui, who helps me find the center, balance, and direction of my life. She sustains me in every one of my endeavors with patience, grace, and wisdom—and she does it all with a minimum of force!

Zhang Yun
Princeton, New Jersey

Master Wang Peisheng

I

JIAN, THE CHINESE DOUBLE-EDGED SWORD

The *jian*, a straight double-edged sword *(fig. 1)*, is the most common weapon in the traditional Chinese martial arts, and at the same time it is also a very special one. It is common because it is used in almost all styles and is practiced by almost all groups. As a result, its technical features have been developed to a very high level. It is special because it is not just a martial arts weapon but also an important symbol central to Chinese culture. It embodies the spirit of the Chinese people and has been celebrated in art and legend for thousands of years. It has come to express the most deeply held Chinese values and moral precepts. People practice it not only to improve their health and fighting skills, but also to develop character and personality. It is treated with great respect in Chinese culture as a pure, sacred, and beloved icon.

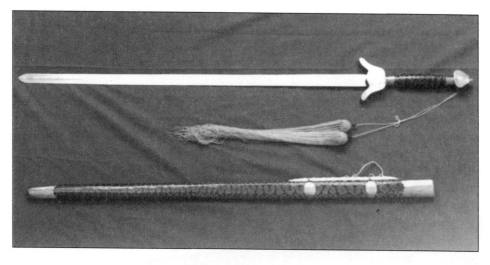

1 The jian and its scabbard

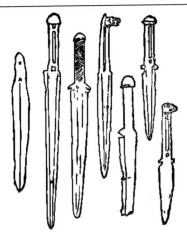

2 Zhou Dynasty jian, excavated from sites near Xian and Beijing

3 Short bronze jian, 7¾ in. (20 cm) by 1⅜ in. (3.5 cm)

HISTORY OF THE JIAN

The jian has a recorded history of more than three thousand years in China. From written records and archaeological discoveries, we know that such swords were first used in northwest China. From there, its use spread to central and southern China. The earliest records of jian date from the Xia Dynasty (2100–1600 BC). By the time of the Zhou Dynasty (1100–256 BC), they had become one of the most popular weapons in use. They were made of bronze, an alloy of copper and tin, and, because of the weight and hardness of this metal, their length was limited to about 15⅝ inches (40 cm). Archaeologists have found many jian that date from this period (*fig. 2*).

About twenty-seven hundred years ago, during the Spring and Autumn period (770–475 BC), the art of making jian was developed to a very high level. At that time, people skilled in this craft were highly regarded and many became widely known and deservedly famous. Some of the jian created by these renowned artisans have been discovered in the last one hundred years. Even after being buried in the earth for more than two thousand years, they are still sharp enough to cut coins. Qualities such as this have amazed modern-day experts and reflect the high degree of technical and artistic skill that went into the manufacture of these weapons.

Although jian from this period were also made of bronze, they were longer than those of the Zhou Dynasty. Their increase in length and their remarkable sharpness were made possible by an increasingly sophisticated knowledge of metallurgy and metal-working techniques. Although these new technologies allowed the production of longer blades, the short jian-like daggers remained popular. *Figure 3* shows a beautiful short jian from this period.

It had become known that when the percentage of tin is higher, bronze becomes harder, but is also more brittle, and that when the percentage of tin is lower, bronze gains tensile strength but becomes soft. With the former type of mix, jian could be made with very sharp edges but had to remain relatively short because of the brittleness

4 King Yue's jian, 21 5/8 in. (55.6 cm)
  by 1 3/4 in. (4.6 cm)

of the alloy. With the second type, jian could be made considerably longer but were too soft to be adequately sharpened. Contemporary experts using modern equipment were surprised to discover that the percentage of tin is lower in the center of these jian, allowing for greater tensile strength in the body, and higher at the edges, allowing for greater sharpness where it was needed. This technical ability to vary the proportions of copper and tin in different parts of jian made it possible to create swords that were both long and sharp. It is difficult to imagine how an ancient people could have acquired the technical expertise that led to the production of such excellent weapons. Jian from this period have proved the accuracy of ancient writings which describe techniques of metallurgy and the art of weapon production thousands of years ago.

Figure 4 shows the famous jian that belong to King Yue, who is known for the war he fought with King Wu. The fighting skills of both kings and the high quality of their jian have been praised in many legends. The accuracy of these stories, however, was not appreciated until the graves of the two Kings were discovered and their actual weapons unearthed.

The fighting principles of jian, still used today, were also developed to very high level in the Spring and Autumn period. These principles were established by Yue Nü, Yuan Gong, Lu Shigong, and some others. Yue Nü, a woman, was a high-level jian master invited by King Yue to train his army. Later, he won the war against King Wu and destroyed Wu's kingdom. Yue Nü's teachings were respected and followed from that time onward. Today, when we read the principles set forth by Yue Nü, we recognize the depth of her knowledge and can fully appreciate how great a master she was. Figure 5 shows a picture of Yue Nü, copied from a two-thousand year old stone carving, as she performs her jian skills for King Yue.

In the Spring and Autumn period, skilled jian masters, jian makers, and jian appraisers were highly respected in Chinese society. People carried jian to express their high status and the presumably noble quality of their characters. Jian skills were widely studied and practiced, and competitions were frequent. Some kings retained

6 A general hunts a tiger with his jian

7 A long bronze jian of the Qin Dynasty, 35 ½ in. (91 cm) by 1 ½ in. (3.3 cm)

thousands of masters and fighters in the imperial palaces so that high-level competitions could be held daily. *Figure 6* shows a general hunting a tiger with a jian. It was copied from the back of a bronze mirror dating from the Spring and Autumn period.

Bronze jian production was developed to its highest level during the Qin Dynasty (221–206 BC). The shape of bronze jian was changed from short, broad, and thick to long, narrow, and thin. Jian of more than 39 inches (100 cm) in length have been discovered from this period. *Figure 7* shows a bronze jian typical of those made in the middle of the Qin Dynasty.

Iron began to be used in the manufacture of jian around two thousand four hundred years ago; it was well developed in the kingdom of Qin, which was the predecessor of the Qin Dynasty. Iron jian were used by the armies of the Qin in the series of wars that were fought among the various kingdoms of this period, so some people believe that the success of the Qin in defeating its rivals and in unifying the country is largely due to the use of iron jian. It was during this dynasty that the jian came to be viewed not just as a weapon but also as a revered symbol of moral values, such as honor and honesty. People started to use jian in dramatic performances, and jian dance became popular. *Figure 8* is taken from an ancient wall painting depicting a jian dance from this period. Four musicians are shown playing their instruments in the upper part of the painting, while the figures below perform the dance.

During the Han Dynasty (206 BC–220 AD), the Jin Dynasty (265–420), and the Southern and the Northern Dynasties (420–581), the process of making jian from iron and steel was further developed. The popularity of the weapon greatly increased, and the publication of books about jian principles became widespread. One of the most famous of these was the *Jian Dao (Way of Jian)*, or "Thirty-eight Topics." Jian forms were also more fully developed during this period and many new jian forms were created.

During these dynasties, the uses of jian and its significance in Chinese society started to change. Gradually, jian were replaced by *dao*, broadswords, as the weapon of choice for soldiers, while only officers carried jian. Government officers also were

8 Jian dance with musical accompaniment

required to carry jian to and from work, and the rank of each government officer was indicated by the type of jian carried. As an indication of one's rank and abilities, jian began to be widely used in official rites and protocols as well as in sacrificial religious ceremonies. Jian came to be respected as holy objects and it was even believed that they could protect people from harm and exorcise devils.

The shape of jian was modified throughout these dynasties, becoming longer and narrower, until by the time of the Tang Dynasty (618–907), they had acquired a shape that is common today. During the Tang also, the influence of jian spread to every area of China and a famous jian form was developed by Gongsun Daniang, a woman who became well-known for this accomplishment. Her form inspired great works of art and poetry; the work of the famous calligrapher Zhang Xu and of the poet Du Fu extol Gongsun Daniang's jian form. Even ordinary citizens came to regard the practice of jian as an important and worthwhile undertaking and it was widely believed that the practice of jian had the power to imbue a person's life with honor and integrity.

In the Song Dynasty (960–1279), jian manufacture was developed to its highest level. Those called Long Quan jian (Dragon Spring jian) made during this period are perhaps the most famous ever made. Long Quan jian were tempered with Dragon Spring water and some could slice through ten large nails at one time. Jian from this period are avidly sought today but very few exist, and those that do are mostly owned by museums or private collectors. Today, many swords are labeled with the Long Quan name but they are not authentic and their quality is not good. And although some martial art shops may claim that their swords come from the Song period, the vast majority of these claims are, unfortunately, not true.

During the Ming Dynasty (1368–1644) and the Qing Dynasty (1644–1911), Chinese martial arts were developed to their highest level, and this era has become known as the Golden Age of martial arts. Many new styles were developed, and because the jian was practiced by a great variety of martial arts groups, the number of different jian forms developed during this period reached several hundred. Many of these forms are

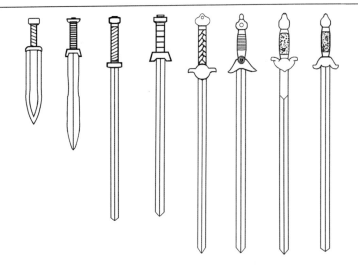

9 Drawings of jian from various historical periods. From left to right: bronze jian, Zhou Dynasty; bronze jian, Spring and Autumn period; bronze jian, Qin Dynasty; iron jian, Han Dynasty; steel jian, Tang Dynasty; steel jian, Song Dynasty; steel jian, Ming Dynasty; steel jian, Qing Dynasty

still practiced today and the jian currently in use are similar in shape and material to those used during these dynasties. *Figure 9* shows several jian shapes from different historical periods. Note that the material used in the manufacture of jian changed over time from bronze to iron to steel.

As we have seen, jian have a long and glorious history in China. In the last one hundred years, especially since the 1950s, however, interest in the martial arts has waned in China and many skills have been lost. High-level masters are few, and the principles of jian have been misunderstood and poorly taught. Low quality weapons have been mass produced and the well-guarded secrets about how to make high-quality jian have not been passed down from master to apprentice. As a result, these secrets are no longer known. Today, when people practice jian, they typically pay attention only to the external movements of the form and overlook the internal aspects of jian training.

This state of affairs has created widespread concern among serious practitioners of jian. In response, some great masters have given up the tradition of keeping secret the knowledge of high-level skills. In the hope of restoring the high-level practice of jian and making it once again widely known and respected, these masters have became more accessible to the public and are reaching out to interested novices and experienced practitioners through teaching and writing. Master Wang Peisheng is one such master.

JIAN AND TRADITIONAL CULTURE

To the Chinese the jian, as has been noted, is not only a martial arts weapon but also a subject and tool of meditation and a symbol of moral uprightness and achievement. Its importance as a symbol is, if anything, even greater than its significance as a weapon.

The jian is known as the "gentleman's weapon," which means that if you practice jian, you must do so with a sense of internal calm and correctness and that your movements must be beautiful. Even in real fighting, you must never be hard or crude in your movements or your manner. Rather, you must use only high-level techniques and you must use them with subtlety and expertise. Your *yi* (mind) and *shen* (spirit), as well as your *qi* (intrinsic energy), must lead your movements and you must never show cruelty or ferocity. Physical ability is always secondary to the skillful use of yi, qi and shen, and even when you are successful in beating your opponents, you must do so in a way that creates in these opponents no anger or resentment towards you but rather a sense of respect, admiration, and even friendship.

Everything you do in your jian practice and in jian fighting should come from your heart, not just from your body. This is an attitude that has characterized jian forms for more than two thousand years and in this respect, the jian is different from any other martial arts weapon. For centuries, it has been a deeply held view in Chinese culture that the better your jian skills are, the finer your character must be. This traditional view holds that only people of superior character, such as heroes or other chivalrous individuals can truly use jian well. The jian, in fact, has come to stand for justice, chivalry, integrity, nobility, purity, gentleness, and wisdom. Because it is also considered to be a sacred and magical talisman capable of exorcising evil, the jian has historically been used in religious ceremonies and has been commemorated in legends, poems and songs. Some even regard the jian as a lover, devoting their lives to its practice. Traditionally, in fact, the jian is always called *baojian* (precious sword) and its practice is one of five special disciplines believed to build character through the development of moral integrity, nobility of mind, emotional sensitivity, and physical well-being. The other four are *guqin* (the skillful playing of a seven-stringed instrument), *weiqi* (Go, a game played with black and white pieces), poetry, and painting.

2

TAIJI QUAN AND TAIJI JIAN

Taiji Jian has two meanings. First, it refers to the straight double-edged swords known as jian which are used in Taiji groups. Second and more commonly, it refers to a jian form and skills that are based on Taiji Quan principles. The jian form of Taiji is beautiful and all of its movements are useful. Its principles derive from Taiji philosophy and the basis of the jian form derives from the empty-handed Taiji Quan form. Unlike ordinary jian, whose long history has been described in the previous chapter, jian forms of Taiji are of more recent origin. It is said that when Master Yang Luchan taught Taiji Quan in Beijing, from about the 1850s to the 1870s, no sword form had yet been developed. Master Yang had only some basic skills and principles available to him but he passed these on to his sons and students, and it was they who developed the jian forms of Taiji. Today, many different forms are practiced under the discipline called Taiji Jian, but all are based on the same fundamental principles and techniques.

REVIEW OF TAIJI PRINCIPLES

All the skills of Taiji Jian follow the principles of Taiji (literally "great ultimate"), which are in turn derived from ancient Chinese philosophy. In this section, some of these important Taiji concepts will be presented for readers who are just beginning their study of Taiji Quan or Taiji Jian. Even those familiar with Taiji Quan and who have been practicing it for some time may want to read through this section, although they will no doubt already be familiar with the ideas presented. However, because translations can differ greatly from one book to another, they will be able to understand the description of the Taiji Jian form presented here more thoroughly if they are familiar with the way that I define its underlying principles and concepts.

1 Diagram of Taiji, symbolizing the interrelatedness of yin and yang

Yin, Yang, and Taiji

Yin and yang are two abstract concepts central to the Taoist philosophy, upon which all jian forms are based. These concepts express the oppositions found in all natural objects and phenomena. Conceptually, yin represents qualities such as negativity, femaleness, passivity, subordination, internality, softness, fullness, quietness, substantiality, and darkness, as well as specific objects such as the moon and earth. Yang represents the opposite qualities of positivity, maleness, initiative, leadership, externality, hardness, emptiness, movement, insubstantiality, and light, as well as objects like the sun and sky.

Taiji is an abstract concept as well, and is commonly symbolized as shown in *figure 1*. It emanates from *wuji*, which is the original undifferentiated state of being. Once Taiji has emerged as a transitional state in the process of differentiation, it changes, in turn, and separates into yin and yang. It is said that Taiji is the mother of yin and yang.

It is also sometimes said that Taiji *is* yin and yang. This statement is not quite correct because it suggests that yin and yang are two separate forces. Rather, Taiji is a state of being in which yin and yang forces are just about to become differentiated. It is a state that encompasses both yin and yang as they interact with each other and one in which each force contains within it an essence of the other. In the Taiji state, yin always contains some yang; and yang, always some yin. Each force is continuously changing and being changed by the other, and both are in eternal flux, always complementing, replenishing, supporting, and transforming each other. In the state of Taiji, yin and yang are in perfect balance and are inextricably related to each other. They should not be confused with the notions of pure yin and pure yang which are expressed by a different conceptual term, *liangyi*. Confusion of this term with Taiji can lead to misunderstandings in the application of Taiji Quan techniques.

Taiji and the Martial Arts

The concept of Taiji influenced many aspects of Chinese culture, including the martial arts, where the concept provided the core of a new and very special style. The martial arts practice of this style, Taiji Quan, is designed to bring the body's internal forces of yin and yang into balance and thus to promote good health. A balance of complementary yin and yang forces in the body's external movements is also sought, so that a relaxed and coordinated physical state can be achieved in which intrinsic energy can move smoothly throughout the body and the body's internal force can be strengthened. When the Taiji concept of balance is realized, fighting skills become faster, more powerful, and more efficient because energy is borrowed from the opponent, who then beats himself with his own force. While the achievement of such balance through the practice of Taiji Quan can result in more effective mastery of fighting skills, the benefits of its practice go well beyond combat.

INTERNAL COMPONENTS

There are important internal components that must be understood and practiced for high-level mastery of Taiji Quan and Taiji Jian. Each of these components is important for understanding the Taiji Jian form that will be presented in Chapter 6.

Spirit

This is a common translation of the term *shen*, although in my view, this definition is close to the true meaning but is not entirely accurate. In fact, shen is very difficult, perhaps impossible to describe in words. It is a subjective feeling that may be essentially nonverbal but that can be sensed internally when it occurs. Sometimes, it is expressed through one's gaze, which has been likened to the almost hypnotic stare of an animal ready to spring at its prey. Shen is the internal component that directs or leads all the other internal and external components in every movement in the form and at all moments of your practice. Your *yi* (mind), your *qi* (intrinsic energy), and all your movements follow the direction and flow of your shen.

Whenever you practice Taiji, you must pay attention to shen and recognize that every movement is informed by this internal component. It is one of the three elements involved in the internal integration described below. Shen can internally gather strength and project itself outward to imbue all movements with increased vigor. Most of the time when you are practicing the Taiji form, shen energy is being gathered internally and this process is reflected through the eyes in a steady gaze. When you are actually performing Taiji techniques, shen is projected outward and this process is reflected through eyes that shine with intensity. Shen is the most fundamental and essential element of Taiji, but it is the last element to be mastered because it is the most difficult to comprehend and use. You should train your shen and seek to increase its intensity at each moment and in every movement of the form.

Mind

The essence of Taiji has been expressed in many different ways: "The mind is the commander," or "First in the mind, then in the body," or "Sometimes the internal force is broken, but never the mind," or "Use the mind but not force." Each of these adages underscores the importance of the concept of yi, or mind, in Taiji. Yi influences all aspects, both internal and external, of Taiji practice. The mind directs or leads the flow of qi, and qi, in turn, leads the external movements. If you want to change your character and your natural way of expressing yourself in body and in spirit, you must have a strong mind to regulate and redirect your energy. The correct practice of Taiji depends on the use of the mind rather than on physical strength. Only by applying the mind, by keeping it focused and calmly alert, can you effectively direct and control your internal force. With a focused mind you will be able to become more aware of all the other internal components and to use them effectively in your practice of Taiji. Training your mind can bring your ability to a high level, especially in Taiji Jian, where more attention should be paid to this component than to any other. Concentrating, or "putting the mind on" the body's acupoints is a helpful way to train your mind so that it can be used to add direction and control to your movements.

Intrinsic Energy

Expressed in Chinese as qi, this is a familiar concept to many people but an especially difficult one to define clearly. Qi has been described as a kind of feeling, or intrinsic energy, spirit, mind, or breath. You cannot see it, but you can feel it, control it, and use it. Sometimes it seems to be related to objective and real physiological processes and sometimes it seems more like a spiritual or metaphorical phenomenon. It can move inside or outside of your body. Because it is difficult to describe and feel, many people are skeptical of the notion, but qi does exist. When you practice Taiji, you will occasionally feel parts of your body become slightly warm or heavy or you will feel as though parts of your body are expanding. These experiences indicate the presence of qi. As your training advances, your qi will become stronger and as this happens, your body will feel very strong, stable, and nimble and your breath will be very comfortable even after vigorous movement.

For three thousand years, the Chinese have applied this concept in many disciplines, especially in medicine and physiological research. Over the centuries, many methods for increasing the intensity and flow of qi have been developed. These methods are called Qigong or Neigong.

Qi can improve all aspects of Taiji practice but if you do not train your qi, you will accomplish nothing. Two of the most important effects of qi are improving your health and increasing your fighting skills. With regard to your health, Taiji practice can train your qi to move more smoothly along the meridians of your body, as though massaging the acupuncture points. In traditional Chinese medicine, this smooth flow of qi is thought to lead to improvement in the body's general well-being.

As for improvement in fighting techniques, qi guides the expression of internal force and of all external movements. If your qi can move continuously and freely throughout your body, your movements will be robust and quick. If your qi is strong, your internal force will likewise be strong. If your qi can move smoothly down through your body, you will be stable; if it can move smoothly up, you will be nimble.

The most efficient way to train your qi is to practice the form. When you practice, you should be relaxed and keep your mind focused. Your movements should be correct in every detail and you should practice the form daily and with great attentiveness. When you practice, do not try consciously to direct or control your qi. Instead, let it emerge and intensify naturally. If you try to sense your qi, you can become aware of it quite quickly, but this will be a superficial and counterproductive experience because it will distract you from developing a deeper and more lasting understanding of the Taiji form.

One of the most important components of qi practice is the *dantian*, which refers to areas or fields of qi. There are three dantian fields on the body: upper (higher), middle, and lower. The upper dantian is inside the head at the vertex of the *baihui* and *xuanguan* acupressure points. (See Appendixes for an introduction to acupoints and their locations.) The middle dantian is inside the abdomen, one-third of the way between the *shenxue* and *mingmen* acupoints. The lower dantian is at the *huiyin* point. Usually, when people speak of "the" dantian, they are referring to the middle one. Different systems or styles may locate dantian in different places and this will lead to different training methods. In all systems, however, qi is considered to be collected, concentrated, developed, and refined in dantian.

Internal Force

Jin, or internal force, is different from *li*, or physical force. In Taiji, "force" refers to your natural force, the force that everyone has and that results from muscle activity. Every movement of the body requires work from the muscles. The harder the muscles have to work, the more difficult it is to relax while the movement is occurring. Movements resulting from muscle activity, as opposed to those resulting from internal force are visible, discontinuous, and relatively short, slow, straight, stiff, unchangeable, undifferentiated, and uncoordinated. They are also pure, that is, they can be either hard or soft but not a mix of both. This is not to say that muscle activity itself cannot be highly complex and subtle, but rather that it is not nearly as finely discriminated and fluid as jin.

Jin refers to the force that results only from the practice of Taiji or other high-level Kungfu (used here to refer to all internal Chinese martial arts). It is not a quality that everyone has naturally, and although it is somewhat related to muscle activity, it has much more to do with qi and with mind, or yi. Through Taiji practice, you can make your muscles work together when you move. Each muscle, then, has to provide just a small amount of work or physical force and this makes it easier for you to relax. If all your muscles work together well, and each is used just enough to maintain a state of relaxation throughout the body, your force becomes internal force or jin. If you develop jin, your energy will be very powerful even if your body is weakened by age or your build is slight.

Unlike physical or muscular force, jin is intermixed (hard and soft), invisible, continuous, long, fast, curved, smooth, relaxed, integrated, changeable (nimble), heavy (stable), and sharp. While physical force operates according to natural reflexes, jin works according to new and acquired reflexes that result from the training of mind and are led by qi as you practice the form. Physical force is exerted in only some parts of the body and is applied in specific directions; jin is always present in all parts of the body and is expressed in all directions.

Practicing the form can lead to the development of jin because practice transforms physical force into internal force. After this first step, however, you must learn how to use jin. This knowledge is very important if you want to develop high level skills. A central tenet of Taiji points out that: "Once you understand jin, the more you practice, the more skill you acquire. You must silently treasure the knowledge and reflect on it. Gradually, you will be able to do whatever you like." The most important elements in using jin successfully are relaxation, timing, direction, mind, and an understanding of yin and yang. In Taiji, whether in empty-handed forms or using jian, there are thirty-six kinds of jin, that is, thirty-six different ways in which your internal force can be used. Once you have achieved jin, you can study how to apply it in each of these ways.

Combining Internal Components
Shen (spirit), yi (mind), qi (intrinsic energy), and jin (internal force) are all important components of Taiji Quan. If you have not acquired and learned to control and direct these components, you will not be able to fight well. Shen is the component that leads all the others, with the complete sequence being: shen, yi, qi, and jin. If shen does not lead correctly, yi cannot follow. If all goes well and yi does follow shen, shen must leave and move to the next point as soon as yi arrives, that is, as soon as the mind has focused wherever shen has led it. If shen does not leave once yi has arrived at a given point, a situation of double-weight occurs and Taiji balance will be lost.

Yi, in turn, is used to lead qi. In a fight, when the opponent touches you at two different points you should forget the heavier of the two touch points and direct yi to the lighter. It is important to forget the first point because if you do not, you will again be double-weighted. The movement of yi to the touch point will cause qi to flow through your body to that point. If only one point is touched, you should create a second touch point in your mind and then direct yi to the lighter of the two. It is important to follow these guidelines even if there is no actual touch point at all but only a point that is simply thought of as having been touched.

The essence of Taiji has been expressed as follows: "If you have qi, you do not have to use physical force; if you do not have qi, you will be purely hard, which is a natural state but not Taiji." You must refine your practice so that qi can move smoothly and freely throughout your body. The movement of qi will, in turn, lead jin to the touch point because when qi moves, jin moves. Once this has occurred, any point you use to touch your opponent can be also be used to release the jin.

When you practice Taiji, the order in which the components are learned and mastered is the reverse of the sequence just described. First, jin or internal force develops as you learn the movements and become adept at performing them. Next, your ability to feel, control, and develop qi increases and as this happens, you begin to understand how to use your mind. Finally, you become aware of shen and learn to direct it so that it leads the whole sequence.

When you have achieved this level of practice, it is said that whatever you accomplish is a result of shen's "reaching" to anywhere you want, then leading yi to reach, followed by qi's reach, then jin's reach, and finally the movement's reach. If you can make all of these components reach simultaneously, your Kungfu is good. Whenever you practice the applications of Taiji, you should strive to let your shen, yi, qi, jin, and movements reach towards the same point.

When your training is advanced, you can practice using just your shen, yi, qi, and jin. You will not need to pay attention to the movements. As you become even better, you can try just to use shen, yi, and qi, and then just shen and yi. Because movements are the slowest component, followed by jin, qi, yi, and finally shen which is the fastest, your skills will increase in speed as you narrow down your attention or "forget" successive components.

At the highest level of Taiji practice, only shen is necessary. You do not need to care about anything else. Here, "not need to care" does not mean that you do not have to know about or use any of the other components. It means, rather, that you will no longer need to think about how to use these components. They will have become so familiar to you and well integrated with each other that they will seem to occur almost automatically. What was once an unnatural progression that had to be thought out at every moment will have become a naturally flowing sequence that occurs without conscious effort. All you have to do is follow your shen and you will have mastered Taiji skills at the highest level.

TECHNIQUES OF TAIJI QUAN

Because Taiji Quan is based on a particular set of philosophical principles, its techniques are different from those of other martial arts, in spite of some apparent similarities. This section presents descriptions of some of the most well-known and essential Taiji Quan techniques.

Relaxation

Relaxation, or *song*, is the most important technique in basic Taiji forms. Relaxation does not mean that you should avoid exerting energy. Rather, it means that you should avoid the use of extra or unnecessary force. The goal of relaxation is to use the minimum force needed to accomplish your purpose. If you can relax, all of your actions will be more effective.

The ability of qi to move smoothly throughout your body depends on your ability to relax. If you are not able to relax, your qi cannot move freely downward, and so you cannot achieve stability. If you are not able to relax, your qi and your shen cannot move freely upward, and so you cannot be nimble.

When you practice fighting skills, relaxation can help you escape from your opponent's control. It can also save energy, allow the release of powerful internal force, and make your body position more comfortable. Relaxation is the first technique you should understand and master. If you cannot relax, you will never truly be able to master Taiji.

Unfortunately, relaxation is much easier to describe than to achieve. It is, in fact, a very difficult technique to acquire, especially when so much attention and effort must be directed to learning how to use each of the five essential components of the Taiji form. In the form, relaxation results from the ability to sense and expend only the amount of physical energy necessary to move correctly from one posture to the next. In push-hands practice, relaxation requires that you be able to "forget" or ignore the spot at which the opponent touches or holds you. The ability to use minimum force and the ability to ignore the point of an opponent's attack are difficult to learn because neither is a natural response. In fact, one's habits and past training in other physical disciplines are usually concerned with using all the force you can muster and directing this force exactly at the point of attack. Both of these habits must be overcome through practice so that all of the Taiji components can be expressed in a completely relaxed way.

Smoothness of Movement

There are two important aspects to the technique of moving smoothly. The first is that all movements must follow an arc or curve. Curvilinear movement increases relaxation, and is more flexible and easily changed. It can also strengthen and activate the flow of qi.

The second aspect of this technique is that all movements must be performed at a steady, even pace. Even more important than maintaining the continuity of movements, however, is the maintenance of an uninterrupted flow of shen, yi, and qi. This is especially necessary in the practice of jian, where pauses occur between some of the movements. Such apparent breaks in the flow of external movements are not a problem if the internal components of shen, yi, and qi remain uninterrupted. A Taiji principle instructs: "Do not make movements that are interrupted, broken, or uneven. If the movements are broken, do not allow the mind to be interrupted. If the mind is interrupted, use shen to provide continuity." Keep this injunction in mind whenever you practice Taiji and you will gain many benefits, including a strengthening of shen, yi, and qi.

Nimbleness of Movement

A famous Taiji principle prescribes that one should: "Move like a great river." In other words, all parts of the body must be light, nimble, and seamlessly connected when the body moves. Other Taiji precepts instruct that: "When moving, there is no place in the body that does not move," one should "walk like a cat," and one must "suddenly appear, suddenly disappear."

Nimbleness means that your steps and the movements of your body should be light, agile, and quick. The movements may be so big that your opponent cannot follow them or so small that your opponent cannot sense them, but whatever the case, nimbleness can help you follow and control the movements of your opponent and confound his attempts to follow or control yours. Nimbleness allows your qi to move with agility and this in turn allows your movements to embody the principle of sudden appearance and disappearance. This quality is especially important when fighting. If qi can be nimble, jin can be nimble and then your movements can be nimble. The nimbleness of jin is considered by some to be even more important than the nimbleness of the other components. If you can achieve overall nimbleness, your opponent will be easily confused by the apparent suddenness with which qi and jin seem to appear and disappear. This will make it difficult for your opponent to keep his jin unbroken and his yi quiet and focused.

To practice nimbleness, imagine that the top of your head is suspended from above at all times. Keep your mind calm and feel your qi moving actively throughout your body.

Stability

The Taiji principle of stability enjoins one to "Be still as a mountain." This requires that the body be upright and comfortable so that it can withstand force from any of the eight directions. A related injunction is to avoid leaning in any direction.

Stability means that you must keep your body centered, a condition referred to as *zhongding*. When engaged in push-hands practice, you will lose your balance if you lose your center. To be stable or to maintain your center, however, does not imply that your body should not move. The goal is to keep your body stable while it is in motion. If your movements are correct, qi will sink down to the dantian and the resulting feeling will be that your feet are extending down into the ground like the roots of a tree. This feeling indicates that you have achieved stability. Just as yin always contains yang and vice versa, stability must always include a sense of nimbleness, and nimbleness, a feeling of stability.

Emptiness

The technique of *kong*, meaning emptiness, or nothing, is the highest level technique in Taiji fighting skills. In your solo practice, kong is usually felt as a drawing back of some part of your body so that it seems as though nothing is there. It is as if the body or part of the body can be seen but not felt. This feeling of emptiness causes other parts of your body to extend or expand. "Empty chest" (kongxiong), for example, means that your chest should draw back, your back should expand and your arms should extend. Kong always results in increased nimbleness and power. In fighting, kong will create an uncomfortably odd feeling in your opponent, as though something strange has suddenly happened to him. He will feel confused and unprepared to respond. His yi will lose continuity and his movements will become stiff and awkward. His heart may pound and he may have the sensation that it is about to jump out of his mouth. Overall, he will feel as though he has just fallen into a trap set in the earth. It will be as though he put his foot down, shifted his weight onto it, and then discovered that the ground beneath him had disappeared. As a result, he will immediately lose his balance.

To use kong effectively, you should let your opponent feel that he can touch you, control you, and even beat you easily. When he commits himself to a movement, your kong will create the sensation in him that he is not really in contact with you. This will cause a break in his qi, yi, and shen. His body will stiffen and his balance will be lost. At this moment, you will have your best opportunity to redirect against him the force he originally directed against you. This use of kong is called "luring into emptiness" (yin jin luo kong). To accomplish it, the critical variables are timing and direction.

Integration

Integration, or harmony, he, means that all parts of the body are working together. This causes the internal force to become relaxed and powerful. As already noted, one never uses unnecessary force in Taiji. All the muscles of the body share in the overall effort and each one exerts only a small amount of force. With all the muscles working together, relaxation is possible and each movement will be more forceful. Clearly, the force that can be exerted by the whole body working together is greater than that of any one part.

To achieve integration, you must practice liuhe, the "six integrations." Through this practice, your movements will become relaxed, smooth, coordinated, and complete and will more fully reflect shen, yi, qi, and jin. The integration of all the Taiji components will make your reactions more consistent across situations. Liuhe practice involves careful attention to the acupuncture points.

The six integrations include neisanhe (three internal integrations) and waisanhe (three external integrations). The order of the three internal integrations is: xin (literally "heart," but here understood to be a center of awareness) or shen (the expression of heart) integrates yi (mind); yi integrates qi; and qi integrates jin (internal force). The order of the three external integrations is: shoulder integrates hip; elbow integrates knee; and hand integrates foot.

When you practice Taiji, you should try to follow this sequence, so that shen leads or directs yi, yi leads qi, and qi in turn leads jin. Finally, jin leads your movements which then fully reflect all of the internal components. In order to insure this sequencing of Taiji components, you must be very attentive when you practice. At every point in the form, you should know where your shen, yi, qi, and jin are directed and how your body should be moving. You should also be aware of the degree to which you are relaxed. This kind of knowledge and awareness does not come naturally for most people, so you must practice thoughtfully and with dedication for a long time to achieve it. You should develop proficiency at empty-handed Taiji and master its integrations before you undertake the study Taiji Jian. In Taiji practice, the internal integrations are even more important than the external ones.

FOUR TAIJI ELEMENTS

There are four important components of all Taiji skills, and all require that you have cultivated good sensitivity.

Adhering
Zhan means that when you and your opponent touch each other, you must maintain contact at all times, never separating from each other's touch and never allowing the energy between you to be blocked. The technique of zhan allows you to borrow your opponent's force and cause him to lose his rootedness. Thus, you can move him, or in Taiji parlance, "stick" him. In high-level practice, zhan applies to shen, yi, and qi as well as to external physical movements. Blocking the flow of energy is a purely yang process and separating from contact is a purely yin process. Zhan is Taiji because it represents a balance between these two forces.

Cohering
Nian means continually guiding the movements of your opponent so that he cannot escape your control. Paradoxically, you do this by following the movements he makes. Controlling him is a purely yang process; following his movements is a purely yin process. Nian represents a balance between the two processes and is, therefore, Taiji.

Linking
Lian means continously using jin, your internal force, never letting it break while you are in contact with your opponent. To use jin is yang; not to use it is yin. Lian is Taiji because when jin is most fully engaged, lian has qualities of both yin and yang. When you touch the opponent, never let him break away from your lian.

Following
Sui means to avoid resisting. That is, you must always follow your opponent's movements so that he cannot beat you or escape from your control. In this process, you should first follow your opponent completely but then occasionally give him a sense that you have the ability to apply some internal force. It is said: "Forget yourself and

just follow your opponent. Then, you can control him." Just following the opponent's movements is a purely yin process. Used alone, it will make you weak or "soft" and too passive. The occasional appearance of internal resistance introduces yang energy, and thus creates sui, which is Taiji.

While these four techniques can be differentiated from each other for purposes of discussion, they are, in fact, inseparable in practice. They are basic elements of all Taiji skills.

FEATURES OF TAIJI JIAN

Taiji Jian skills and principles include many special features in addition to those of the jian itself, which were discussed in the previous chapter. In this section, these additional features will be described.

Because Taiji Jian is derived from Taiji thought and practice, the two share deep philosophical roots and a detailed and complete set of principles. The depth and strength of this foundation makes possible a high level of mastery. In addition to training your movements so that they are correct, your should always be guided by these central Taiji Quan ideals.

First, you must understand clearly the difference between the concepts of "empty" and "full." These concepts correspond respectively to a feeling of lightness, almost to the point of feeling insubstantial or even nonexistent, and a feeling of being weighted or heavily substantial. Understanding this difference between empty and full will help you perceive how your waist, legs, and feet should move and how these movements should relate to each other.

Second, you must keep moving at all times so that your body feels as though it is in a constant state of change or flux. This will increase your ability to feel the flow of the internal components. Even if there is an occasional pause in your outer movements, you should have the sensation that there is always movement occurring inside your body.

Third, you must observe nine key points regarding the position of your body. These key points are as follows: (1) relax your shoulders and do not raise them during the movements; (2) drop your elbows; (3) keep your chest slightly concave and empty; (4) keep your back erect; (5) relax your waist; (6) draw in your hips; (7) keep your crotch curved and expanded; (8) keep your lower spine straight so that your buttocks do not protrude; and (9) hold your head up as though it were suspended from above.

The fourth Taiji ideal is that all your movements must be graceful. This is a very important feature of all Taiji practice. Never think that the beauty of your movements is irrelevant or useless. When you understand jian deeply and thoroughly, you will understand why this is so.

Fifth, your movements must maintain a rhythmic flow throughout the jian form. Unlike the empty-handed form, it is not important in the jian form that the speed of your movements be constant. Some of your movements can be slightly quicker than others and some a little bit slower. Occasionally, you even can pause and hold one position for a few moments. The important point is to maintain a feeling of comfort and rhythm. Your movements should have a quality of smoothness even though there may be variations in tempo.

Two other important features of jian practice involve the movements of the upper and lower parts of the body and the internal and external components. The movements of the upper body are usually called "hand skills" and those of the lower body are called "step skills" or "footwork." For every movement or technique, the hand skills and the step skills must be fully coordinated with each other. If the hand extends before the foot, or the foot before the hand, the movement is incorrect and cannot be effectively applied. If the hand and step skills are coordinated, the movements of the whole body are likely to be coordinated.

Similarly, for every movement and technique, the internal and external components must be coordinated with each other. Any lack of coordination among these components will interfere with your technique. When fighting, you should try to disturb the coordination between your opponent's internal and external components. This will cause his shen to be disturbed, his yi to be confused, his qi to break, his jin to be scattered, and his balance to be lost. It should be noted that while shen, yi, and qi are internal components and movements are external components, jin has elements of both internality and externality. This is because jin occurs internally but is expressed through external movements.

In all jian fighting skills, you should always act in accordance with the central Taiji tenet of "minimum force," whether in your practice or in combat. You should use zhan, nian, lian, and sui techniques in jian fighting, as well as shen, yi, qi, and jin instead of physical force. You should also include kong or "luring into emptiness" among your fighting skills. Learn to apply your skills efficiently, to find the best body positions, and to use the smallest movements possible.

There are several important points to keep in mind about the jian itself. It should be regarded as a precious and fragile object that must always be used in a careful and gentle way. Never use your jian, especially its edges, to block hard and never let your jian be hit hard by your opponent.

Finally, you must be sensitive to the movements and internal characteristics of your opponent. Always try to avoid his strengths and attack his weak points and take advantage of every opportunity offered. Observe all of these points if you want to develop high-level jian skills.

BASIC TRAINING SEQUENCE

When you begin your study of jian, you should first learn each movement of the form in great detail. The ability to perform the movements correctly is basic to all other skills. It is usually best to study the form several times through from beginning to end at increasing levels of detail. After you have learned the basic movements, you should focus your attention on your footwork and stances and then become adept at control-ling the range, direction, and level of your movements.

Next, you should perfect the ways you hold the sword and practice changing grips quickly and comfortably so that you can correctly execute the different movements. Jian must be held very flexibly so that the angle and thrust of the sword, especially at the edges, can be adeptly changed. An understanding of the application of the differ-ent movements can be very helpful at this point in your training.

Once your movements are correct and can be smoothly performed, you should turn your attention to the training of the internal components, shen, yi, and qi. Let your movements reflect your inner feelings. The inclusion of fighting skills in your prac-tice at this point can help you become more aware of your feelings.

This part of your training will require a lot of time and discipline. Do not rush or become impatient. Practice regularly and with devotion and take one step at a time. It is counterproductive and dangerous to seek shortcuts. There are none to be found and the futile search for them will distract you and will make it less likely that you will ever achieve a high level of expertise.

Finally, do not forget to study Taiji principles. They are the essential foundation of the form and if you do not understand them, it will be impossible to attain high-level mastery.

BENEFITS OF PRACTICE

Taiji Jian is good for your internal Taiji martial arts training. First, it will help you understand the principles of Taiji Quan. Taiji Jian is more complex than the empty-handed Taiji Quan form because of the relationship between the number of touch points and the continuously changing nature of yin and yang. In push-hands, there are two touch points, so yin and yang can be separately associated with each of the two points and changes in yin and yang can be clearly felt. In the jian form, however, there is only one touch point and yin and yang both center on this singular point. In order to create balance, you must use your empty hand and your mind to create a second touch point. Then, yin and yang can be separately associated with the one actual touch point and the touch point created by your mind. To create the second touch point and distribute yin and yang correctly, you must have a sound understanding of Taiji prin-ciples. Because of this, the practice of Taiji Jian will enhance your knowledge of Taiji.

Second, Taiji Jian practice will help in the training of your body, especially your legs and waist. Many requirements of the jian form, such as the balance positions, the footwork and the larger range of movement, are more difficult than those in the empty-handed form. As a result, you must practice harder to master the jian form. In sum, the jian form presents the body with a more demanding set of challenges than does the empty-handed form.

Third, Taiji Jian practice will help in your movement coordination training. Because the movements of the jian form are more difficult than those of the empty-handed form, the timing is also more difficult. Furthermore, in the jian form you have to hold and manipulate a sword. This makes hand skills, step skills, and the coordination of internal and external components more complex. As a result, you may feel uncomfortable at the beginning of your study of Taiji Jian. Gradually your skills and coordination will improve, and you will begin to feel better. Jian practice can yield clear and quite rapid increases in the strength of the internal components shen, yi, and qi.

The fourth effect of Taiji Jian practice is an improvement in stability and nimbleness. While the Taiji empty-handed form is very effective in improving stability of motion for many practitioners, it does not typically lead to similarly great improvements in nimbleness. Because Taiji Jian practice requires many complex step changes and intensive training of shen, yi, qi, and jin, it is more effective than the empty-handed form for helping the body become nimble.

Fifth, Taiji Jian is very good for Qigong training and for improving and maintaining one's health. Because the range of the movements is greater in Taiji Jian than in the empty-handed form and because the sword extends the energy of the body, Qi can move more smoothly and more extensively. Also, the circles of yi can be larger and shen can be projected out to a greater distance. All of these differences contribute directly to an improvement in Qigong training. A sixth result of Taiji Jian practice is an improvement in health. This outcome is a consequence of the concentrated physical training that Taiji Jian demands.

Traditionally, students did not begin weapons training until they had already achieved some expertise in the Taiji empty-handed form. The weapons chosen first were always the short ones, like the dao (broadsword) and jian, but dao and jian forms are different in several ways. The dao form is more nimble and flexible than the jian form. On the other hand, jian training is much more demanding than dao training. Dao practice involves more exclusive attention to fighting skills; jian practice requires concentration on a wider variety of elements, some of which have little if any application to combat situations. Usually, masters suggest that students who want to begin weapons training study the jian form first because its style is closer to empty-handed form and because jian training helps students improve their skills in every respect. It contributes to your fighting skills, your health, your character, and your knowledge of Daoism.

3

FUNDAMENTALS OF THE JIAN

Before studying Taiji Jian, you should be familiar with the characteristics of the jian, the weapon used in the Taiji Jian form. There are many special terms that distinguish the parts and movements of the jian. If you are not familiar with these terms or do not use them correctly, you will not be considered properly trained in the Taiji Jian tradition.

PARTS OF THE JIAN

A traditional Chinese martial arts short weapon, the jian is a straight double-edged sword with a very sharp tip *(fig. 1)*. Generally, only one sword is used in practice but sometimes two swords may be used. In traditional Taiji Jian, only one sword is used but it is changed from hand to hand several times during the form. Although there are different jian designs, the names for the parts of the sword are the same, regardless of stylistic variation.

Body of the Jian
The body, *jianshen,* is usually referred to simply as jian, and has four parts. These are separately made and then assembled by a craftsman or manufacturer.

Jianti refers to the blade, usually made of high-quality steel. The jianti in turn has three main parts, each of which has several alternative names. The tip of the jian is called *jian jian'er,* sometimes *jianfeng* or *biduan.* These terms can be used interchangeably, but sometimes jian jian'er refers exclusively to the tip of the blade, while jianfeng refers to the top two inches of the blade, including the tip. The ridge or spine that extends down the center of jianti is called *jianji, jianbei,* or *jian e'er.*

The edges of the sword are called *jianren.* Because the jian is a straight sword, both sides or edges are identical. Each edge, however, has its own name depending on the relationship between it and the hand holding it. The edge that is on the same side as

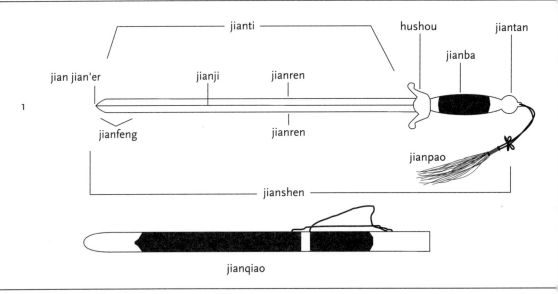

the thumb of the hand holding the sword is called *shangren*, which means the "upper edge." The shangren is considered the upper edge of the jian regardless of the sword's orientation. The edge on the finger side of the hand holding the jian is called *xiaren*, or "lower edge." As with the shangren, the definition of xiaren is unaffected by the sword's orientation. In *figure 2*, shangren is facing up and xiaren is facing down, as one might expect. In *figure 3*, however, shangren is facing down and xiaren is facing up because the hand holding the sword has turned over.

The blade of the jian is usually considered to have three distinct sections *(fig. 4)*. The section extending six inches downward from the tip is called *qianren* or "front edge," which includes the *jianfeng*, the tip. The qianren is extremely sharp and is always used for moves that are quick and light. The six-inch section at the bottom of the blade is referred to as *jiangen* or "jian root." Here, the edges are blunt and can be used to provide a strong defense against attacks from an opponent's weapon. The midsection of the jian is called the *zhongren* or "middle edge." The edges of zhongren are of intermediate sharpness and have varied uses.

The other three parts of the jian body are called the *hushou*, the *jianba*, and the *jiantan*. The first of these, the hushou, is the hand shield or hand guard of the jian. Often beautifully decorated, it is also called *jianshou, tunkou, jiange*, or *yuntou*.

The *jianba*, also called *jianbing* or *jianjing*, is the handle of the jian. Typically made of hardwood, it is usually wrapped in animal skin or some other material to make it more comfortable to hold. The *jiantan* is the end or tassel holder of the jian. Like the hushou, it is often beautifully embellished and, in addition to anchoring the tassel, provides proper balance to the sword.

The Tassel

The *jianpao*, the tassel of the jian, is also known as *jiansui, wanshou, suitou*, or *liubing*. There are two kinds of tassels: *changsui*, which is as long as the body of the jian; and

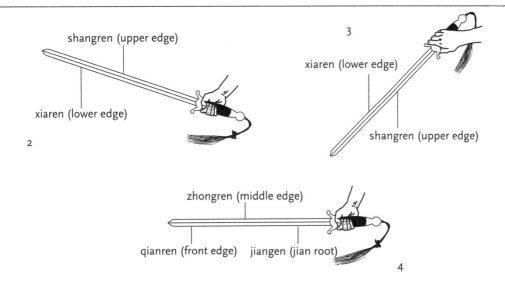

shangren (upper edge)

xiaren (lower edge)

2

xiaren (lower edge)

shangren (upper edge)

3

zhongren (middle edge)

qianren (front edge)   jiangen (jian root)

4

duansui, which is half the length of the jian. Originally made of rope that connected the jian to the practitioner's wrist, the tassels of contemporary jian are always made of beautiful materials. Historically, the jianpao allowed the jian to be thrown outward by the practitioner and then pulled back into his grasp. Today, jianpao are used primarily for show, not combat.

It is not advisable for beginners to use jianpao because the fluttering of the tassel can distract from the task of learning the basic movements of the form. When you have mastered the form, a short tassel may be used, but some movements will have to be altered slightly to allow for the tassel's motion.

The Sheath

Jianqiao or *jianke* refers to the sheath of the jian. A good jianqiao will have a key that can eject the jian automatically. Historically, the jianqiao was adorned with beautiful and expensive ornamentation meant to display the wealth and position of the sword's owner.

LENGTH, WEIGHT, AND BALANCE

The proper length, weight, and balance of the jian vary according to the stature of the practitioner. The standard length of the jian is measured when the sword is held in *fanwo,* or reversed holding position. In this position, your arm should extend down along the side of your torso and the body of the jian should rest along the outside of your arm with the tip pointing up. The tip of a standard-length jian held in fanwo should be level with the top of your ear.

Many practitioners prefer their jian to be slightly longer than this standard. The longer sword allows shen, yi, and qi to extend farther and helps develop jin, internal force. The longer jian can also increase the efficiency of your practice and the sense

of inner balance and comfort. Although a longer sword is more difficult for beginners to control, it is generally recommended for advanced study. Most Taiji swords are longer than regular jian.

There is no standard weight for the jian; the proper weight depends on the feeling the practitioner has when he holds the sword, and relative weights have advantages and disadvantages. Heavy swords, for example, are particularly well suited to techniques that involve chopping, pressing, or thrusting. Practitioners should select swords that are comfortable to hold and that allow them to perform the widest range of techniques with maximum ease and effectiveness.

Correct balance also depends on the practitioner's judgment. A common indication of improper balance is the feeling that the tip of the sword is heavy. This situation is called *zhuishou* or "weighted hand," and will quickly result in fatigue in the wrist. If the sword is properly balanced, the tip will feel just slightly heavy when the jian is held with a very relaxed hand. The center of balance will typically be no more than ten centimeters in front of the hand shield, and you will feel as though the angle of the sword can be adjusted with only slight pressure from the fingers. It is sometimes possible to modify the balance of the sword by replacing a light jiantan, the tassel holder, with a heavier one; even more effective is replacing the handle, the jianba. Attaining the proper balance will create an increased sense of comfort and control when the jian is held and used.

Whatever the length, weight, and balance of the jian, you must feel comfortable when you hold it. If the balance is correct and you practice with discipline, your skills and qi can develop quickly. If the balance is not good, the smooth flow of qi will be impeded. Years ago, it was common practice for Taiji Jian masters and students to specify the desired length, weight, and balance of their swords, which were, as a rule, made to order. Today, it is often difficult to find a good sword that is well matched to the particular requirements of an individual practitioner. In your search for a good jian, consider balance first, then length, and finally weight.

HOLDING POSITIONS

In learning the Taiji Jian form, it is very important to know how to hold the jian. If you hold it correctly, you can wield it much more easily, powerfully, and nimbly. Using the correct grip also allows qi to flow more smoothly and will have a positive influence on the overall development of your skill. The Chinese word *wo* means to hold something in your hand. The two basic hand positions for holding jian are *zhengwo* and *fanwo*. In the form which we will describe in Chapter 6, the jian is sometimes held in one hand and sometimes in the other. The description of grips provided in this section will indicate which hand the sword is held in. It is important to pay close attention to this variable.

Extended Holding Position

In this position, called zhengwo, the sword is held in a handshake grip and is extended away from the body *(fig. 5)*. The "tiger mouth" of the hand (the area between thumb and index finger) is closed at the base of the hand shield (hushou), and faces the tip of the jian (jian jian'er). The zhengwo position is the most frequently used in the form, and has seven grip variations, explained in the next section.

Reversed Holding Position

Called fanwo, in this position the hand shield is held in the palm of the hand. Use the thumb, middle, ring, and little fingers to grasp the hand shield and put the index finger on the handle. The blade of jian is held alongside the forearm and should stay in touch with the elbow. The tiger mouth faces the tassel holder (jiantan) of the sword. When held in this position, the blade of the sword rests against the back of the forearm rather than along the front. *Figure 6* and *figure 7* show both sides of the reversed holding position. In traditional Chinese martial arts, regardless of the style or group, the sword is always held in the left hand in the fanwo position at the beginning and end of the form. Fanwo is also used at several points in the middle of some jian forms.

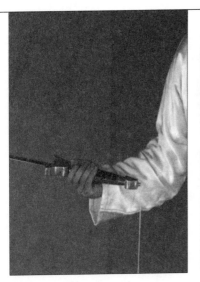
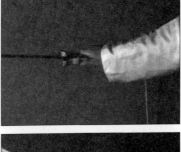

| 8 | 9, 10 | 11 |

JIAN GRIPS

The seven *jianba* or "sword grips" used to hold the sword in zhengwo position are described in this section. The techniques which most commonly use each of the grips will also be indicated. A fuller description of all Taiji Jian techniques will be presented in Chapter 5.

Palm-up grip
In this grip, *yinba*, the palm of the hand holding the sword is facing up while the blade is horizontal *(fig 8)*. The wrist can be flexible or firm, depending on which technique is being used. The palm-up grip is commonly used to press down on or slide along and push the opponent's weapon, as well as to strike at the opponent from the side or to cut from side to side.

Palm-Down Grip
Yangba means the palm of the hand holding the sword is facing down *(fig. 9)*. The blade of the sword is horizontal and, as with yinba, the wrist can be flexible or firm. Both may be used with the same techniques, but when the sword is held in the right hand, applications with yangba are generally executed to the front or left of the body, while with yinba, they are executed to the right.

Thumb-Up Grip
In *shunba* the palm of the sword hand is facing to the left if the sword is held in the right hand or to the right if the sword is held in the left hand *(fig. 10)*. In either case, the thumb of the hand holding the jian is positioned above the handle. The upper edge, shangren, which is always the edge on the thumb-side of the sword hand, is facing up. The lower edge, xiaren, is facing down. The blade of the sword is vertical and

 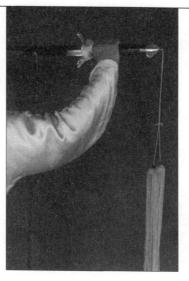 

12   13   14

the wrist must be very flexible so that the jian can be quickly changed without a loss of control. Shunba is used in almost every technique, including pointing, hitting, chopping, cutting, blocking, stirring, and thrusting.

Thumb-Down Grip

In this grip, *niba*, the palm of the sword hand faces to the right if the sword is held in the right hand and to the left if it is held in the left hand *(fig. 11)*. In either case, the thumb of the hand holding the sword is positioned below the handle. In this grip, the upper edge faces down and the lower edge faces up, while the wrist is not flexible. This grip is often used with techniques that require the sword tip to be pointed down.

Palm-Inward Grip

In *neiba*, the palm of the sword hand faces inward, toward the body *(fig. 12)*. This grip is commonly used when the sword must be raised to block a strike from above or to thrust upward at an opponent.

Palm-Outward Grip

In this grip, *waiba*, the palm of the sword hand faces outward, away from the body *(fig. 13)*. Like neiba, the waiba grip is used to block or thrust upward or to raise the sword tip to strike an opponent from above.

Two-Handed Grip

In *heba*, both hands are used to hold the handle of the jian *(fig. 14)*. The wrists should not be flexible. The purpose of this grip is to provide extra power when chopping or thrusting techniques are used.

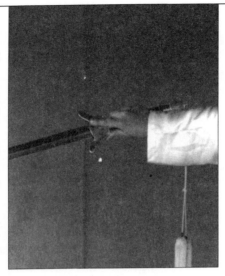

15   16   17

GENERAL GUIDELINES FOR HOLDING THE JIAN

Regardless of the grip used, there are general rules for holding the jian that should always be followed. The first of these is to relax and maintain a feeling of "emptiness" in the palm of your sword hand. Never hold the jian tightly, or qi will be unable to move freely to the sword tip, which will then never acquire concentrated power.

Second, the fingers of the hand that holds the sword must be nimble and flexible at all times. To accomplish this, use only your thumb and middle finger to hold the jian. The tips of these digits should touch so that they form a ring around the handle. When correctly held in this manner *(fig. 15)*, the jian is said to be "wearing a bracelet." The other fingers should remain very flexible, always ready to grasp or release the handle of the jian.

The third general guideline for holding the jian is to keep the fingers of your sword hand nimble so that your grip can be easily and quickly changed at any time. Your thumb should usually be on one side of the handle and your fingers on the opposite side. Occasionally, however, the thumb and index finger may be placed on the side of the hushou, the hand shield *(fig. 16)*, to lend more power and control to the movements.

There are several other variants of the most frequently used hand grips. If you want to turn your hand over and let the palm face outward so that the tip of the jian points down, for example, you need to release the tension in your index, ring, and little fingers almost completely, holding the sword with just your thumb and middle finger *(fig. 17)*. If you want to raise the handle and point the tip down, using the neiba position to make the base, the jiangen, or midsection, zhongren, of the blade more powerful, you need to relax your ring and little fingers and turn your wrist slightly *(fig. 18)*. Alternatively, if you want to raise the handle and point the tip down, using the shunba grip so that the tip becomes more powerful, you need to relax your index finger and

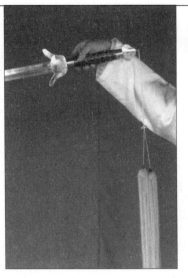

| 18 | 19 | 20 |

move your thumb up on the handle of the sword while turning your wrist slightly down *(fig. 19)*.

FINGER SWORD AND SWORD HELPER

Jianjue, also known as *qijian* or "finger sword," and *jianfa*, also known as *liangzhangjue*, or "sword helper," are the two positions for the hand not holding the jian. Most of the time when you practice, you hold the sword with only one hand. The other hand should then be in either jianjue or jianfa position. The jianjue position adjusts or balances qi and adds direction to the sword. The jianfa position increases the control and leverage of the sword and also adds extra power.

Finger Sword
In the jianjue position, the index and middle fingers of the hand not holding the jian are thought of as forming a second sword. This "finger sword" acts as a balance for the jian, which is held in the other hand. The jianjue position requires that your index and middle fingers remain straight while your thumb, ring, and little fingers are closed to the center of your palm until the nails are almost hidden from view *(fig. 20)*. This position allows qi to flow smoothly through the fingers of the hand holding the jian and then outward to the tip.

Jianjue is often a difficult and uncomfortable position for beginners to master. It requires careful practice and attention. Even some experienced practitioners do not form jianjue correctly. This can result either from the difficulty associated with maintaining the correct position or from a lack of proper instruction. Information about jianjue has been a guarded secret in some groups and so it has not been widely taught. Nevertheless, the finger sword is very important in jian practice, for it adjusts qi, balances the jian, and develops yi. Most of the time, the jianjue is placed behind the tassel holder, the jiantan.

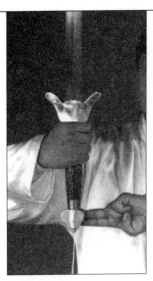

21   22   23

The index and middle fingers of the jianjue sometimes remain in contact with the jiantan to help adjust the angle of the sword so that the tip points in the correct direction (figs. 21–23). The finger sword should never be placed in front of the tip of the sword, nor should it ever move along the jianren, the edges of the sword.

Sword Helper

The jianfa, or sword helper, position requires that your index and middle fingers remain straight while your thumb is bent and put behind your index finger. The ring and little fingers should be bent so that their tips touch at the center of your palm (fig. 24). Although jianfa is very different from jianjue, failure to distinguish between these two positions is a common error. Unlike jianjue, jianfa is used to provide additional control and leverage, and is always placed on the tassel holder, the jiantan. The index and middle fingers wrap around one side of the jiantan and the thumb wraps around the other. In this position, the sword appears to be held by both hands but it is actually being held by only one hand and supported by three fingers of the other. If the tip of the sword needs to be moved downward or forward with extra power, you can use the index and middle fingers to push the jiantan up (fig. 25). Alternatively, when you want to move the tip upward or backward with additional force, you can use your thumb to push the jiantan down (fig. 26).

When using the sword helper, your thumb, index, and middle fingers may be placed on the jiantan at same time (fig. 27), making it easy to control the movement of the sword tip in any direction. Be careful to distinguish this position from the two-handed grip, heba, in which all the fingers of the second hand wrap around the handle of the sword and hold it snugly against the palm. This grip is used for powerful chopping or thrusting. Unlike heba, jianfa is used when the sword must be moved nimbly and with agility, to make small, quick, and suddenly forceful blocks or thrusts. Jianfa is the hand position you should be using most of the time.

| 24 | 25, 26 | 27 |

JIAN CIRCLES AND JIAN FLOWERS

Jian circles, called *jianquan*, or jian flowers, *jianhua* (also known as *wan jianhua*, making flowers), involves moving the jian in circles. The three basic configurations in which the jian can be moved are a point, a straight line, and a circle. The most common of these is the circle. Circular movements allow the jian to be manipulated in an agile, smooth, and flexible manner. Circles facilitate transitions between all jian techniques and occur at several different points throughout the form. You should carefully and thoroughly practice jian circles before you begin to learn the postures of the form.

Some of the most common jianquan movements are front circles, horizontal, or overhead circles, and vertical, or side circles. Jianquan can be large or small, the size depending upon the amount of internal force released by your body, the part of the body from which the internal force is released, and the size of your steps. If the internal force is released from your waist and your steps are large, you can make very big circles. If the internal force is released from your wrist, you can make circles so small that they will be almost invisible even to the most attentive observer. Side circles can be made by using the internal force from your elbows and shoulders. Jianquan are always combined in sequences and trace the outlines of an imaginary ball turning around your body. It is said of jianquan that "Your body follows your jian and your jian makes circles to cover your body."

The descriptions and illustrations below present only a few types and basic variations of jian circles, which are infinitely variable. When jian circles are used in fighting, they need not be completely formed; rather, they can appear as arcs that flow seamlessly into one another. You should, however, feel as though you are drawing a set of complete circles instead of just arcs. This will help you practice your movements and focus your mind. When you practice circles and circle changing, the most important point to keep in mind is that all your movements must be smooth.

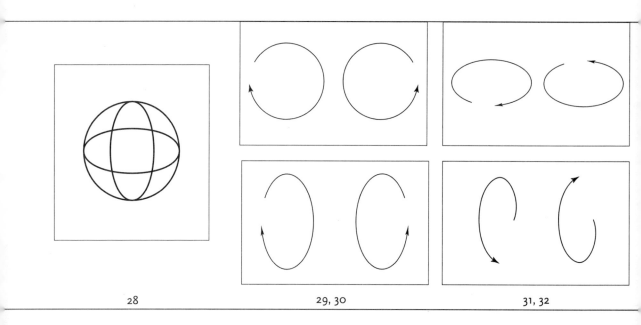

28   29, 30   31, 32

Practicing jian circles can help you develop your footwork and increase your coordination and integration. It can also improve your fighting techniques by increasing your ability to conserve energy and gain good position, especially when using defense skills. Additionally, it can increase the directness and efficiency of your attack skills.

The Basic Jianquan Ball

The jianquan ball *(fig. 28)* is formed by circles in three planes: front circles, vertical circles, and horizontal circles. Jianquan circles are based on the same principles as "random circles" in Taiji Quan. Each of the three basic circles can be created in front of, or to either side of the body. Taken together, the three planes in which circles can be drawn allow jianquan to be changed in any direction. When the jian is held in your right hand, a circle drawn in a counterclockwise direction is referred to as *zhengzhuan* or a "normal" circle; a circle drawn in a clockwise direction is referred to as *nizhuan* or a "reversed" circle. If the jian is held in your left hand, a circle drawn in a clockwise direction is a normal circle, while a circle drawn in a counterclockwise direction is a reversed circle. Jian circles can be linked together in many different combinations, but every combination, regardless of complexity, is derived from the central notion of the jianquan ball.

Front Circles

Circles can be drawn in front of your body with the jian in either a clockwise or counterclockwise direction. Front circles *(fig. 29)* are most commonly used in fighting, especially for attacks that are launched straight ahead. You should practice front circles to increase the speed and agility of your movements.

Vertical Circles

Clockwise and counterclockwise vertical circles *(fig. 30)* can be drawn by the jian on either side of your body. These circles are always used to create smooth transitions

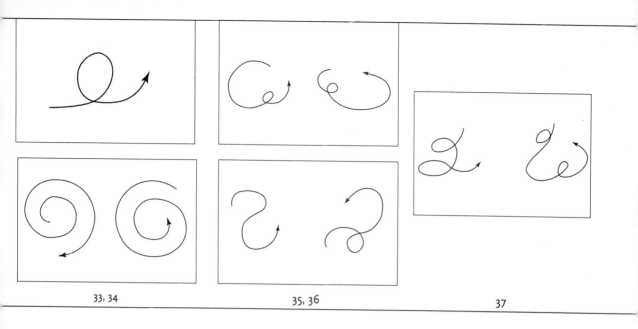

between attack and defense or defense and attack. Good footwork is necessary for the effective use of vertical circles in fighting situations.

Horizontal Circles

Horizontal circles *(fig. 31)* can be drawn by the jian over or in front of your head. This kind of circle is always used as a transition between attack and defense or defense and attack. The ability to turn smoothly and quickly from your waist is an essential skill for the proper application of horizontal circles.

Turnover Circles

These circles *(fig. 32)* are made by turning over your wrist or forearm. They allow the jian to change direction very quickly and for this reason, are used in many jian techniques.

Chain Circles

This circle *(fig. 33)* is actually a sequence of circles drawn one by one, as in a chain. Any of the jianquan circles can be arrayed as a chain.

Spiral Circles

Spiral circles *(fig. 34)* are very useful. When you move the jian backwards, you should usually do so by making spiral circles that get progressively larger. This is illustrated in the picture on the left. If you move the jian forward, you should do so by making spiral circles that get progressively smaller. This is shown in the picture on the right.

Changes in Size and Direction of Circles

Jian circles may be changed in size, from large to small or from small to large *(fig. 35)*. Circles may be also be used to change the direction of the jian *(fig. 36)*, upward, down-

38 39, 40 41, 42

ward, or to the left or right. The circles of the jian should be made smoothly during these transitions.

Linking Circles

Changing from one kind of circle to another *(fig. 37)* can be accomplished in a variety of ways. It is best to keep the circular movements small when making these transitions, especially if you are making several in quick succession. As with the random circles of Taiji Quan, all transitions should be smooth and the combination of circles should be inventive.

HOW TO CARRY AND PREPARE TO USE THE JIAN

Traditionally, there are several ways to carry the jian, depending upon your role and situation. In the past, when people routinely walked long distances, jian were usually carried on the backs of their owners. Generals, however, have always carried their jian at the waist. Although this looks impressive and is fine for ceremonial purposes, it is rather impractical for combat, especially if the jian is long and must be unsheathed quickly. So most practitioners find that simply carrying the jian in the hand is the most practical way.

However, there are several rules for carrying the jian by hand correctly. If the jian is sheathed, you should hold the sheath in your left hand. The left arm should be bent so that the jiantan points up *(fig. 38)*. The sheath should stay in touch with the inside of your left forearm and should be held along the side of your torso.

When the jian is held in this manner, it can be unsheathed quickly and used immediately. Simply grasp the jian with your right hand in zhengwo position to remove it from its sheath *(figs. 39, 40)*. However, when using the jian for any purpose, whether practicing, fighting, or performing, the more common rule is always to start by holding the sheathed jian in your left hand *(fig. 41)*. Grasp the handle of the jian with your

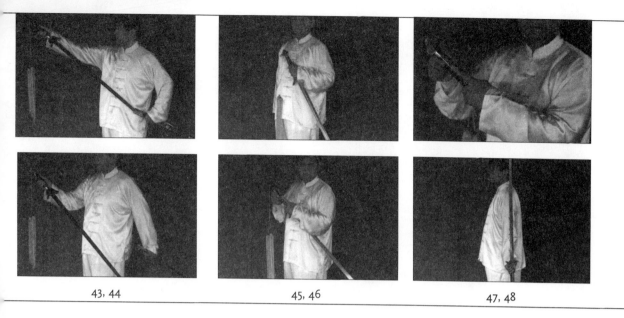

43, 44 45, 46 47, 48

right hand *(fig. 42)*, and remove it from its sheath *(fig. 43)*. Put the sheath down *(fig. 44)*, and transfer the jian to your left hand *(fig. 45)*. This is also the correct position for carrying the unsheathed jian. Once the jian is unsheathed for any purpose, be careful never to let its edges touch your body.

To use the jian, observe the following sequence of movements: First, use your right hand on the jiantan to help your left hand change to the fanwo position *(fig. 46)*. If the jian has a tassel, you will need to use your middle finger to hold it for more control *(fig. 47)*. Then, lower your left arm down along the side of your torso *(fig. 48)*, so that the jiantan points down and the jian tip points up. Maintain this position until you start to use the jian. It is said: "Always begin to use the jian from the reversed holding position in the left hand."

Although knowledge of how to carry and unsheathe the jian will not affect your training, it is important for improving the overall quality of your practice. It will add to your respect for the weapon and the traditions of training. It will also increase your understanding of the details that comprise high-level skill. It is from knowledge such as this that you will gradually gain a sense of the courage, honesty, and worthiness that holding and using the jian can bring. With attentive study, respect for this noble weapon will grow in your heart and your understanding of the art of Taiji Jian will deepen. Without proper knowledge of how to carry, unsheathe, and prepare the jian for use, you will never be considered well educated and properly trained, regardless of how adept you may become at the jian form.

4

BASIC MOVEMENTS OF TAIJI JIAN

While some of the basic movements of the Taiji Jian form are similar to those of the Taiji Quan form, others are unique. Each basic jian movement can be combined with the techniques that will be described in the next chapter. If you understand the basic movements and can combine them appropriately with the techniques, your Taiji Jian form will improve. If you lack this understanding, you will develop habits that can interfere with your progress and make it increasingly difficult for you to improve your form.

Learning to perform the basic movements correctly is the first step in traditional jian training. Such proficiency is crucial because it provides the foundation for all later learning. Without it, high-level mastery is difficult, if not impossible to achieve. Nevertheless, many people today do not devote nearly enough time and attention to this essential stage of the training process.

Each basic movement has its own standard for correct execution. Until relatively recently, these were kept secret by the groups who developed and practiced them. Even within groups, these standards were often not clearly and directly explained to students. Instead, movements were demonstrated by the master and then each student was left to perfect them and to infer the standards for himself by diligent and focused practice. In the traditional view, if you do not perform the basic movements of Taiji Jian form correctly, it will be assumed either that you did not receive serious training from your master or that you never had a real master at all.

PRINCIPLES OF BODY MOVEMENT

In the Taiji Jian form, the movements of the body must always adhere to the basic Taiji Quan principles expressed in what are called the Nine Key Points. Each of these principles refers to a particular kind of movement and focuses on a key acupoint or pair of acupoints. To locate these acupoints, refer to the charts in the Appendixes.

Relax the Shoulders

Relaxed shoulders, *songjian*, will help you relax your arms and allow your qi and internal force to extend through your arms. If you cannot relax your shoulders, the muscles of your arms and hands will tighten and you will be unable to move with strength and fluidity. Your mind should be focused on the *jianjing* acupoints of the shoulders.

Drop the Elbows

Dropping your elbows, *zhuizhou*, will allow your qi and internal force to extend to your hands. As a result, your wrists will acquire greater power and will move more nimbly. Dropping your elbows will also increase the integration of your movements. Your mind should be focused on the *quchi* acupoints of the elbows.

Empty the Chest

To empty the chest, *hanxiong*, means to draw your chest back slightly to create a feeling of hollowness on your torso. This movement will cause your qi to sink smoothly and easily down to dantian along *renmei*, the acupuncture meridian which is the centerline on the front of your torso. It will also improve your footwork. Focus your mind on the key acupoint *tanzhong*, which is on the center of your chest.

Straighten the Back

You must always keep your back straight, an action called *babei*. Never let it hunch forward or sway backward. Proper alignment will help your qi ascend smoothly and easily along *dumei*, the acupuncture meridian which is the centerline on the back of your torso. When combined with the empty chest, babei will allow your qi to move around your body in a circle, extending from your head down to your toes and back up again. This circular movement of qi facilitates the release of internal force and is the most important element in your basic internal training. You should focus on *jiaji*, the acupoint located at the center of the back, to help you align this part of your body.

Relax the Waist

Called *songyao*, this is one of the most important points because it involves your waist, the center of your body and the locus of control for all movements. If your waist is tight, you will not be able to relax any other part of your body. Your qi will not be able to move smoothly through your body, your internal force will not be sustained, your arms will not be flexible, and your footwork will not be nimble. The key acupoints for relaxing your waist are the *mingmen* on the center of your lower back and *shenque* on your navel. You should alternate your focus between these two points.

Draw in the Hips

Called *choukua*, this means that when you are about to take a step, you should feel as though the hip that is above the unweighted leg (the leg which will be moved) is being raised up and placed on top of the hip that is over the weighted leg. This will make all your footwork quick, nimble, stable, and powerful. In choukua, the key acupoints are the *huantiao* on the hips. When you step, focus on the unweighted side, and then on the other, when it becomes the unweighted side.

Curve and Expand the Crotch
The inside of both your legs and crotch should curve and expand. These adjustments, called *guodang*, will help your qi sink smoothly to your legs without becoming dissipated. Guodang will also increase your root and the power in your legs. It will make your whole body very nimble. The key acupoints for this are the *yonglingquan* points on your knees. To curve and expand your crotch correctly, put your mind on these acupoints and make sure that each knee is aligned directly above the toes of the corresponding foot.

Tuck the Buttocks under the Lower Back
Liutun means to keep your lower spine straight so that your buttocks do not protrude. This movement will allow your waist to remain relaxed and your shen to rise. The key acupoint for liutun is *weilu*, on the tailbone. Weilu should be aligned above an imaginary line drawn between your heels.

Suspend the Head
Dingtouxuan means that you must always hold your head erect, as though it were suspended from above. This is one of the most important points. If it is not followed, none of the Taiji Jian movements, skills, or techniques can be effectively executed. Correctly performed, dingtouxuan will enhance the development of your shen, yi, and qi and will make your body alert and nimble. It will also adjust the balance of your body and increase your ability to focus your mind on the acupoints. The key acupoint for dingtouxuan is *baihui*, which is on top of the head. Imagine that you are using baihui to hang your whole body up. Put your mind on this acupoint and make sure that it is aligned directly above the *huiyin* acupoint, which is midway between the sexual organs and the anus.

Additional Points to Note
There are three other important aspects of movement that should always be observed in the practice of Taiji Jian form. The first of these concerns the angle at which the body is held. Several jian techniques require that the body lean in one direction or another. Great care should be taken that when your body does lean, the baihui point and the huiyin point remain aligned. As long as these two points are aligned, your form will be correct even if your body is leaning forward or back. If these two points are not aligned, you will easily lose balance and power. A general tenet of Taiji forms is that whenever the internal components are correct, the external movements are of

relatively little importance. For high-level masters who have perfected the use of the internal components, the external movements are always correct, even if they do not conform exactly to standard configurations.

The second aspect of body movement that must be observed for proper practice of Taiji Jian concerns the waist. In the jian form, the movements of the waist should be larger than they are in the empty-handed form. Because of this distinction, the jian form provides an especially good opportunity to increase your awareness of the movements of your waist. In all Taiji forms, the waist is the main locus of control for all body movements and it must always remain relaxed and nimble. When the waist moves, be careful to keep your hips as stationary as possible.

The third aspect of Taiji Jian that should be carefully studied is the movement of the lower body. The Taiji Jian form includes many postures in which the body must assume a crouched position. To master this position you must practice diligently to develop a good sense of balance and to increase the strength of your legs.

HAND MOVEMENTS

Although the jian is held in one hand throughout most of Taiji Jian form, it is important always to be aware of the other hand as well. Your attention should be evenly divided between the two hands. The empty hand and the jian hand should always be symmetrical in movement and in your mind. There are, as described in Chapter 2, many different hand positions that can be used to hold the jian. Despite the variety of grips, however, the basic Taiji injunction to remain relaxed at all times applies to all hand positions. Relaxing your hands allows jian movements to be changed with agility, speed, and nimbleness. Relaxing your hands allows qi and the internal force to flow more easily to the jian and thereby increases the power and quickness of sword movements.

The ability to enhance the flow of qi to the tip of the jian is the most important skill in Taiji Jian and the hands are the most important part of the body for the development of this ability. The free and smooth movement of qi depends as much on the empty hand, whether held in jianjue or jianfa, as on the hand that holds the sword. Attention to the empty hand will create a balance among the Taiji elements of qi, internal force, mind, and movement.

Paying close attention to the empty hand will also prevent injuries that might be caused by allowing it to move along the edges of the jian or over the tip. You should also be careful never to pass the jian over your head or around your body.

STANCES

A stance, or *buxing*, refers to the position of the feet and legs when a stationary posture is assumed. It is a very important aspect of Taiji Jian training. If your stances are not correct, you will never achieve high-level skills and you may injure yourself. If

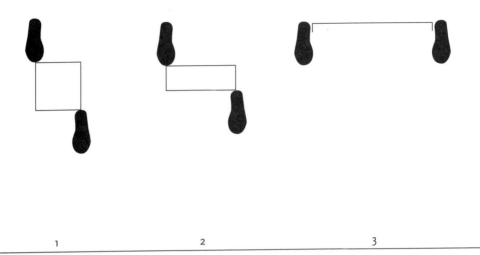

your stances are correct, your rooting and balance will be improved. Proficiency in assuming correct stances will increase your ability to relax, to enhance the flow of qi, to sense the internal Taiji components, and to acquire good fighting skills. It is said that when you stand in front of a master, he can tell immediately from your stance what your Kungfu level is.

As with the basic movements, there are some aspects of Taiji Jian stances that are similar to those of Taiji Quan. In both forms, the distance between the feet is important and the measure of distance is the length of the practitioner's foot. In the standard stance, called *zhengbu*, both the distance between the heel of the front foot and the toes of the back foot and the horizontal distance between the feet are one foot-length (*fig. 1*). In the wide stance, called *yubu*, the distance between the heel of the front foot and the toes of the back foot is half the length of the practitioner's foot, while the horizontal distance between the feet is one-and-a-half foot-lengths (*fig. 2*). In the side stance, called *hengkaibu*, the feet are parallel to each other and the distance between them is two-and-a-half foot-lengths (*fig. 3*).

In most stances, all or most of the body's weight is borne by only one leg. The name of the stance often includes an indication of which leg bears the weight. A left bow stance, for example, is a bow stance in which the weight is borne by the left leg. In the case of the insubstantial stances, the left-right distinction can lead to some confusion. A left insubstantial stance is one in which the weight is borne by the left leg; the right leg is insubstantial. Careful attention to this point will help you avoid mistakes. Because the stance definitions in this chapter are not dependent on which leg bears the weight, the indication of "left" or "right" will not be used.

Each stance will be described in terms of traditional standards. These standards have been developed over the years to help practitioners learn the basic movements and skills of Taiji Jian. Once the Taiji Jian form has been well learned and the skills mastered, the standards become unimportant and you can let all your movements be guided by your feelings rather than by a set of traditional conventions.

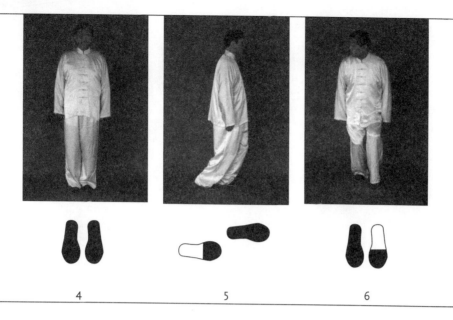

| 4 | 5 | 6 |

The standards also become less important in fighting situations. Generally, your stances should be smaller than the standard specifications when you are fighting because smaller stances allow you to move more nimbly. Nevertheless, it is still important for you to be familiar with the proper standards even if your goal is primarily to develop fighting skills. Because knowledge of the standards is necessary for mastery of Taiji Jian form, it is also fundamental to the training of fighting skills. The relevance of standards at different stages of your Taiji Jian practice and for different purposes applies not only to stances but also to the step practice that will be described later.

The stances used in Taiji Jian form are described and illustrated in this section. The photographs show the body position for each stance and the line drawings show the foot positions. In the latter illustrations, the white part of the outline indicates the part of the foot that is not touching the ground and the black part of the outline indicates the part of the foot that is touching the ground.

Merging Stance

In *bingbu*, or merging stance, the feet are close and parallel and the weight of the body is placed evenly on both legs (*fig. 4*). In this position, the feet are said to be "merged," or closed. Despite the even weight distribution, your mind should be focused on only one leg at a time so that you do not become "double-weighted."

Following Stance

In *genbu*, or following stance, the feet are almost merged but actually the weight is on just one of the legs and only the ball of the empty or non-weight-bearing foot touches the ground. There are two different following stances. In the back following stance *hou genbu*, the ball of the empty foot is placed just behind the "full" or weighted foot and usually the legs are slightly bent (*fig. 5*). In the side following stance *ce genbu*, the ball of the empty foot touches the ground beside the weighted foot and the legs are always bent (*fig. 6*).

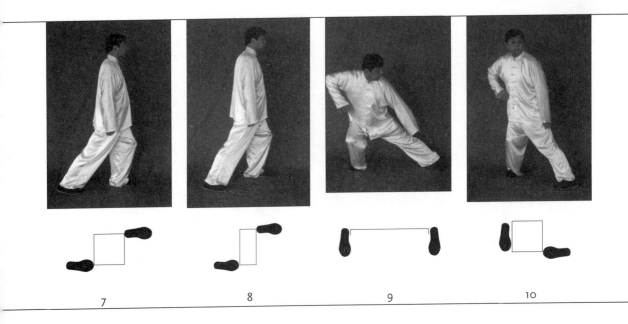

7   8   9   10

Bow Stance

In *gongbu*, the bow stance, one leg is bent and bears the full weight of the body while the other leg is straight and empty. There are four different bow stances: the standard bow stance, the wide bow stance, the side bow stance, and the dingba bow stance. In the standard bow stance, *zheng gongbu*, the front leg is bent and bears the full weight of the body, the back leg is straight and empty, and the toes of both feet point forward *(fig. 7)*. The feet are placed one foot-length apart horizontally and one foot-length apart from front to back to form a standard distance stance.

The wide bow stance, *yu gongbu*, is the same as the standard bow stance except that the feet are placed in the wide distance position, which is one-and-a-half foot-lengths apart horizontally and one-half foot-length apart from front to back *(fig. 8)*.

In the side bow stance, *ce gongbu*, also called the lay-down stance, *pubu*, the feet are parallel to each other and are placed two-and-a-half foot-lengths apart to form a side distance stance *(fig. 9)*. The full or weight-bearing leg is bent and the empty leg is straight.

The *dingba* bow stance, or *dingbabu*, is a hybrid of the standard bow stance and the side bow stance. The standard bow stance is taken first and then the front foot is turned inward on the heel ninety degrees *(fig. 10)*. The back foot is not moved. The front leg is kept bent and bears the full weight of the body, while the back leg is straight and empty.

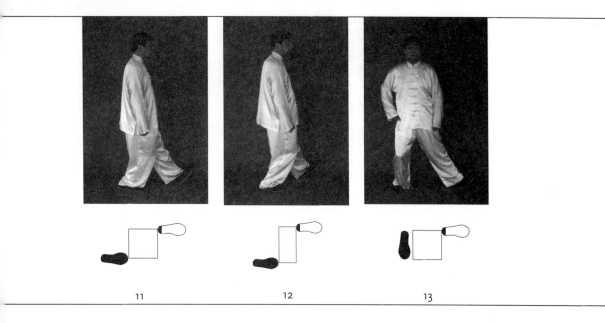

11   12   13

Sitting Stance

In *zuobu*, or sitting stance, the back leg is bent and bears the full weight of the body, while the front leg is straight and empty with the heel touching the ground and the toes pointing upward. There are three different sitting stances: the standard sitting stance, or *zheng zuobu*, in which the distance between the two feet is the standard distance of one foot-length *(fig. 11)*; the wide sitting stance, *yu zuobu*, in which the distance between the feet is the wide distance of one-and-a-half foot-lengths *(fig. 12)*; and the side sitting stance, *ce zuobu*, in which the empty leg is extended to the side of the fully weighted leg *(fig. 13)*.

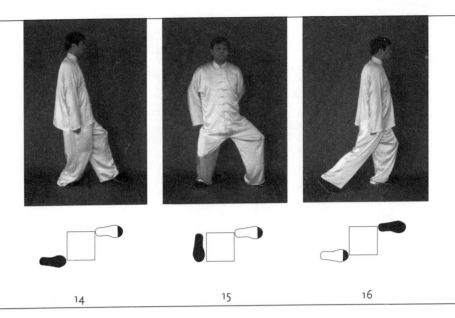

14   15   16

Insubstantial Stance

In *xubu*, the insubstantial stance, one leg is bent and bears all or most of the body's weight. The foot of this leg is flat on the ground. The other leg, which is called the "empty" or "insubstantial" leg, is also bent and carries little or none of the body's weight. Only the ball or the toes of this foot touches the ground. In the xubu stance, the usual weight differences between the legs are: one hundred-to-zero percent; eighty-to-twenty percent; seventy-to-thirty percent; or even sixty-to-forty percent.

There are three xubu stances. In the standard insubstantial stance, also called the sitting insubstantial stance, *zuo xubu*, the empty leg is extended in front of the body *(fig. 14)*. In the side insubstantial stance, *ce xubu*, the empty leg is extended to the side of the body and the knee and toes of this leg point out to the side *(fig. 15)*. In the back insubstantial stance, *hou xubu*, the empty leg is positioned behind the body *(fig. 16)*. It is important in the insubstantial stances always to keep the knee and ankle of the empty leg vertically aligned.

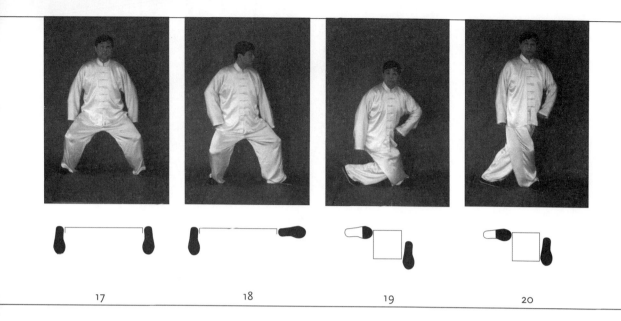

17   18   19   20

Horse Stance

In *mabu*, the horse stance (more accurately, the riding-horse stance), also called *zheng mabu*, the feet are parallel to each other and separated by two-and-a-half foot-lengths to form a side distance stance *(fig. 17)*. Both legs are bent and each knee should be directly above the toes of the corresponding foot. There are two different horse stances. In the variation typically referred to as mabu, the weight is evenly divided between the two legs. In the half-horse stance, called *ban mabu*, one foot points forward and bears sixty percent of the body's weight, while the second foot points to the side *(fig. 18)*. In both horse stances, the mind should always be focused on only one leg.

Rest Stance

In *xiebu*, or the rest stance, the legs are crossed and bent. The front foot is always pointed away from the body and bears almost all of the body's weight. Only the ball of the back foot touches the ground. The knee of the back leg should touch the back of the front leg as though the back leg were resting on the front leg.

There are two different rest stances: the low rest stance, which is usually referred to as xiebu, and the high rest stance (or twist stance), known as *gao xiebu*. In the low rest stance, the body is in a squatting position and the body's full weight is usually on the front foot *(fig. 19)*. In the high rest stance, the legs are only slightly bent and the body's weight is divided, but not evenly, between the two legs *(fig. 20)*.

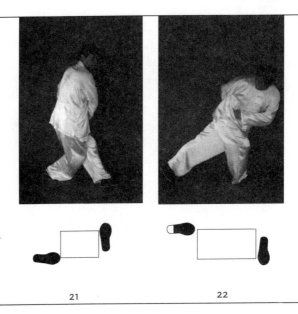

21   22

Cover Stance

In *gaibu*, the cover stance, the legs are crossed. The front foot is always pointed outward from the body. One leg is bent and bears most of the body's weight, while the other leg is almost straight. *Figure 21* shows gaibu with the front leg straight, while *Figure 22* shows the stance with the back leg straight. Unlike the variations of other stances, the two different cover stances do not have separate names. To add to the confusion, the step that one takes to form gaibu stance is also called gaibu. This step will be described later in the chapter.

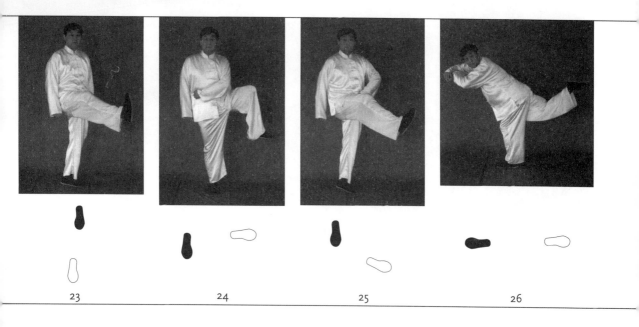

23   24   25   26

Single-Leg Stance

In *dulibu*, the single-leg stance, for obvious reasons sometimes called the balance stance, one leg is raised off the ground and the full weight of the body is balanced on the other leg. There are many different kinds of single-leg stance. The leg which supports the body can be straight or bent and the raised leg can be held in a variety of positions *(figs. 23–26)*. Single-leg stances can be very helpful in developing an awareness of internal force and an increased ability to use this force skillfully. In general, the balance stances are used more for the practice of Kungfu than for direct application to fighting situations.

27

STEPS

The term *bufa* refers to the movement of the feet or to footwork in general, which is a very important part of Taiji Jian training. A traditional view holds that thirty percent of Taiji Jian skill is in the hands and seventy percent is in the feet. This difference between the importance of step skills and that of hand skills is especially marked in fighting.

Footwork provides the foundation for all the other movements. If your steps are not correct and well executed, none of your other movements will be adequate. Good footwork is a basic component of the ability to relax and to move with agility and stability. It can also improve your use of jian techniques and strengthen your internal force.

The steps used in Taiji Jian form are described and illustrated in this section. The photographs show the movement of steps and the line drawings show the route of the feet for each movement. In these illustrations, the white, unshaded foot indicates the position of the foot before a step is taken and the solid black foot indicates the foot position either after a step has been taken or when it has never been moved. The arrows indicate the directions in which the feet are moving. The numerals indicate the sequence in which the steps should be taken.

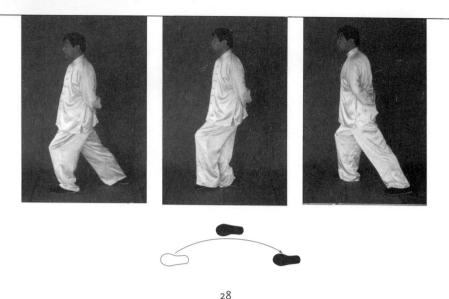

28

Step Forward with the Back Foot

Called *shangbu*, this is a step in which the back foot moves forward and is placed in front of the fixed foot *(fig. 27)*. As the back foot moves forward, it follows a curved path, first being placed alongside the fixed foot and then moved forward to a position ahead of the fixed foot. The distance between the two feet at the end of the step is either one or one-and-a-half foot-lengths, depending on the kind of stance that is being formed. Because shangbu is a big step, it is taken slightly more slowly than smaller steps and is used only when you need to move far forward.

Step Backward with the Front Foot

Chebu is a step in which the front foot moves back so that it is behind the fixed foot *(fig. 28)*. Again, the moving foot must follow a curved path, moving first alongside the fixed foot and then to the front and side of the fixed foot. Like shangbu, chebu is a large and slow step, used when you need to move back a long distance.

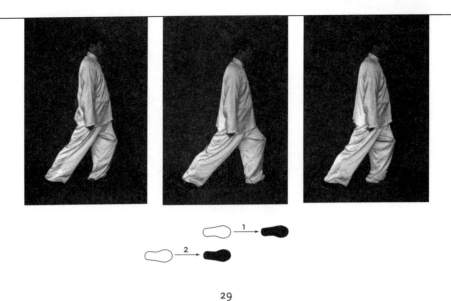

29

Step Forward with the Front Foot

Jinbu is a step in which the front foot moves further forward, with the back foot usually just following *(fig. 29)*. It is a quick step that is used frequently and in situations that require you to move forward swiftly.

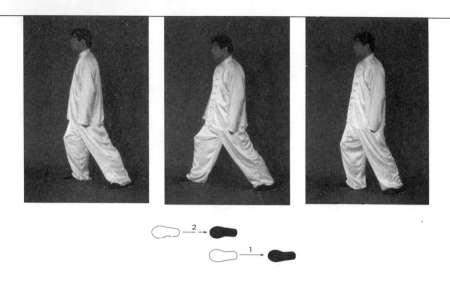

30

Step Backward with the Back Foot

Tuibu is a step in which the back foot moves further back, with the front foot usually just following *(fig. 30)*. Like jinbu, it is a quick step often used in situations that require you to move back swiftly.

31

Side Step

Hengkaibu is a step in which the left foot moves to the left while the right foot remains stationary or the right foot moves to the right while the left foot remains stationary *(fig. 31)*. Hengkaibu is used very often for moving quickly to the side.

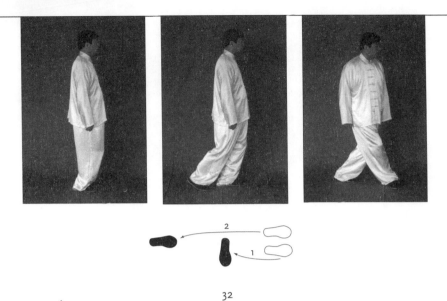

32

Back Insert Step and Sneak Step

Daochabu is a step in which one foot moves back and is inserted behind the other foot *(fig. 32)*. The first foot usually takes a half-step back and is turned on its heel so that the toes of this foot point outward. The other foot moves straight back, coming to a rest behind the first foot, with only the ball of the foot touching the ground. This step always terminates in a rest stance.

In daochabu, the step back is taken with the body facing forward. If the backward step is taken to change the direction in which the body faces, the step is referred to as *toubu,* meaning "sneak step," because the opponent does not know that it will lead to a sudden turn. Daochabu is a fast and frequently used step for moving backward and turning quickly to the side.

33

Cover Step

Gaibu, or cover step, is one in which the back foot moves forward. As it moves forward and passes in front of the front foot, it turns outward and comes to rest alongside the fixed foot *(fig. 33)*. Having made the step, the foot is placed flat on the ground. This step can result in a rest stance, in which most of the body's weight is on only one leg, or a cover stance, in which the body's weight is usually more evenly divided between the two legs. Gaibu is a fast step and is used very often for moving forward and for turning the body to the side quickly.

34

Buckle Step

Koubu is a step in which the back foot moves forward *(fig. 34)*. This foot touches the ground heel first and then the toes turn in so that they face the toes of the other foot and are closer to each other than the heels are. The knees should be close to each other and may even touch. Koubu is a frequently used and fast step for turning the body inward.

35

Swing Step

In *baibu*, the back foot moves forward, then swings to the outside and touches the ground heel-first *(fig. 35)*. The toes of this foot point outward so that the heels are at right angles to each other. Baibu is a very commonly used fast step for turning the body outward.

36

Pad Step

Dianbu is a half-step that sometimes has the appearance of a jump. It is taken before or just after any one of the other steps *(fig. 36)*. If, for example, a step forward is taken with the back foot, the front foot may take a half-step forward just before the back foot is moved. If the back foot steps next to the front foot, the front foot may take a half-step forward just as the back foot moves alongside. Dianbu does not involve either a change in stance and or a shift of weight. It is a common and quick step that is very useful for the development of nimble footwork and for maintaining your posture as you move.

INTEGRATION OF MOVEMENTS
AND INTERNAL COMPONENTS

The hands, eyes, body, and step are considered to be "outside," or external components of the Taiji Jian form, and they must be seamlessly coordinated. Shen, yi, qi, and internal force are considered to be "inside," or internal components, and they, too, must be integrated. Taiji Jian training of the external and internal components will lead to the development of "six integrations," which you will be able to feel more clearly as your practice progresses. The internal components and external components should be acquired and practiced together so that they become coordinated and integrated.

In integration training, the movement of the jian must be coordinated with the movements of your body. Your body's movements, in turn, should follow your jin or internal force and your jin should follow your qi. With practice, jin and qi will be able to shift to any part of your body and move in any direction instantaneously. As integration increases, these two components will move around your body smoothly and agilely as they follow your mind, yi, and its focus points. Finally, yi follows shen, which is the lead component in the entire sequence.

When you begin your practice of the jian, you will be most aware of the outside movements of your body. These movements will become more smoothly coordinated as your training continues. Gradually, you will begin to feel the internal components and these, too, will become stronger and more concentrated as your training progresses. As you become aware of each component, it is important that you work to integrate it with the others. The integration between external and internal components is one of the most important aspects of internal Kungfu training and only by achieving this kind of integration will you be able to advance to a new and higher level of skill.

Integration training is easy to describe but difficult to accomplish. It not only depends on concentrated practice but also requires that you think deeply about the fundamental principles of Taiji. You must be alert to every detail until all your movements can be done with ease and naturalness and until they seem simply to be following feelings that come directly from your heart.

5

BASIC TECHNIQUES OF TAIJI JIAN

All Taiji Jian skills consist of one or more basic techniques. Because some of the basic techniques are similar to those of other styles, it is important to keep Taiji principles in mind during your training. You should work on the techniques separately until you have developed a thorough understanding of each one. This kind of practice will help you become familiar with the details of all jian movements and will allow you to hold the sword more comfortably and use it more effectively. It will also be of great benefit to you when you reach an advanced level of study. Traditionally, masters required that students practice only one technique until it could be performed with a high degree of expertise. Sequential training of techniques makes it easier to understand Taiji Jian postures and to perform them well.

THIRTEEN KEY TERMS

The document known as *The Thirteen Key Terms (Shisan Zhijue)* describes the thirteen basic principles and techniques of Taiji Jian. It provides explanations for how to use the jian and how to apply internal force, jin. It reminds practitioners that the Taiji principles of using mind, yi, and minimum force should always be carefully observed in Taiji Jian practice and that the proper application of Taiji Jian techniques depends far more on accuracy than on force.

The thirteen classic jian techniques will be presented in this section, accompanied by photographs and, in some cases, by references to illustrations from the next chapter, which depict applications of the techniques. In the photographs, please pay particular attention to the position of the sword, the direction of jian movements, and the part of the jian used in each application.

1 Move close to your opponent

2 Dodge to the left and raise sword

3 Make downward hit and step forward

4 The upward hit (a)

5 The upward hit (b)

Hit

The Chinese word for hit, *ji,* means to strike a bell, throw a stone, or hit something with a hammer. In the ji technique, the tip and front part of the jian are used to attack the opponent. In executing ji, the tip of the sword can be moved in one of three kinds of curves. In *zhengji*, the tip is moved in a downward curve and the jian is held in *shunba*, the thumb-up grip *(fig. 1–3 and Chapter 6 fig. 22.2.2)*. In *fanji*, the tip is moved in an upward curve and jian is held in *niba*, the thumb-down grip *(fig. 4, 5, and Chapter 6 fig. 3.2.2)*. In *ceji*, the tip is moved from side-to-side and the jian is held in *yinba*, the palm-up grip or *yangba*, the palm-down grip *(fig. 6–9 and Chapter 6 fig. 20.4.2)*.

6 Step to the right and forward

7 Make a sideways hit right to left

8 Step to the left and forward

9 Make a sideways hit left to right

In all ji variations, the internal force comes from and is released by the forearm. As a result, the ji movement is not particularly large or powerful but rather very quick. You must practice letting the tip of the sword follow your shen, your spirit, so that any target on which you focus your gaze can be hit precisely and immediately. Ji is the most useful attack technique and is frequently applied.

10 Dodge and raise sword

11 Thrust downward

12 Focus the mind and wait for an opening

13 Step forward and thrust upward

14 Focus the mind and wait for an opening

15 Step forward and thrust forward

Thrust

Ci, meaning to thrust, prick, or poke, is a frequently used technique. In this technique, the tip of jian is thrust quickly and powerfully to attack the opponent. The thrust can be directed downward *(fig. 10, 11* and Chapter 6 *17.1.2)* or upward *(fig. 12, 13* and Chapter 6 *fig. 8.2.2)*, forward *(fig. 14, 15* and Chapter 6 *fig. 27.4.2)* or sideways *(fig. 16, 17* and Chapter 6 *fig. 29.1.2)*. The most important aspect of the technique is that the tip of jian always be moved in a straight line. If the line of attack is not straight, the sword is likely to bend or break.

16 Focus the mind and wait for an opportunity

17 Step left and thrust sideways

18 Thrust with two-handed grip

19 With two-handed grip thrust, press sword downward slightly

20 Thrust with horizontal blade

21 Thrust with vertical blade

The internal force for ci comes from the back and the legs. Some times *heba,* the two-handed grip, is used to lend additional force *(fig. 18, 19)*. The blade can be either horizontal *(fig. 20)* or vertical *(fig. 21)* depending on the part of the opponent's body that is targeted. The attack must always be carefully directed at a particular part of the body. Because of the scope and power of the ci thrust, it is a difficult movement to change once begun. If the target of the initial thrust is missed, the attacker is very vulnerable to counterattack. Consequently, it is essential to aim carefully.

22 Use the ridge to block opponent's weapon

23 Follow opponent's weapon with yours and step forward quickly

24 Use the ridge to block opponent's weapon

25 Follow opponent's weapon with yours and step forward quickly

26 Turn hand over and use ridge to block opponent's weapon to left

27 Turn hand over and use ridge to block opponent's weapon to right

Block with the Ridge

Ge means to use just the ridge of the sword, jianji, to block the opponent's weapon. The jian can be moved in a curve or a straight line and the internal force should come from the waist. The most important aspect of this technique is that the sword "stick to" or follow the opponent's weapon lightly, never with force. It is also important never to use the edges of the jian to apply a block, which would reveal a basic lack of appreciation for the nature of the sword.

Ge, the most common sword technique for blocking an opponent's weapon, has two variations, each of which can be performed on either side of the body. In the zhengge variation, the tip of the jian points up *(fig. 22–25* and Chapter 6 *fig. 11.1.2).* In fange, the tip points down *(fig. 26, 27* and Chapter 6 *fig. 19.1.4).*

The most important component of the ge technique is footwork. Your step must be nimble so that you can dodge quickly. The jian is used primarily to provide cover for the body; that is, its importance is not so much in blocking the attacking weapon as in protecting the body as you dodge the attack and change position and momentum to prepare for a counterattack.

Ge is a also dangerous technique because it can be effectively used only when the opponent's weapon strikes very close to your body. This makes timing the most difficult aspect of the technique. As soon as the blade of your sword touches the opponent's weapon, your movements and footwork must be nimble and quick so that your jian can touch and closely follow the opponent's weapon. This provides the time needed to prepare your counterattack. Ge is a very typical Taiji Jian technique and has traditionally been regarded as a measure of one's Taiji Jian skill.

28 Move sword upward

29 Move sword forward

30 Move sword downward

31 Move sword backward

32 Move sword forward

Wash

Xi literally means to wash, a frequently used jian technique in which the sword tip is moved smoothly and continuously in alternating upward and downward circles around the body. The movement of the tip should create the impression that it is being dipped into water to be washed or that it is a sprinkling can scattering water. The xi technique uses the ridge of the jian as well as the tip and can be used for both attack and defense *(fig. 28–32* and Chapter 6 *fig. 19.4.3, 4)*. Its most common use, however, is to provide a smooth and nimble transition from one movement or technique to the next.

The internal force for xi comes from the legs and waist. The body is said to "follow the jian," which means that the movement of the torso follows or "chases" the jiantan. This strengthens the qi and creates the smoothly flowing motion characteristic of the technique. Practicing xi is very helpful for increasing the coordination between the jian and the movements of the body.

33 Touch opponent's wrist
with sword

34 Pull sword to the left to
produce a horizontal cut

Draw

Chou means to pull, take out, or draw along. In the chou technique, the edge of the jian is used to touch the opponent and is then pulled to create a cut *(fig. 33, 34* and Chapter 6 *fig. 10.4.2)*. Generally, this movement should be quick and produce a horizontal cut. The internal force for chou comes from the body and should be released quickly. The touch of the sword must be so light and nimble that the opponent is unaware of being touched. The ensuing pull and cut must be made with speed and agility.

35 Move tip of sword in same direction as opponent's movement

36 Move tip of sword to cut opponent's wrist in direction it is moving

37 Use the ridge of the sword to touch opponent's weapon

38 Move sword with opponent's weapon and lure him

39 Use sword to touch opponent's arm from the right side

40 Draw edge of sword back in direction of opponent's movement

Take Back

Dai means to take something back, without effort. It involves following or anticipating the opponent's movement and then causing him to fall in the direction of his own movement. The dai technique, in which the jian is moved straight back, can use either the tip, ridge, or edge of the sword. There are three kinds of dai attack. The tip of the jian can be used to strike at the opponent's wrist (*fig. 35, 36* and Chapter 6 *fig. 4.2.2*). Or, the ridge of the jian can be used to "stick to" the opponent's weapon (*fig. 37, 38* and Chapter 6 *fig. 26.2.2*). Thirdly, the edge of the jian can be used to cut the opponent's body (*fig. 39, 40,* and Chapter 6 *fig. 25.3.2*). The internal force for dai comes from the forearm and wrist. To apply this technique properly, the body must move very nimbly.

Direction is the most important aspect of the dai technique. Applying dai in the correct direction will make the technique more efficient and will reduce the amount of force needed to complete the movement. To protect your body, try to keep your sword positioned across your opponent's weapon throughout the movement.

Try also to use the expanding force, *pengjin*, when applying the dai technique. This will allow you to avoid the risk you create by your initially feigning weakness to lure your opponent into using more force. Once the lure has worked and your opponent is exerting excess force, it will be easy to defend against his attack. This technique exemplifies the classical Taiji principle of "borrowing force from your opponent."

41 Move sword under
opponent's weapon

42 Raise sword with palm-outward
grip and cut opponent's wrist

43 Dodge to left and move sword to
close opponent

44 Raise sword with palm-inward
grip and cut opponent's wrist

Raise

Ti means to raise or move up. In this technique, the tip of the jian is turned over and moved upward to cut the opponent, usually on the wrist. The movement of the jian can be small or large and it must always be quick and nimble. There are two variations of ti. When waiba, the palm-outward grip, is used, the ti technique is called *zhengti* (*fig. 41, 42* and Chapter 6 *fig. 16.2.3*). When neiba, the palm-inward grip, is used, the ti technique is called *fanti* (*fig. 43, 44* and Chapter 6 *fig. 24.2.2*). The internal force for ti comes from the arm and the body. Its effectiveness depends much more on its accuracy than its power.

45 Wait for opponent's weapon
to strike close

46 Use tip of sword to attack
opponent's wrist suddenly

Explode

Beng means to explode or burst. The beng technique consists of an upward movement of the sword tip *(fig. 45, 46* and Chapter 6 *fig. 9.2.3)*. The movement should be sudden, quick, and small but also powerful. The internal force for beng comes from the wrist and the forearm.

This technique is always used when the opponent's weapon strikes very close. Consequently, it is a dangerous move that requires a highly accurate sense of distance and timing. Diligent training is needed to use this technique effectively and to acquire the necessary explosiveness.

47 Raise sword up from the back

48 Chop straight down

49 Raise sword up from the back and right side

50 Chop downward at slant

51 Block to the right and press down

52 Chop down with two-handed grip

Chop

Pi means to chop. In the pi technique, the middle part of the sword edge is used to chop powerfully down at the opponent. The internal force moves from the legs to the waist, and then to the back and arm. There are two pi variations. In *zhengpi*, the chop is directed straight down *(fig. 47, 48* and Chapter 6 *fig. 18.9.2)*. In *xiepi*, the chop slants downward *(fig. 49,50* and Chapter 6 *fig. 18.6.2)*. Heba, the two-handed grip, is sometimes used with pi to increase the power of the technique *(fig. 51, 52* and Chapter 6 *fig. 26.4.2)*.

Because pi involves a large movement, it is slower than many of the other techniques and is not often used. It requires excellent footwork and must be thoroughly practiced if it is to be used comfortably and reliably.

53 Wait for opponent's weapon to move close

54 Point quickly to opponent's forearm

Point

Dian means to point, poke, or jab. In this technique, the sword tip is used to strike straight down, usually at one of the opponent's acupoints *(fig. 53, 54* and Chapter 6 *fig. 7.4.3)*. The movement of the jian should be small but sudden, powerful, and quick. The internal force for dian comes only from the wrist; the sword arm does not need to move.

Dian is a commonly used technique. Its goal is to cause the opponent to drop his weapon as a result of the attack to the front part of his wrist. To achieve this end, the dian strike must be very accurate and the jian must be held in a relaxed grip to insure that the small movement of the sword will be agile as well as powerful.

55 Touch opponent's weapon from right

56 Turn sword around opponent's weapon

57 Unbalance opponent, pull away, and circle sword back to attack

58 Touch opponent's weapon from left

59 Turn sword around opponent's weapon

60 Unbalance opponent, pull away, and circle sword back to attack

Stir

Jiao means to stir or mix. In this technique, the jian is either held vertically and moved in horizontal circles or is held horizontally and moved in vertical circles. In both cases, the internal force comes from the waist and then moves through the forearm and the wrist. There are two jiao variations. In *zhengjiao*, for example, the circle is vertical and the jian moves in a counterclockwise direction *(fig. 55–57* and Chapter 6 *fig. 23.4.2).* In *fanjiao*, also a vertical circle, the sword moves in a clockwise direction *(fig. 58–60* and Chapter 6 *fig. 23.2.2).*

This technique requires powerful internal force and good integration of the external and internal components. Ideally, when the jian touches the opponent's weapon, the internal force should "shake his root," thus causing him to lose balance and drop his weapon. If the target is missed, however, your own balance can be easily lost, so sensitivity is important for effective application of the technique. The jiao circles should be as small as possible, and intensive practice is necessary to achieve this.

61 Press opponent's weapon down
with palm-down grip

62 Press opponent's weapon down
with palm-up grip

63 Press opponent's weapon down
and left with thumb-up grip

64 Press opponent's weapon down
and right with two-handed grip

Press

Ya means to press down. In this technique, the opponent's weapon is pressed down upon so that it is immobilized and can be brought under your control. The internal force for ya comes from the whole body, making it a powerful technique. Either the jianji, the ridge of the blade, or the jiangen, the root of blade, can be used.

There are three variations of this technique. *Zhengya* is a variation in which the sword is held in yangba, the palm-down grip, and the ridge of the blade is used. The sword is referred to as *yangba jian (fig. 61* and Chapter 6 *fig. 24.3.5)*. *Fanya* is a variation in which the sword is held in yinba, the palm-up grip, and the ridge of the blade is used. The sword is referred to as *yinba jian (fig. 62* and Chapter 6 *fig. 20.3.2)*. In the third variation, called *xiaya*, shunba, the thumb-up grip, or heba, the two-handed grip, is used to hold the sword and the root of the blade is used *(fig. 63, 64* and Chapter 6 *fig. 8.1.2)*.

Ya is not a very common technique. When you use it, be careful not to hold the position for a long time. Rather, change very quickly to another technique so that the tempo of your movements is not impeded. Although force from the whole body is used in ya, it is important to maintain complete relaxation. Practice is needed to insure that your hips stay relaxed and that your step remains nimble.

65 Dodge to the left and intercept upward

66 Dodge to the right and intercept upward

67 Step back and intercept upward

68 Step forward and intercept downward

69 Dodge to the left and intercept forward

70 Intercept side-to-side

Intercept with the Edge

Jie means to block, cut off, or intercept with the edge of the sword, the jianren. This technique usually involves dodging a frontal attack and then defending against the attack once it has reached the midway point. Because the edge of the jian is used, this technique should never be applied to block the opponent's weapon but only to block or cut his body, usually his wrists or arms. The internal force for jie comes from the waist and moves through the arm.

Jie has four variations. In *shangjie*, the movement of the jian is upward *(fig. 65–67 and Chapter 6 fig. 2.2.3)*. In *xiajie*, the movement is downward *(fig. 68 and Chapter 6 fig. 2.3.3)*. In *hengjie*, the movement is forward *(fig. 69 and Chapter 6 fig. 20.3.2)*, while in *cejie*, the movement is from side-to-side *(fig. 70 and Chapter 6 fig. 25.1.2)*.

Jie is a common and useful technique. It requires that you watch very carefully and wait until your opponent has committed to an attack. Then you must dodge the attack and interrupt the flow of your opponent's movements. To use jie successfully, both your mind and your step must be extremely nimble and your sense of timing must be very good.

COMBINED TECHNIQUES

Although the thirteen basic jian techniques can be used individually, they are often used in combination with each other. In these combinations, the individual techniques have been so smoothly and seamlessly joined that they are no longer separately identifiable. The combined techniques described in this section are so commonly used that they have been given their own names. All numbers below refer to figures to be found in Chapter 6.

Block and Cut at Midway

Lan means to block, stop, or break something off in the middle. It is a combination of ge, ya, and jie and is always used to block or stop the opponent's attack before his force is released. Sometimes, a side-to-side chopping movement at mid-level can also be called lan. Lan is a common and useful defensive technique *(fig. 10.3.2)*.

Thrust and Cut Upward

In *tiao,* the tip of the sword is used to thrust, prick, or poke in at the opponent and then cut upward. It is a combination of ci and ti. Because it is a small but quick and strong movement, this common and useful attack technique requires powerful internal force from the wrist and forearm *(fig. 13.2.2)*.

Peel Quickly

Xiao means to peel or cut, and is a combination of jiao, dai, ya, and ji. It is a quick and subtle technique rather than a powerful one. The goal is to find a gap or a vulnerable point of the opponent's movement and cut in towards the opponent. Usually the gap is around the opponent's weapon. In xiao, the sword moves first in a curve or circle and then straight ahead *(fig. 5.2.2)*. It is important that the two parts of the xiao movement be smoothly connected and combined. The internal force for xiao comes from the waist. The qianren, the sharp edges of the upper section of the sword, are used in this technique.

   Xiao is always used following a defensive technique and is often combined with ge or ya. The sword is usually used to cut in along your opponent's weapon, but this common and adaptable technique can be used in many different ways.

Cut Lightly and Quickly

Liao means to sprinkle. This technique is a combination of ji, tiao, and xiao, and involves a quick, smooth, small upward cut with the tip or front edge of the sword. In this technique, the jian is usually moved along the opponent's weapon. There are two variations of liao. In *zhengliao*, the sword is held in either yinba, the palm-up grip, or neiba, the palm-inward grip *(fig.22.3.2)*. In *fanliao,* the jian is held in either yangba, the palm-down grip, or waiba, the palm-outward grip *(fig. 22.6.2)*. Liao is not a powerful technique but it is very effective for disturbing the opponent and interfering with his concentration.

Hang

Gua means to hang something. This technique is a combination of ji, dian, lan, and dai. When using gua, you should think of your target as though it were a hook and your sword as though it were going to hang something on the hook *(fig. 15.1.2)*. Gua is not a very common technique. To do it well, your footwork and the movements of your body must be very nimble.

Cut Off

Zhan means to cut off. This technique is a combination of pi, jie, ya, and ji, and uses the edge of the sword. The movement must be quick and hard. Zhan is similar to pi (chop) but the movement of the sword in zhan is smaller, quicker, and more sudden. There are two variations. In *hengzhan*, the jian cuts horizontally *(fig. 29.3.2)*, while in *shuzhan*, the cut is vertical *(fig. 23.2.2)*. When executing zhan, imagine that you are really about to cut something off. Although not a common technique, zhan is a very useful one.

Point with the Tassel Holder

Tandian means to point, hit, or poke with jiantan, the tassel holder. In this technique, the sword is held in the left hand with fanwo, the reversed holding position, and the tassel holder is used to attack the opponent *(fig. 1.17.2)*.

Block with the Handle

Jianbing lange means to use jianbing, the handle of the sword, to block the opponent's attack. In this technique, jian should be held by the left hand in fanwo, the reversed holding position *(fig. 1.11.4)*.

Point with the Finger Sword

Juedian means to use jianjue, the finger sword, to attack the opponent *(fig. 1.12.3)*. With intensive practice, this technique can increase the flow of qi to your fingertips. Training in *dianxue* techniques, which involve attacking acupoints with your fingers, will help you develop the ability to use juedian effectively.

HOW TO BRANDISH THE JIAN

To use the techniques and skills of Taiji Jian correctly you must understand the basic rules for brandishing the jian and be able to apply these rules in your practice. If your sword movements are not guided by knowledge of these rules, it will be assumed that you have never received serious training.

There are three basic movements that the jian can make. It can point; it can be moved in a straight line; and it can follow a circular path. The pointing movement is small and needs to be very precise. The tip must be made powerful by the movement of qi from the sword hand through the entire jian to the tip. If the flow of qi is complete, the tip can be used to attack any part of your opponent's body accurately and swiftly. In fighting, the target should always be an acupoint.

The straight-line jian movement is easy to execute but it must be done quickly. The sword should move directly forward as soon as you have an opportunity to attack. Keep your wrist straight and let your internal force move to the tip of the jian in a straight line. If you cannot keep the jian straight, there will be a break in the flow of qi and internal force. If you feel that the sword tip is too light and cannot be well controlled, your wrist has become too tight and is impeding the flow of qi to the tip of the jian.

The circular movement of jian, called jianquan, is used more frequently than the other two movements. As mentioned in Chapter 3, jianquan must be smooth, relaxed, steady, and yet able to be quickly changed when necessary. Circular movements of the jian promote the smooth flow of qi throughout the body. In fighting, circular movements allow you to change techniques easily and to follow the movements of your opponent using only minimum force. You must use your sensitivity to anticipate the intentions of your opponent and then follow his movements with circular movements of your sword. Be ready to change the direction of the circles quickly to gain and maintain control. To use circular movements skillfully, your body must remain flexible and nimble and your footwork must be good. Circular movements are pervasive throughout the Taiji Jian form.

While some of the basic skills and techniques of Taiji Jian are subtle and agile, others are powerful and sudden. How can such a wide array of requirements be mastered? Relaxation is the key. This may sound like a simple solution but do not be deceived. Learning how to relax from your feet to your legs, hips, waist, back, shoulders, elbows, wrists and finally to your hands, requires much careful study. If, from your practice of empty-handed Taiji Quan, you have already learned how to relax, just apply this ability to Taiji Jian. In Taiji Jian, you should pay particular attention to relaxing your shoulders and elbows and especially your hands. If you have not yet learned how to remain thoroughly relaxed in the empty-handed form, continue to practice diligently. In Taiji Quan form it is important to give special attention to relaxing your legs and waist.

The wrist is one of the most important parts of the body for the practice of Taiji Jian. It must be nimble and powerful. The wrist determines your ability to control the jian. If you cannot relax your wrist, qi will be blocked at that point and will not be able to reach the jian, which will then lose power and accuracy. When this occurs, the jian is said to have "flapped," in Chinese, piao.

If you know some dao (broadsword) skills, you should pay very close attention to keeping these skills separate from those of the jian. The techniques for these two short weapons are similar in some respects but they should never be mixed. Although both weapons are short and look somewhat alike, their qualities and uses are very different. Many dao movements, like raising the dao over your head and passing it around your body, are never done with the jian. Because the jian is a double-edged weapon, it would be very easy to cut yourself if you tried to perform such dao movements. Also, unlike the dao with its blunt edge that can be used for blocking, the jian should never be used to execute a hard block. In general, dao skills are more powerful, while jian skills are more subtle.

Three more important rules to keep in mind for your Taiji Jian practice are as follows. Jianjue, the finger sword, should never move past the jiantan, or tassel holder, when both hands are close together on the handle of jian. Jianjue should never be moved along the jianren, the edge of the sword, but should remain behind the jiantan most of the time. Finally, your body should always follow the jiantan, which will cause the tip of the sword to become powerful. Traditional advice states that one should "pay attention to the jiantan when practicing the jian." It is thought that a person's skill level can be accurately judged simply by looking at the movements of his jiantan.

In brandishing the jian, you should feel that the sword and your body have been joined into a single unit. Your whole body should be involved in every movement you make. Your internal force should flow smoothly and continuously from your feet to the tip of the jian without any variation in speed.

In Taiji Jian as with all Taiji training, qi should move freely and continuously through all parts of your body. Your waist should function as the locus of control for all your movements. You should remain relaxed so that your movements can be nimble, powerful and quickly changed when necessary. You should practice yi so that wherever your mind focuses, the jian can instantly follow. Finally, you should use shen to lead the elements of mind, qi, internal force, and movement. The ability to use shen in this way will eventually allow you to achieve a deep understanding of Taiji Jian and a high degree of skill.

6

THE THIRTY-TWO POSTURE TAIJI JIAN FORM

This chapter presents the Wu style thirty-two posture Taiji Jian form. The presentation is very detailed so that readers of all levels will be able to benefit from it. If you are a beginner, we suggest that you study the physical movements first. Do not worry about the internal components or applications. Once you have learned the physical movements well, you can address the other elements one by one. This gradual process will make it easier for you to understand and master the form. Take your time and you will do well.

BASIC INFORMATION

Taiji Jian forms have not had a long history. No Taiji Jian form had yet been developed when Master Yang Luchan taught Taiji Quan in Beijing in the mid-nineteenth century. He taught only some basic sword skills and principles to his sons and students and it was they who later developed the original Taiji Jian form. Today, many different Taiji Jian forms are practiced but all are based on the same basic principles.

About the Traditional Sixty-four Posture (Long) Form
There are sixty-four postures in the traditional Wu style Taiji Jian form that was developed by famous masters one hundred years ago in Beijing. At that time, many renowned masters in Beijing taught martial arts. Some of them, like Quan You, Liu Dekuan, Ji Zixiu, and Chang Yuanting were good friends and practiced together, always exchanging their ideas and skills. They worked together to recreate traditional forms and to invent new ones. Then they taught these variations to their students. The late Master Xu Yusheng founded a famous martial arts school, the Beiping (as Beijing was then called) Physical Institute, and invited masters from different groups to teach there. A wide variety of forms was taught at this school and many became popular. When Master Quan You's son, Ai Shen, also well known as Wu Jianquan, taught Taiji

Quan at the school, he taught the sixty-four posture form created by his father and his father's friends. This variation of the form became popularly known as Wu style.

Wu style Taiji Jian is a beautiful and useful form that was made even more popular by Master Quan You's most famous disciple, Wang Maozhai, who was the leader of the largest Taiji group in northern China at the time. Wang Maozhai founded the Beijing Tai Miao Taiji Quan Association and taught several thousand students. In the next generation of this group, Master Yang Yuting was the foremost master. He passed on his skill to his senior pupil Wang Peisheng who also studied directly with Master Wang Maozhai. Today, Master Wang Peishang has become one of the most widely known and justly famous Wu style masters. He has published a book and videotape of this traditional form.

The Wu style sixty-four posture form is complex and difficult. Many movements require that the practitioner have very good basic Kungfu. Complete mastery requires a great deal of practice and just to do the form from beginning to end takes about twenty minutes. Although this jian form is well-suited to the needs of some people, many do not have the time or interest for the prolonged practice that it requires. For this reason, Master Wang decided to create a short form that most people could study easily. His main goals in developing this form were: to make the form shorter (only five to seven minutes); to remove some of the complex and difficult postures while retaining all the basic features of the form; and to make the form accessible to people for use as a martial art as well as an an aid to meditation and health. The final form, designed under the instruction of Master Wang, has thirty-two postures and can be of benefit to almost everyone.

About the Thirty-two Posture (Short) Form

The thirty-two posture Taiji Jian form is comprised of one hundred forty-four movements. The first and last postures, called "Preparation" and "Return to Original Position," include a total of four additional movements, but these postures are not technically considered part of the form.

This chapter presents detailed and illustrated descriptions of the movements for each posture. The descriptions include guidelines for enhancing shen and yi by describing, respectively, where your eyes should look during each movement and where your mind should be focused. This, in turn, will help you develop qi and internal force. In addition, descriptions of the internal feelings that should be experienced as the movements are executed and information about how to correct mistakes are given.

As with Taiji Quan, the Taiji Jian form should be practiced smoothly and as a continuous whole in order to allow for the full expression of shen, yi, and qi. Because of their difficulty, however, jian techniques sometimes result in an interruption of the smooth flow of the external movements and in these instances, the internal components of shen, yi, and qi must provide continuity so that no internal interruptions occur. The inner experience of the practitioner must always be of each movement flowing smoothly into the next so that the whole form is like one complete movement. The points in the form where special care must be taken to insure that even the external movements are absolutely continuous will be indicated in the "Movements" sections by phrases such as "in a continuous motion" or "continuing from the previous movement."

Acupuncture points are frequently mentioned in the description of "key points" for each movement. Such acupoint information will help you develop internal feeling and qi by indicating where you should focus your mind as you perform each movement. If you are not familiar with acupoints, please refer to the acupoint location charts in Appendixes.

To help you deepen your understanding of the jian form, the description of each posture also includes information about how the movements of that posture can be applied. Because applied movements often differ from the standards prescribed for those same movements when they are practiced in the form, the descriptions in the "Application" sections may be different from the information provided in the "Movements" sections. Specifically, applied movements are usually smaller than the movements of the form and the steps or stances of applied movements are often simpler and more quickly done than those of the form. (So that these may be clearly distinguished, some photographs which show the applications are taken at different angles from the photographs which show the movements of same posture.)

Despite these differences, the expectation is that the more diligently and carefully you practice the movements of the form, the more easily and effectively you will be able to execute jian movements in fighting situations. It should always be remembered that successful application depends more on your internal Kungfu than on your movement techniques. Because Taiji Jian is an internal skill, successful application depends on how well you use the internal components shen, yi, and qi and the composite component jinshen. Even movements that are outwardly the same will generate different techniques if the configurations of internal components associated with the movements differ.

In the "Application" section for each movement, particular techniques or combinations of techniques, as described in Chapter 5, are presented. Although the "Application" sections discuss examples of how the basic techniques are used to defend against different weapons, do not assume that the techniques are limited to the described purposes. Each technique can be used in many ways. Remember that the proper use of all techniques requires close attention to basic principles and to the internal components.

Important principles for the application of Taiji Jian techniques in fighting will be discussed in detail in Chapter 8. Briefly summarized here, Taiji Jian can be used to defend against any kind of weapon. Techniques vary, however, in the degree to which they are effective against different weapons. In the Wu style thirty-two posture form, some techniques are designed for use against long weapons, like the *qiang* (spear) or *gun* (staff), and others are designed for use against short weapons, like the dao (broadsword) or jian.

Because spear attacks are usually made in a straight line and because they consist of movements that are quick and changeable, you should try to dodge the forward thrust of the spear and direct your defense to the middle part of the weapon, as close as possible to your opponent's front hand. In defending against a staff attack, try to find an opportunity to move close to your opponent's body. While a staff is very powerful at its front end, its thrust is not quickly or easily changed. The relative sluggishness of this weapon will give you an advantage if you can avoid the forward attack and with a ready jian move past the front end of the staff towards your opponent. By contrast, the dao, or broadsword, is a quick and powerful weapon. You should never block it directly with the jian but rather try to cut off its root, that is, attack the arm which holds the dao. Finally, the use of the jian to defend against a jian is very interesting and knowledge of this aspect of jian training will deepen your appreciation and respect for the weapon.

According to Chinese tradition, idioms and special phrases are always used to name the postures and movements of a form. Unfortunately, these idioms and phrases are often difficult to translate. In this book, the meanings of the original words for the posture names have been used, even though at times this may make the posture titles somewhat difficult to comprehend. For the movement names, descriptions of the movements have been used rather than translations of the Chinese characters that comprise the original titles. As a result, the movement names may sometimes differ from traditional designations.

DESCRIPTIONS AND ILLUSTRATIONS OF THE FORM

The following section presents detailed descriptions and photographs of the entire thirty-two-part form. So that all movements can be seen clearly, some were shot at different angles. These photographs will be labeled with the same number but will have an additional, letter designation, (a) indicating the "standard" view (as other photos in the series), and (b) indicating a shot from another angle. The thirty-two posture Taiji Jian form includes one hundred forty-four movements. The names of all postures and movements are listed below for easy reference.

PREPARATION *(yubei shi)*
    Take sword in left hand and quiet the mind
    Merge steps and hold sword along outside of left arm

1. COMMENCING FORM *(qi shi)*
    1.1   Immortal points direction
    1.2   Hold seven stars
    1.3   Press and strike while in bow stance
    1.4   Point and prick with right jianjue
    1.5   Horizontal block in bow stance

1.6   Wait to fight in sitting stance

1.7   Horizontal block in sitting stance

1.8   Press forward in bow stance

1.9   Turn back sword in sitting stance

1.10 Point to neck or eye with right jianjue

1.11 Low block in insubstantial stance

1.12 Point right jianjue to armpit in bow stance

1.13 Block up to the left and down to the right

1.14 Point to armpit with jiantan

1.15 Block up to the right and down to the left

1.16 Point to armpit with right jianjue

1.17 Stretch arm and point with jiantan

1.18 Spread arms and assume side bow stance

1.19 Make a closed circle with arms

1.20 Change sword from left hand to right hand

2. SPREAD-EAGLED SWORD PASSES BY SEVEN STARS (*fenjian qixing*)

2.1   Spread arms outward

2.2   Raise sword to block up and assume bow stance

2.3   Block down while taking a back insert step

2.4   Pull sword from side to side and assume balance stance

3. STEP FORWARD AND SHELTER KNEE (*jinbu zhexi*)

3.1   Low block backward while in sitting stance

3.2   Turn sword over and strike up while in bow stance

4. TIGER CROUCHES AT THE FRONT DOOR (*wohu dangmen*)

4.1   Raise body forward and block wrist

4.2   Hold sword horizontally and assume insubstantial stance

5. BOATMAN ROWS A SCULL (*shaogong yaolu*)

5.1   Turn around and block back with sword

5.2   Raise body forward and cut up

6. PUSH A BOAT WITH THE TIDE (*shunshui tuizhou*)

6.1   Sink down with sword and assume rest stance

6.2   Step forward and thrust at side of chest

7. PAINT A RED DOT BETWEEN THE EYEBROWS (*meizhong dianchi*)

7.1   Relax crotch and block up

7.2   Cut attacker's wrist while in sitting stance

7.3   Pursue and strike while in bow stance

7.4   Step forward and point to *xuanguan*

8. THRUST SWORD IN THE OPPOSITE DIRECTION (*ni lin jian*)
8.1   Sink body down with sword and step forward

8.2   Thrust straight ahead with sword while in bow stance

9. TURN BACK WHILE PRICKING LIGHTLY UP (*huishen dian*)
9.1   Turn back and hide sword

9.2   Step forward and point at attacker's wrist

10. PEI GONG CHOPS A SNAKE (*Pei Gong zhanshe*)
10.1   Block up with sword and make back insert step

10.2   Step back and make a horizontal circle with sword

10.3   Step forward and cut attacker's waist

10.4   Pull sword back while in insubstantial stance

11. BRUSH DUST IN THE BREEZE (*yingfeng danchen*)
11.1   Make a closed circle with arms and assume insubstantial stance

11.2   Hold sword vertically and assume rest stance

11.3   Raise sword and assume sitting stance

11.4   Thrust straight ahead and assume bow stance

11.5   Make a closed circle with arms and assume insubstantial stance

11.6   Hold sword vertically and assume rest stance

11.7   Raise sword and assume sitting stance

11.8   Thrust straight ahead and assume bow stance

12. DRAGONFLY SKIMS THE WATER (*qingting dianshui*)
12.1   Turn to the left and use sword to block back

12.2   Point at the ankle

13. WASP FLIES THROUGH A HOLE (*huangfeng rudong*)
13.1   Thrust to the leg

13.2   Hold sword vertically and assume insubstantial stance

14. SCOOP THE MOON FROM THE OCEAN DEPTHS (*haidi laoyue*)
14.1   Block up and take cover step

14.2   Turn to the right and pull sword

14.3   Raise a flag

14.4   Tree roots twine around each other

15. TURN AROUND AND HANG A GOLDEN BELL (daogua jinling)
15.1 Turn around and block left side and back
15.2 Merge steps and block down

16. KUI XING RAISES HIS BRUSH (Kui Xing tibi)
16.1 Turn around and block side to side
16.2 Raise sword and assume single leg stance

17. THRUST SWORD DOWNWARD (zhidang jian)
17.1 Put foot and sword down
17.2 Unicorn exploration

18. STEP BACK WITH THREE REVERSE HITS (tuibu liaoyin sanjian)
18.1 Raise sword and turn it over while assuming bow stance
18.2 Turn and point sword back
18.3 Chop forward and assume bow stance
18.4 Turn sword over and strike back while taking cover step
18.5 Raise sword and assume insubstantial stance
18.6 Chop forward and assume bow stance
18.7 Turn sword over and strike back while taking cover step
18.8 Raise sword and assume insubstantial stance
18.9 Chop forward and assume bow stance
18.10 Raise knee and push sword
18.11 Straighten body and thrust forward with sword
18.12 Turn sword over and strike back while in bow stance

19. CAPTURE A LEGENDARY TURTLE IN THE OCEAN DEPTHS (haidi qin'ao)
19.1 Block down while taking a back insert step
19.2 Raise and straighten waist and move sword up
19.3 Raise knee and push sword
19.4 Turn back and strike down

20. GODDESS SPREADS FLOWERS (Shen Niu sanhua)
20.1 Hold sword horizontally and assume rest stance
20.2 Block arm and assume insubstantial stance
20.3 Lower sword and assume side bow stance
20.4 Strike knee while taking back insert step

21. PICK UP STARS WITH AN UNERRING HAND (miaoshou zuixing)
21.1 Turn hand over to pick up star
21.2 Step forward and thrust straight ahead with sword

22. RAISE WHIP AND ATTACK WRIST (*tibian liaowan*)

22.1 Raise whip back and assume insubstantial stance
22.2 Chop back while taking pad step
22.3 Cut upward at attacker's wrist and assume bow stance
22.4 Raise whip back and assume insubstantial stance
22.5 Chop back while taking pad step
22.6 Cut upward at attacker's wrist and assume bow stance

23. BLACK DRAGON STIRS ITS TAIL (*canglong jiaowei*)

23.1 Look back at the tail
23.2 Step back and strike forward
23.3 Look back at the tail
23.4 Step back and strike forward
23.5 Look back at the tail
23.6 Step back and strike forward
23.7 Look back at the tail
23.8 Step back and strike forward

24. JUMP OVER A RAVINE TO BLOCK AND INTERCEPT (*tiaojian jielan*)

24.1 Turn back and block down
24.2 Raise knee and block outside
24.3 Chop and block with jump step
24.4 Block down and reverse hit using cover step

25. FISH LYING AT THE BOTTOM OF A POND (*zuoyou woyu*)

25.1 Raise the body and block up
25.2 Wave whip and take a back insert step
25.3 White crane spreads wings
25.4 Swallow settles down on duckweed

26. TURN AROUND AND CHOP THE FACE (*zuoyou fanshen pimian*)

26.1 Turn sword over and cut up while assuming bow stance
26.2 Feign escape and pull sword back
26.3 Turn around and raise knee
26.4 Assume bow stance and chop at face
26.5 Feign loss and take sword back
26.6 Turn around and chop at face

27. WHITE SNAKE FLICKS ITS TONGUE (*baishe tuxin*)

27.1 Take sword back and assume sitting stance
27.2 Thrust sword upward

27.3 Take sword back and assume sitting stance
27.4 Thrust sword forward
27.5 Take sword back and assume sitting stance
27.6 Thrust sword down

28. LI GUANG SHOOTS A STONE (*Li Guang sheshi*)
28.1 Make a back insert step and lower sword
28.2 Turn around and strike back
28.3 Raise knee and hide tip of sword
28.4 Hold bow and arrow

29. HOLD THE MOON IN YOUR ARMS (*baoyue shi*)
29.1 Move sword around and thrust forward while in bow stance
29.2 Turn and make a horizontal circle
29.3 Block side to side while taking a step forward
29.4 Circle block and cut to waist

30. SINGLE WHIP (*danbian shi*)
30.1 Step back and sweep sword to the left
30.2 Turn around and sweep sword back

31. GOLDEN COMPASS POINTS SOUTH (*jinzhen zhinan*)
31.1 Encircle arms
31.2 Change hand that holds sword
31.3 Turn left and point to the sky
31.4 Hold sword and block horizontally
31.5 Block down as if to draw a line on the earth
31.6 Stretch arm and point forward while in bow stance
31.7 Turn around and poke from side to side
31.8 Strike with handle while in bow stance

32. MERGE STEPS AND CLOSE THE FORM (*binbu guiyuan*)
32.1 Merge hands and feet
32.2 Push up with jianjue finger
32.3 Right hand stretches to the right
32.4 Lower right jianjue

RETURN TO ORIGINAL POSITION (*huan yuanshi*)
Hold sword in left hand
Adjust breath and relax whole body

1

PREPARATION

Before practicing the form, you should prepare yourself by adjusting your breath and mind and by orienting your body in a direction that will be the beginning and ending position of your form practice. The direction you face when you begin and end is always considered to be "south" regardless of its relationship to the actual compass point. This convention will help you remember the relationship among the movements of the form and is also useful for practicing Bagua positions, which are oriented in eight different directions. Finally, you should be sure that you are holding the sword properly.

Take sword in left hand and quiet the mind

Movements   Face "south" and stand erect. Keep your feet parallel and close together. Bend your left elbow slightly and hold the hushou, hand shield, of the sword in your left hand. The jiantan, the tassel holder, should point up and be level with your chest. Keep your right arm relaxed and let it rest along the right side of your torso *(fig.1)*.

Internal Components   Keep your whole body relaxed and look straight ahead but "see nothing," that is, do not let your eyes rest on any particular object. Keep your mind quiet and untroubled. Breathe deeply and smoothly. This will help qi sink down to dantian (between the navel and mingmen point, which is on center of the lower back).

Key Points   This movement should create a sense of comfort and relaxation throughout your whole body and in your mind. It is the standard position for carrying the sword before and after practice.

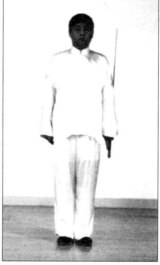

2   3

Merge steps and hold sword along outside of left arm

Movements   Keep your body erect. Use your right hand to help the left hand hold the sword with fanwo, the reversed holding position *(fig. 2)*. Then put both arms down along the sides of your torso. Holding the sword with your left hand, turn it so that jiantan points toward the earth. The jianran, the edges of the sword, should face north and south. Keep the body of the sword resting along the outside of your left arm and in touch with your left elbow. Let your right hand form the jianjue, finger sword, and then point the jianjue down *(fig. 3)*.

Internal Components   Keep looking forward. Your mind should be alert and concentrated but still relaxed and quiet. Feel qi extend throughout your body.

Key Points   Before starting to move, establish a sense of physical and mental relaxation. Maintain a feeling of readiness to fight and at the same time a sense of meditative calm. Let your breathing become smooth, deep, and slow. Try to be neither too excited nor too relaxed.

Application   Imagine that you are surrounded by many people who want to attack you. You must concentrate your attention in every direction and be ready to fight at any moment. Internally, though, you must remain quiet, receptive, and comfortable. Focus your mind on the yuzhen acupoint (on the back of the head). This will cause you to be very watchful and able to change direction quickly.

1.1.1   1.1.2   1.1.3

1. COMMENCING FORM

This is the beginning posture. It is traditional to start one's practice by holding the sword in the left hand and in a reversed holding position, a stance called "modestly declining." This position signifies that you are a gentle, well-mannered person and a high level practitioner who would never initiate fighting. It indicates that you respect everyone, including your opponents, and that you will not use the blade of your sword for attack until you have been attacked more than three times by an adversary. The beginning posture provides practice in using the jiantan and forming jianjue. After this posture, you begin using the sword to apply Taiji Jian skills and techniques.

1.1 Immortal points direction

Movements   Relax your left shoulder and drop your left elbow. At the same time, push your right hand down slightly and point the right jianjue forward *(fig. 1.1.1)*. These movements will cause both knees to relax and bend, and your whole body to sink down. As your body sinks, raise your left hand and hold the jiantan in front of your body and opposite your nose. Point the jiantan up and slightly to the right and forward *(fig. 1.1.2)*.

Internal Components   Look forward and concentrate. Your mind should be quiet and alert and focused on your right hand. Feel qi extend through your left arm to the jiantan.

Key Points   Keep your body erect, with both knees touching each other at the yinlingquan acupoint (inside of the knees). Your weight should start to shift to the right. Feel as though your left foot wants to take a large step and the right jianjue wants to move up and forward. Keep your abdomen pulled slightly back but feel as though your whole body wants to move forward.

1.2.1

1.2.2

1.2.3

Application If the opponent attacks you from above, move your body down slightly and use the jiantan to attack his right wrist, armpit, or ribs *(fig. 1.1.3)*. Here, the basic technique is dianchuo, a pricking point, with the jiantan.

1.2 Hold seven stars

Movements Shift your weight to your right leg and at the same time move your right hand up until the right jianjue is touching the inside of your left elbow *(fig. 1.2.1)*. Step forward with your left foot, using a standard step and let your left heel touch the ground while the toes of your left foot point to the sky. This forms a right sitting stance *(fig. 1.2.2)*.

Internal Components Keep looking forward and concentrate. Focus your mind on your right elbow. Feel as though your body wants to move down and forward and as though your left elbow is sinking and the jiantan wants to move up. Feel the qi moving from the dantian to the jiantan in a steady stream.

Key Points Keep your body erect. The right jianjue should touch the quechi point on your left elbow. Inside, your body should feel as though it is sinking further down and causing increasingly powerful internal force to go to the jiantan.

Application This is a continuation of the last movement and results in the jiantan becoming more powerful *(fig. 1.2.3)*.

1.3.1   1.3.2   1.3.3

1.3 Press and strike while in bow stance

Movements   Shift your weight forward and turn your left foot to the right (west), making a left bow stance. At the same time, move your left hand down until the jiantan and your left elbow are in a horizontal line, and move the right jianjue up and then forward along the inside of your left forearm until both wrists cross. Turn your head to the right and face west *(fig. 1.3.1, 2)*.

Internal Components   Look from south to southwest and then to the west. Focus your mind on moving your body to the left and then forward. Feel qi extending fully throughout your left arm.

Key Points   During the weight shifts, your left foot should turn by pivoting on the left heel. When your weight has shifted fully to your left leg, your left foot should point west. At this point, your tailbone should be directly above your left heel and your torso should be erect. Keep the sword on the outside of your left forearm and feel your internal force pushing to the south.

Application   When the opponent attacks from above, you can step to his right side and use the jiantan to attack the side of his body. Also, you can use your left forearm to press against him and push him *(fig. 1.3.3)*.

1.4.1

1.4.2

1.4 Point and prick with right jianjue

Movements   Continuing without interruption from the last movement, move the right jianjue toward the west until your right wrist touches the jiantan. At the same time, relax your right hip and knee and adjust your right foot, letting the heel touch the ground while the toes of your right foot point to the sky. This forms a standard left sitting stance *(fig. 1.4.1)*.

Internal Components   Keep looking west and focus your mind first on mingmen acupoint (at the center of the lower back) and then on your right hand. Feel qi extend to the right jianjue.

Key Points   Your body should move slightly forward and then turn to the right in a continuous movement. Your right shoulder should relax and your right elbow should drop down. This will cause the right jianjue to gain power as it points to the west. You should feel as though your left forearm is pushing to the south.

Application   After using the jiantan to attack your opponent's right side, you can use the right jianjue in a continuous movement to attack his neck or eye *(fig. 1.4.2)*.

1.5.1   1.5.2

1.5 Horizontal block in bow stance

Movements   Shift your weight forward to make a right bow stance. At the same time, move your left arm so that it is horizontal and at chest level and then push it forward. Keep the sword in front of your left forearm and in touch with your arm. The right jianjue should point to the west *(fig. 1.5.1)*.

Internal Components   Look to the west and focus your mind on your left elbow. Feel qi extending fully throughout your arms. This will cause your arms and the sword to become powerful. Then change your mental focus to the jiaji point (at the center of the back).

Key Points   Be careful not to let your body lean forward. Feel as though your body is sinking down and becoming stable. Keep your left leg very nimble.

Application   When the opponent is very close to you, you can use the right jianjue to block his attack and your left arm with the sword pressed alongside it to attack him *(fig. 1.5.2)*.

1.6.1

1.6.2

1.6 Wait to fight in sitting stance

Movements   Shift your weight back to the your left leg. Let your right leg become empty (non-weight-bearing) and keep your right heel on the ground and the toes of your right foot pointing to the sky. This is a left sitting stance. At the same time, move your right hand back to the right side of your torso in front of your abdomen. Keep the right jianjue pointing toward the west and let your left hand holding the sword follow the right hand so that the jiantan stays in touch with your right wrist and the tip of the sword points to the southwest *(fig. 1.6.1)*.

Internal Components   Look to the southwest and focus your mind on the right jianjue as it moves. Think about pulling your body back as though to dodge and about moving your left elbow forward. Feel qi extending to your left elbow. This will cause the tip of the sword to become powerful.

Key Points   Keep your torso erect and never let your body move up or down during the weight shift. Turn your body slightly to the right. Keep the sword vertical and in touch with your left elbow.

Application   If the opponent moves vigorously towards you, you can dodge back and attack him with the tip of your sword. Your sword should be under your left arm when you attack *(fig. 1.6.2)*.

1.7.1   1.7.2

1.7 Horizontal block in sitting stance

Movements Remain in the sitting stance and turn your body to the left. At the same time, turn your right forearm over so that your right palm faces up. Then move your upturned right hand across the front of your abdomen toward the left side of your torso. Let your left hand holding the sword follow your right hand so that the jiantan maintains contact with your right wrist. Continue to hold the sword on the outside of your left forearm and keep the tip of the sword pointing toward the southeast *(fig. 1.7.1)*.

Internal Components Look at the right jianjue as it crosses your torso. Imagine that your body is sinking slightly down. This will cause the back of your body to be strong and your shoulders and elbows to become heavy. Focus your mind on your right hand. and feel qi in your right arm. This will cause your body to sink down. Then, feel qi moving up to your head. This will cause your body to be erect.

Key Points When turning your body, let your waist turn but do not move your hips. Your abdomen should be pulled back slightly. When you feel your whole body sink down, think of qi moving up to the baihui point (on top of the head). As your body becomes erect, feel as though you want to move forward.

Application If the opponent attacks your abdomen, you can move back and turn. At the same time, you can use the handle of the sword to block his attack *(fig. 1.7.2)*.

| 1.8.1 | 1.8.2 | 1.8.3 |

1.8 Press forward in bow stance

Movements Move the right jianjue forward and point it toward the southwest at shoulder level. Let the left hand holding the sword follow your right hand so that the jiantan stays in touch with your right wrist. At the same time, shift your weight forward to form a standard right bow stance *(fig. 1.8.1)*.

Keep moving the right jianjue to the right, in a horizontal arc, until it points to the northwest. At the same time, let your body sink down slightly and turn your torso to the right *(fig. 1.8.2)*.

Internal Components Look from southwest to northwest. Focus your mind on your right hand and imagine that you are using that hand to hold something. Feel qi in the right jianjue and let it extend outward in a large circle.

Key Points Let the right jianjue follow the movement of your eyes. Feel heaviness in your right hand.

Application When the opponent attacks you at chest level, you can move your body slightly sideways and use your right arm to block his arm, or use the handle of the jian to block and the right jianjue to attack *(fig. 1.8.3)*.

1.9.1a   1.9.1b   1.9.2

1.9 Turn back sword in sitting stance

Movements Move the right jianjue in a horizontal arc from northwest to north and then to northeast. At the same time, shift one hundred percent of your weight to your left leg to form a standard left sitting stance with your right heel touching the ground and the toes of your right foot pointing to the sky. Let your left hand holding the sword follow the movement of your right hand so that the jiantan stays in touch with your right wrist and the tip of the sword points to the southwest. Let your torso follow your right hand by turning to the right *(fig. 1.9.1a, b)*.

Internal Components Look from northwest to north and then to northeast. Let the movements of the right jianjue follow the movements of your eyes. Imagine that your body is sinking down but inside qi should be moving up. Focus your mind on your left elbow and then on the baihui point (on top of the head).

Key Points Keep your torso erect and be careful not to lean to the right or backward. Make sure that your left shoulder is relaxed and that your left elbow drops down.

Application If the opponent attacks your face, you can use your right forearm or the handle of the sword to block him *(fig. 1.9.2)*.

| 1.10.1 | 1.10.2 | 1.10.3 |

1.10 Point to neck or eye with right jianjue

Movements Turn your body to the left and move the right jianjue across the front of your body toward the south *(fig. 1.10.1)*. At the same time, turn your right foot until it faces south and let it fully touch the ground. Then shift your weight to your right foot as it turns so that one hundred percent of your weight is on your right leg when the right foot comes to rest on the ground. Let your left hand holding the sword follow the movement of your right arm. As the movement ends, your left leg is empty (non-weight-bearing) and has not moved. The right jianjue points up and your right palm faces to the south *(fig. 1.10.2)*.

Internal Components Look first toward the northeast and then to the south. Think that your chest is empty, that it is relaxed and that nothing can touch it. This will cause your arms to become extended. Then, as your body sinks slightly, think about your right elbow dropping down and forward. This will make the right jianjue point to the southwest. Focus your mind on your right hand and feel qi in your arms and back and extending outward into a large circle.

Key Points When your weight shifts to your right leg, make sure that your tailbone is above your right heel. When your whole body feels stable, relax your waist. This will cause your right jianjue to point quickly to the southwest.

Application If the opponent attacks your face or the left part of your body, you can use the handle of the sword or your right arm to block his attack. Then you can use the right jianjue to attack his neck or eyes *(fig. 1.10.3)*.

| 1.11.1 | 1.11.2 | 1.11.3 | 1.11.4 |

1.11 Low block in insubstantial stance

Movements   Stretch your right arm out and point the right jianjue up and toward the southwest. This will cause your body to turn slightly to the right *(fig. 1.11.1)*. Then, sweep your left hand holding the sword downward. At the same time, move the right jianjue back and put the "tiger mouth" of your right hand opposite your right ear *(fig. 1.11.2)*.

Continuing without interruption, turn your body to the left, and sweep your left hand downward toward the left side of your body. As your left hand moves to the left (north), the jiantan should point to the ground *(fig. 1.11.3)*.

Internal Components   Look down first and then to the left. Focus your mind on the right "tiger mouth" and think about pulling your body back a little. Feel qi reaching to the jiantan and causing your left arm to become powerful.

Key Points   Relax your right shoulder and drop your right elbow. Let your body dodge slightly to the right. This will make your left hand sink and feel heavy and will cause the handle of the sword to become very powerful.

Application   If the opponent attacks you on the lower left side, you can use the handle of the sword to block his weapon *(fig. 1.11.4)*.

1.12.1   1.12.2   1.12.3

1.12 Point right jianjue to armpit in bow stance

Movements Relax your left hip and knee and move your left foot to the northeast with the heel touching the ground and the toes pointing up. At the same time, turn your body to the left and face the east. Keep all of your weight on the right leg *(fig. 1.12.1)*.

Then, shift your weight forward and when most of the weight has shifted to your left leg, turn your right foot using the ball of the foot and assume a standard left bow stance. At the same time, move the right jianjue forward while it points to the east. Keep your right arm slightly curved. Holding the sword in your left hand, keep it positioned vertically along the outside of your left arm and parallel with the left side of your body. The jiantan should point toward the ground *(fig. 1.12.2)*.

Internal Components Look forward, toward the east. Focus your mind first on the jianjue and then on the jiantan. Feel qi extending to the jianjue and to the jiantan.

Key Points Keep your body erect and relax your shoulders. When your left foot moves toward the northeast, make sure that it passes your right heel before coming to rest on the ground. When shifting your weight forward onto your left leg, the timing of the turn made by your right foot is important because it allows the internal force to move smoothly to right jianjue.

Application In this movement, you can use the handle of the sword to block your left side and the right jianjue to attack the opponent *(fig. 1.12.3)*.

1.13 Block up to the left and down to the right

Movements Move the right jianjue down and point it diagonally toward the ground in front of your body until it is opposite your left knee. At the same time, move your left hand holding the sword in an arc forward, up and then slightly back toward the left side of your head *(fig. 1.13.1)*.

Internal Components Follow the movement of the right jianjue with your eyes and focus your mind on your left hand. Feel qi extending fully throughout both arms.

Key Points Your body can lean forward a little but it must be kept straight from the baihui point (on top of the head) to the huiyin point (at the base of the crotch). You should feel as though you can make a very nimble step with your right foot.

Application If the opponent attacks your upper left side, you can use the handle of the sword to block him and use right jianjue to attack him *(fig. 1.13.2)*.

| 1.14.2 | 1.14.3 | 1.14.4 |

1.14 Point to armpit with jiantan

Movements Move the right jianjue slightly to the right until it is opposite your right knee. Relax your right hip and knee and step forward with your right foot, letting the heel touch the ground and the toes of your right foot point to the sky. This forms a standard left sitting stance *(fig. 1.14.1)*.

Continuing without interruption, shift your weight forward to a standard right bow stance and move the jiantan forward. At the same time, move the right jianjue back and down slightly until it is on the right side of your right leg. It should still to point to the east *(fig. 1.14.2)*.

Internal Components Look first at the jiantan but after you step forward, look straight ahead. Focus your mind first on your left hand and then on your right hand. Feel qi extending through both arms.

Key Points When your body is very stable and can make a very nimble step, take the step. After stepping forward, make sure your body is erect. Throughout the weight shift, be sure to keep your body at the same level.

Application After the right jianjue blocks the opponent's attack *(fig. 1.14.3)*, you can use the jiantan to attack the opponent *(fig. 1.14.4)*.

1.15.1   1.15.2

1.15 Block up to the right and down to the left

Movements   Move your left hand holding the sword so that the jiantan points diagonally down to the ground in front of your body and your left hand is opposite your
right knee. At the same time, move the right jianjue in an arc forward, up and then
slightly back toward the right side of your head. The right jianjue should point toward
the east and up but the palm of your right hand should be turning to face the north.
Then, move your left hand with the sword to the left until it is opposite your left knee
(fig. 1.15.1).

Internal Components   Look at the right jianjue and focus your mind on it as you feel
qi extending to it.

Key Points   Your body can lean forward slightly but keep the baihui point (on top of
the head) and the huiyin point (at the base of the crotch) in a straight line. The feeling inside your body should be of turning slightly to the right. Your right leg should
feel stable and your left foot nimble.

Application   In this movement, you can use the handle of the sword to block an attack
coming from the lower left side of your body and you can use the right jianjue to protect your right side *(fig. 1.15.2)*.

| 1.16.1 | 1.16.2 | 1.16.3 |

1.16 Point to armpit with right jianjue

Movements   Relax your left hip and knee and step forward with your left foot into a standard right sitting stance with your left heel touching the ground and the toes of your left foot pointing up *(fig. 1.16.1)*.

Continuing without interruption, shift your weight forward to form a standard left bow stance. At the same time, turn your right hand so that the palm faces down and move the right jianjue forward, letting it point to the east. Your left hand holding the sword should be alongside your left leg and the sword should be held vertically *(fig. 1.16.2)*.

Internal Components   Change your gaze from the right jianjue to straight ahead and think of the jianjue as following the movement of your eyes to attack forward. Then focus your mind on your left hand. Feel qi reaching to the right jianjue.

Key Points   Your right foot must be stable and the left foot nimble. Your left hand with the sword must sink down and feel heavy. This will generate a feeling of power on the left side of your body.

Application   If the opponent attacks the lower left side of your body, you can use the handle of the sword to block his attack and use the right jianjue to attack him *(fig. 1.16.3)*.

1.17.1   1.17.2

1.17 Stretch arm and point with jiantan

Movements   Move your left arm with the sword up until it is parallel with your right arm. Then turn your body slightly to the right and stretch your left arm forward (eastward) so that the jiantan points in that direction *(fig. 1.17.1)*.

Internal Components   Look forward and focus your mind on your left hand. Feel qi reaching to the jiantan and surging forward.

Key Points   Relax your left shoulder and drop your left elbow. This will cause your left arm to move up and forward. When your body turns right, feel it sinking slightly. This will cause the jiantan to be very powerful and to thrust forward.

Application   When the opponent attacks you at chest level, you can dodge back and use the jiantan to attack his body *(fig. 1.17.2)*.

| 1.18.1 | 1.18.2 | 1.18.3 |

1.18 Spread arms and assume side bow stance

Movements Keep both arms straight and then separate them. Do not move your left hand with the sword but make a half circle with your right arm, moving it in a horizontal arc from east to south to west *(fig. 1.18.1)*. While your right arm is moving, shift your weight to your right leg to form a right side bow stance. During the shifting of the weight, turn your right foot using the ball of the foot and then turn your left foot in the same manner. Both feet should now point to the south. The right jianjue should point to the west and the jiantan should continue to point to the east *(fig. 1.18.2)*.

Internal Components Look back toward the west. Shift your mind from the left hand to the right hand and think of your right hand as being able to extend far into the distance. Feel qi reaching to both the jiantan and jian jianjue and causing your arms to stretch out.

Key Points Keep both arms in the horizontal plane. When starting to shift your weight, first turn your right foot on the ball of the foot. Then, after more than fifty percent of your weight has shifted to your right leg, turn your left foot using the ball of that foot.

Application When the opponent is on your right side, you can use your left hand to block his attack and your right leg and hand to attack *(fig. 1.18.3)*.

1.19.1

1.19 Make a closed circle with arms

Movements Bend both arms forward in front of the chest. Keep the sword on the out-side of your left forearm and the tip of the sword pointing to the east. Your right palm should face out (south) and the jianjue should be opposite your left middle finger on the inside of the handle of the sword. At the same time, keep your torso erect and turn to the left until your body faces south. Turn your head to the left continuously until it faces east. At the same time, relax your left hip and left knee and move your left foot back a half-step. Bend your left knee and let it point it to the east. The toes of your left foot should touch the ground and the heel should be raised. Keep your left knee in a vertical line with your left heel *(fig. 1.19.1)*.

Internal Components Look from west to south to east. Focus your mind on the center of your chest and then on your left knee. Feel qi sink down to the dantian (lower abdomen).

Key Points You should have a feeling of emptiness in your chest and of power in both arms. Feel as though your body is sinking and as though your left knee is coming up. This will create an internal feeling of lightness and readiness to move in all directions quickly and easily.

Application This movement is designed to create a sense of alertness and to help you prepare for fighting in whatever way necessary.

1.20.1

1.20 Change sword from left hand to right hand

Movements   Keeping your body stable, move your right hand to the outside of the handle of the sword. Let your left hand release the handle of the sword and make the jianjue on the inside of the sword while your right hand takes hold of the sword handle *(fig. 1.20.1)*. Then, turn the head to face south.

Internal Components   Look to the south and shift the focus of your mind from your right hand to your left hand. Feel qi extending through both arms.

Key Points   The changing of the sword from the left hand to the right hand must be nimbly done.

Application   None. After again "modestly declining," you should be ready to use your sword quickly to attack or defend.

2.1.1   2.1.2   2.1.3

2. SPREAD-EAGLED SWORD PASSES BY SEVEN STARS

"Seven stars" represents an important concept in the martial arts. Specifically, the seven stars are: the "head star" on the baihui point; the "shoulder star" on the jianjing point; the "elbow star" on the qiuchi point; the "hand star" on the laogong point; the "hip star" on the huantiao point; the "knee star" on the yanglingquan point; and the "foot star" on the yongquan point. All seven stars will be practiced during the form but more attention is paid to them in this posture than in others. Except for the last two postures, all movements from this point on are made with the sword in zhengwo, extended holding, position.

2.1 Spread arms outward

Movements   Push forward with both hands and keep your palms turned down until both the left jianjue and the sword point to the south. The blade of the sword should be horizontal *(fig. 2.1.1)*.

    Let your arms separate continuously as they move outward in a horizontal arc until the tip of the sword points to the west and the left jianjue points to the east *(fig. 2.1.2)*.

Internal Components   Look from south to west. Shift the focus of your mind from the left jianjue to the tip of the sword. Feel as though qi can reach to the tip of the sword.

Key Points   Let both arms stretch outward and let your body sink down slightly. Think of the top of your head as being suspended from above at the baihui point (top of the head). This will cause your body to be stable and nimble and to feel as though it can move around quickly and easily in a circle.

Application   If the opponent attacks from your right side or your back, you can turn your body quickly and use your sword to chop at his waist *(fig. 2.1.3)*. Here, the basic technique is hengzhan, side-cutting.

2.2.1   2.2.2   2.2.3

2.2 Raise sword to block up and assume bow stance

Movements   Relax both arms and with the left jianjue pointing east and the tip of the sword pointing west. Drop your arms down to the sides of your body. Let your body sink down slightly and at the same time, turn your head to the south. then step forward with your left foot by putting the heel on the ground and letting the toes point up *(fig. 2.2.1)*.

Continuing without interruption, shift your weight forward to make a left wide bow stance. At the same time, move both arms forward and up until your hands are in front of your face. Hold the sword in your right hand with neiba, the palm-inward grip, so that it is parallel to the ground and so that the edges of the blade are oriented vertically, that is, with the xiaren, the bottom edge, facing up and shangren, the top edge, facing down. The tip of the sword should point to the west. Keep the left jianjue in touch with the jiantan and your left palm facing south *(fig. 2.2.2)*.

Internal Components   As you relax your arms and bring them to your sides at the beginning of this movement, look from west to south. Focus your mind first on the back of your waist and then on the baihui point (on top of the head). Feel qi extending to both hands. This will cause your body to sink down slightly and your hands to push the sword upward.

Key Points   Relax your shoulders, elbows, hips, and knees. This will cause your body to sink down. As it sinks, keep the baihui point high, as though it were suspended from above. Your hands and feet will then feel nimble and ready to move forward as your weight shifts onto your left leg.

Application   When the opponent attacks you from above, you can lower your body a little bit and shift slightly to the left. Then, you can quickly move in close to him and use your sword to strike horizontally under his arm *(fig. 2.2.3)*. This application, a basic technique, is called shangjie, or blocking up.

2.3.1   2.3.2   2.3.3

2.3 Block down while taking back insert step

Movements   Gradually turn your right hand so that the tip of the sword moves up in a half circle until it points to the sky. Keep the left jianjue in touch with the jiantan. Then, turn your left foot to the right, pivoting on the heel until the toes of your left foot point to the west. At the same time, turn your body to the right but keep your head and shoulders facing south *(fig. 2.3.1)*.

Continuing without interruption, turn your head to the left and continue moving the tip of the sword counterclockwise until it points to the east and the sword is parallel to the ground. At the same time, bend your left leg and step back on the ball of your right foot as you place that foot behind the left foot. This is a back insert step. Crouch down but keep your torso straight. Hold the sword near your left knee with your right hand, and position the left jianjue near the right wrist *(fig. 2.3.2)*.

Internal Components   Look forward and then let your gaze follow the tip of the sword as it moves counterclockwise. Focus your mind on the baihui point (on top of the head) and then change the focus of your mind to the left hand. Feel qi in both hands and sinking down

Key Points   When moving the sword up, your body should remain erect. When stepping back, be careful to maintain balance and keep a steady pace. Feel as though you are pressing down heavily on the sword with both hands.

Application   If the opponent is on your left, you can use a back insert step to get close to him and then use your sword to block his thrust and attack his arm *(fig. 2.3.3)*. This is a basic technique called xiajie, blocking down.

2.4.1   2.4.2   2.4.3

2.4 Pull sword from side to side and assume balance stance

Movements Move both hands up until they are in front of your face. At the same time, turn your right hand outward so that the palm faces south and keep the left jianjue near your right wrist. Raise your body about halfway up from the crouch position and make sure that your legs remain partially bent *(fig. 2.4.1)*.

Continuing without interruption, turn your body slightly to the northwest. Lift your right foot off the ground behind your body. Keep your right knee bent and continue to raise your right foot until it is at the level of your hips and the ball of your right foot faces up. Let your body lean forward slightly. At the same time, move both hands up above your head, and then move your right hand, holding the sword, to the northwest so that the jiantan points to the northwest and the tip of the sword points to the southeast. Move the left jianjue parallel to the blade and toward the tip of the sword and then point it toward the southeast *(fig. 2.4.2)*.

Internal Components Look to the southeast and focus your mind on the left jianjue. Feel qi reaching your hands, feet, and the top of your head.

Key Points Move your body up and then separate your hands and raise your right leg behind your body. Your whole body should feel stable. This is a balance movement. Try to do it slowly and to keep your body and leg from shaking.

Application When you are close to the opponent and he is attacking you from above, you can use your sword to block him at his armpit and your jianjue to attack his ribs *(fig. 2.4.3)*. Here, the basic technique is chou, pull-cutting. You can also kick him if he attacks you from behind. Note that there are several balance movements in the form. These are used for basic Kungfu training, especially for the legs and waist, but they are not often used in actual fighting.

3.1.1   3.1.2

3. STEP FORWARD AND SHELTER KNEE

This posture provides good practice for turning the body around to protect the shoulder and the knee and to ji, hammer-hit, the opponent's knee.

3.1 Low block backward while in sitting stance

Movements Step forward toward the northwest with your right foot. Touch the ground with your right heel and let the toes of your right foot point to the sky. This is a left wide sitting stance. At the same time, move both hands down to the left side of your waist with your right hand holding the sword so that the tip points slightly upward and toward the southeast. Keep the left jianjue near your right wrist *(fig. 3.1.1)*.

Internal Components Face the southeast and look at the tip of the sword. Focus your mind on your left shoulder and then change the focus to your left hand. Feel qi return to the dantian, in the lower abdomen.

Key Points Step to the northwest but turn your body slightly to the southeast. Feel as though your body is about to move forward, while your right hand is ready with the sword to protect your left shoulder and to strike backward if necessary.

Application If the opponent attacks your left shoulder, you can dodge to the right and use the sword to block his attack *(fig. 3.1.2)*. Here, the basic technique is fanjie, blocking back.

3.2.1   3.2.2

3.2 Turn sword over and strike up while in bow stance

Movements   Turn your head to the northwest and shift your weight forward, making a right standard bow stance. At the same time, sweep the sword down, edge first, from your left shoulder to the front of your right knee. Keep your right arm extended throughout the arc. This movement traces a half circle, with the tip of the sword traveling from the southeast, then down toward the ground and finally up again to point toward the northwest at knee level. Keep both arms straight and hold the sword with the right hand in niba, the thumb-down grip. At this point, xiaren, the bottom edge of the sword, should face up. Keep the left jianjue under and close to your right wrist *(fig. 3.2.1)*.

Internal Components   Look from the southeast to the northwest and let the sword follow the movement of your eyes. Focus your mind first on your right hand and then on the tip of the sword. Feel as though qi can reach the tip of the sword quickly.

Key Points   When fifty percent of your weight has shifted forward, turn your left foot by pivoting on the ball of the foot and make both feet point to the northwest. Each of the next five postures is oriented toward the northwest.

Application   When the opponent attacks your right knee, you can use the sword to block his weapon and attack his knee or his forward hand with fanji, a curving, upward hammer hit *(fig. 3.2.2)*. Other basic techniques include jie, blocking with the edge, and lan, blocking at mid-level.

4.1.1   4.1.2

4. TIGER CROUCHES AT THE FRONT DOOR

As its name suggests, this posture is meant to make people afraid of coming toward you because the sword, metaphorically the tiger, is ready to attack forward. Although used for attack, this posture is even more commonly used for defense. Shen is very important here and must be used to make the opponent feel afraid to advance.

4.1 Raise body forward and block wrist

Movements Turn your right hand with the sword over 360 degrees clockwise. This causes xiaren, the bottom edge, to face up again. Let the tip of the sword point to the northwest at face level. Put the left jianjue behind the jiantan. Stretch your right arm slightly forward *(fig. 4.1.1)*.

Internal Components Look up slightly and then forward to the northwest. Focus your mind on the tip of the sword. Feel qi going continuously to the tip of the sword.

Key Points Your body should sink down slightly and your left leg should stretch back a little bit as your right arm stretches forward. The movement should feel very nimble.

Application When the opponent attacks your face and your sword is below his weapon, you can turn over your sword and attack him under his front wrist or arm *(fig. 4.1.2)*. Here, the basic techniques are shangjie, upward interception with the sword edge; tiao, to thrust and cut up; and liao, to cut down with the tip or edge of the sword.

4.2.1   4.2.2

4.2 Hold sword horizontally and assume insubstantial stance

Movements   Shift your weight back to the left leg and move your right foot back in a half-step, letting the toes of your right foot touch the ground. This is a left insubstantial stance, xubu. At the same time, turn your body to the left slightly and pull your right hand with the sword back to the left side of your head. Keep the tip of the sword in the center of your body and pointed to the northwest at face level. The jiantan should point to the southeast. Touch the jiantan with the left jianjue *(fig. 4.2.1)*.

Internal Components   Look forward toward the northwest. Focus your mind on your left hand. Feel qi in your right elbow. This will cause your right hand with the sword to be powerful.

Key Points   Although your body dodges back in this movement, you should feel inside as though you want to go forward. Your body should be stable and ready to turn in any direction nimbly. The left jianjue can be changed to jianfa to help control the sword and make it more nimble and powerful.

Application   When the opponent comes in with ferocity, you can dodge slightly to the side and prepare to attack him from this angle *(fig. 4.2.2)*. Also, you can use the sword to cut his wrist or arm from below. Here, the basic techniques are chou, pull-cutting, and dai, moving straight back.

5.1.1a   5.1.1b   5.1.2

5. BOATMAN ROWS A SCULL

The "boatman rows a scull" is a very coordinated and integrated movement. When the body turns and moves up and down, the movement must be agile and smooth, just like a boatman's stroke.

5.1 Turn around and block back with sword

Movements   Move your right foot forward in a half-step and turn it to the right so that the toes of your right foot point to the northeast. At the same time, shift your weight forward and make your body turn to the right and sink down. Raise the heel of your left foot and keep about thirty percent of your weight on your left foot. As your body turns to the right, move the sword in a half circle to the right side of your body until the tip points to the southeast and your right hand is in front of the upper right side of your right knee. Hold the sword in your right hand with yinba, the palm-up grip. Hold the jiantan a little higher than the tip of the sword. Keep your left jianjue touching the jiantan, as shown here in these front and back views *(fig. 5.1.1a, b)*.

Internal Components   Look at the tip of the sword as it moves in a half circle to the right side of your body. Keep your mind focused on your left hand. Feel as though qi is on the jianshen, the body of the sword, which will cause the sword to be heavy.

Key Points   The change of step should be agile and stable. Keep your right heel and the toes of your left foot on a diagonal line from northwest to southeast.

Application   When the opponent attacks you in the center of your body or on the right side, you can dodge slightly to the left and use your sword to press his weapon upward and follow his force as your body turns to the right *(see fig. 5.1.2)*. Here, the basic techniques are ge, blocking with the ridge of the blade; ya, pressing down; and dai, moving straight back.

5.2.1   5.2.2

5.2 Raise body forward and cut up

Movements   Raise your body gradually as you turn to the left and face the northwest. Keep both legs bent slightly while your weight shifts completely to your right leg. At the same time, change the left jianjue to jianfa and use it to hold the jiantan. Move the sword with your right hand up and forward in a half circle until the tip of the sword points to the northwest and is level with the top of your head and until the jiantan points to the center of your chest *(fig. 5.2.1)*.

Internal Components   Look from back to front, just ahead of the tip of the sword as it moves from southeast to northwest. Focus your mind first on your right hand and then on your left hand. Feel qi going to the tip of the sword. This will cause your body to feel as though it is stretching out.

Key Points   When your body is erect, the sword should feel heavy in your hands. Do not fully straighten your legs. You should feel that you can make a nimble step.

Application   Continuing from the last movement, keep your sword in contact with the opponent's weapon and relax your arms. This will cause the sword to become heavy. Then, move the sword up along the opponent's weapon to cut his hand or neck *(fig. 5.2.2)*. Here, the basic techniques are ya, pressing down, and xiao, the quick cut.

6.1.1   6.1.2

6. PUSH A BOAT WITH THE TIDE

In this movement, you should just relax and follow your opponent's force and direction. The techniques used should be done in a smooth and easy manner. Here, the boat is the sword and the water is the opponent's force or movements.

6.1 Sink down with sword and assume rest stance

Movements   Step forward with your left foot, touch the ground with your left heel and then turn your foot to the left so that it points to the southwest. Shift your weight forward and at the same time, turn your body to the left and sink down, keeping your weight evenly distributed on both legs. Your right knee should touch your left knee from behind and your right heel should be raised off the ground. As your left heel touches the ground, move the sword down to the front of your left knee using both hands. The tip of the sword should point to the northwest and the jiantan should point to the left yinlingquan point (inner side of left knee). Keep the sword parallel to the ground and keep the blade horizontal *(fig. 6.1.1)*.

Internal Components   Keep looking forward and focus your mind on your right hand. Feel as though qi is on the body of the sword, which will cause the sword to sink down and be heavy.

Key Points   Move the sword directly down but be careful not to move it forward or backward. Although your weight is on both feet, you should feel that the back foot is nimble and can move quickly. Turn your body to the left about ninety degrees but keep your head facing toward the northwest.

Application   If the opponent attacks you from below, you can drop your sword to block his weapon. Turning your body to the left allows your internal force to change direc-

| 6.2.1 | 6.2.2 |

tion easily *(fig. 6.1.2)*. Here, the basic techniques are ya, pressing down, and ge, blocking with the ridge of the sword.

6.2 Step forward and thrust at side of chest

Movements Step forward with your right foot and make a right standard bow stance. At the same time, move the sword forward with your right hand as if to pierce an oncoming opponent. Keep the blade of the sword flat. Move your left arm back and point the left jianjue toward the southeast *(fig. 6.2.1)*.

Internal Components Continue to look forward. Focus your mind first on your right hand and then on the left hand. Feel as though qi can reach to the tip of the sword.

Key Points Keep your torso erect and be prepared to make a forward step that is quick and big. Your body should be raised slightly but the sword should be kept at the same level as in the previous movement. Relaxing your whole body will cause the sword to feel heavy.

Application Continuing from the last movement, allow the sword to adhere to the opponent's weapon. With this movement you can prick the opponent on the side of his chest between his ribs *(fig. 6.2.2)*. Here, the basic techniques are ya, pressing down, and ci, thrusting.

7.1.1   7.1.2

7. PAINT A RED DOT BETWEEN THE EYEBROWS

Painting red dots between the eyebrows of children is a traditional way of wishing them good luck. This posture involves using the sword to point at and attack the opponent's face, like using a brushpen to draw a red dot between his eyebrows. It is a skill that requires quickness and agility.

7.1 Relax crotch and block up

Movements   Relax your left hip and knee and make a half-step with your left foot, letting the ball of that foot touch the ground. At this point, your left foot should still be behind the right foot. At the same time, move your right hand, which holds the sword in neiba, the palm-inward grip, back to the left side of your head so that the jiantan is near your forehead. The tip of the sword should be in front of the centerline of your body at chest level and the jiantan should point to the southeast and be higher than the tip. Move your left hand back until it is near the left side of your waist. The palm of your left hand should face up and the left jianjue should point toward your body *(fig. 7.1.1)*.

Internal Components   First look forward, then at the tip of the sword and finally, to a point beyond the tip. Focus your mind on your left hand. Feel qi extend around both arms.

Key Points   Continue to keep about ninety percent of your weight on the right leg. Your torso should be erect and turned slightly to the left. Feel as though both hands are pulling the sword up and to the left side of your body.

Application   When the opponent attacks your chest or head, you can move in toward him and slightly to the left. Then, you can use the tip of the sword to block and cut his front wrist from below *(fig. 7.1.2)*. Here, the basic techniques are shangjie, blocking and cutting up, and chou, the pull-cut.

7.2.1

7.2.2

7.2 Cut attacker's wrist while in sitting stance

Movements Put your left heel down and shift your weight to the left leg. As your weight shifts, relax your right leg and take a half-step forward, letting your right heel touch the ground and the toes of your right foot point to the sky. This forms a standard left sitting stance. At the same time, turn both arms outward and move your right hand holding the sword across to the right side of your body and slightly forward. Your right hand should hold the sword using waiba, the palm-outward grip. Point the tip of the sword forward and slightly down so that it is level with your chest. The jiantan should point toward the southeast and be higher than the tip and the tip should point toward northwest. Rotate your left hand so that it pushes outward and slightly down in a small arc and so that the jianjue points toward the north *(fig. 7.2.1)*.

Internal Components Keep looking forward and focus your mind on your left hand. Feel qi extending like a circle through both arms.

Key points Your body turns to the right slightly as your right hand pulls the sword. The tip of the sword remains almost at the same place as in the last movement. As your hands turn outward, feel as though they are pushing to the sides of your body. This will cause the internal force to be powerful. When your weight shifts to the left leg, your right foot should step forward quickly and smoothly.

Application Continuing from the last technique, if the opponent slightly changes the direction of his attack, you can move in a little bit and continue to use the tip of the sword to attack his wrist *(fig. 7.2.2)*. Here, the basic techniques are ti, the upward cut, and chou, the pull-cut.

7.3.1   7.4.1

7.3 Pursue and strike while in bow stance

Movements   Relax your shoulders and elbows and let both arms drop down to the sides of your body. At the same time, relax your hips and knees and shift your weight forward to your right leg. Keep your left leg bent and raise your left heel so that only the ball of your left foot touches the ground *(fig. 7.3.1)*.

Internal Components   Keep looking forward (northwest) and focus your mind on mingmen point, at the center of the lower back. Feel qi reaching to the top of your head.

Key Points   Keep your body relaxed and feel as though it is sinking slightly down. Your right leg should feel like a spring which can make your body move forward with force and speed.

Application   If the opponent wants to move back, you can compress your body by sinking down slightly in readiness to spring forward in pursuit.

7.4.2   7.4.3

7.4 Step forward and point to *xuanguan*

Movements   Step forward with your left foot, using a step that is slightly bigger than normal. Shift your weight to the left leg but keep your leg slightly bent so that your body is a little higher than in the normal bow stance. Take a half-step forward with your right foot, letting that foot follow your left foot. Keep your right leg slightly bent and raise your right heel so that only the ball of your right foot touches the ground. At the same time, move both hands to the front of your chest, with the jianjue and the tip of the sword pointing forward *(fig. 7.4.1)*.

Continuing without interruption, move your left hand up and to the left so that it points to the west. Move the sword up and forward with your right hand so that the tip first points straight ahead and then arcs slightly down as your right arm finishes its extension. At the end of the movement, the tip of the sword should be level with the top of your head *(fig. 7.4.2)*.

Internal Components   Look forward and then slightly up. Focus your mind first on the jiaji point, at the center of the upper back, and then on the tip of the sword. Feel qi sink down to the dantian, the lower abdomen, and then shift to the left jianjue and the tip of the sword.

Key Points   Keep your torso erect. When your right hand points forward with the sword, you should feel the internal force coming up from your wrist to the tip of the sword. The tip of the sword should move with a pricking motion, first forward, then up, and finally down.

Application   When the opponent wants to block your upward attack, you can relax your right wrist to prick at a point on his face. Imagine that the force of your sword goes around his weapon and that you do not want to allow contact between his weapon and your sword *(fig. 7.4.3)*. Here, the basic technique is dian, pointing with the tip.

8.1.1   8.1.2

8. THRUST SWORD IN THE OPPOSITE DIRECTION

In this movement, your sword should move along your opponent's weapon in a direction opposite to that in which the opponent's weapon is moving.

8.1 Sink body down with sword and step forward

Movements   Let your body sink down and then step forward with your right foot. Let your right heel touch the ground and the toes of your right foot point up to make a standard left sitting stance. At the same time, move both hands down and back to the sides of your body. Hold the sword in your right hand with the tip pointing up and forward. Touch the the jiantan with the jianfa of the left hand and place the jiantan in front of your left knee *(fig. 8.1.1)*.

Internal Components   Look forward and focus your mind first on your right hand and then on your left hand. Feel qi sink down to the dantian, in the lower abdomen.

Key Points   Keep your body erect. Feel as though your whole body is sinking down and becoming stable and as though the sword is very heavy.

Application   If the opponent attacks you at the middle or lower part of your body, you can drop your sword down to touch his weapon and press on it *(fig. 8.1.2)*. Here, the basic technique is ya, pressing down.

8.2.1   8.2.2

8.2 Thrust straight ahead with sword while in bow stance

Movements   Shift your weight forward to your right leg to make a standard right bow stance. At the same time, thrust forward with the sword, using your right hand to hold the jianbing, the handle, while your left hand is in the jianfa position to hold the jiantan. The tip of sword should be at throat level *(fig. 8.2.1)*.

Internal Components   Keep looking forward and focus your mind on the tip of the sword. Feel as though qi can reach from the tip of the sword directly to the dantian, in the lower abdomen.

Key Points   Keep your body relaxed and low as though it were sinking down. Feel that the sword is heavy and keep pressing down on it as it moves forward to prick at the opponent. The sword should move forward in a straight, quick, and powerful movement.

Application   Continuing from the last movement, keep your sword on top of the opponent's weapon and press down. Then, strike forward to prick his chest or throat *(fig. 8.2.2)*. Here, the basic techniques are ya, pressing down, and ci, thrusting.

9.1.1a   9.1.1b   9.1.2

9. TURN BACK WHILE PRICKING LIGHTLY UP

Two skills are developed in this posture. One is turning the body to the back and the other is dodging to the left while using the sword to point up.

9.1 Turn back and hide sword

Movements   Pivot your on right foot toward the south using the right heel and turn counterclockwise until you face southeast. Keep your weight on your right leg. At the same time, relax your right shoulder and turn your right hand until the tiger-mouth of the right hand faces down. This will cause the sword to point vertically to the ground. Move the left jianjue first to your right shoulder and then to your left shoulder *(fig. 9.1.1a, b)*.

Continuing without interruption, move the left jianjue past your left shoulder until it points to the southeast. At the same time, move your left foot counterclockwise and let only the ball of the left foot rest on the ground at the end of the step. This forms a insubstantial right sitting stance *(fig. 9.1.2)*.

Internal Components   Look from the northwest to the southeast. Focus your mind on your right hand. Feel qi reaching to the left jianjue.

Key Points   When your body turns to the back, maintain good balance. After turning, you should pull your abdomen in a little bit so that you feel as though your body is dodging slightly back.

Application   When the opponent is behind your back, you can turn your body and dodge back slightly while directing shen forward in the direction the jianjue is pointing. This will make the opponent feel nervous.

| 9.2.1 | 9.2.2a, b | 9.2.3 |

9.2 Step forward and point at attacker's wrist

Movements   Move your right hand holding the sword from the back of your body to the front until it is parallel to the left jianjue and points to the southeast (*fig. 9.2.1*).

Continuing without interruption from the previous movement, move your left foot to the left (counterclockwise) until the toes point to the east. This will cause your body to turn to the left. Then, shift your weight forward to form a wide left bow stance and at the same time turn your right foot using only the toes so that they, too, point to the east. While turning your right foot, separate your hands. Extend the left jianjue in front of your body and slightly to the left of center and let it point with an upward tilt toward the northeast. Do not move your right hand. Relax your right shoulder, drop your right elbow down, and let your right wrist sink down. These adjustments will cause the tip of the sword to point to the southeast and to slant slightly upward, ready to attack (*fig. 9.2.2a, b*).

Internal Components   Look forward. When your body turns to the left, continue to look toward the southeast. Focus your mind first on your right hand and then on the left hand. Feel qi fully in your right wrist.

Key Points   Feel as though your body is about to move quickly and nimbly forward and to the left. The sinking down of your right wrist should cause the tip of the sword to point upward suddenly, powerfully and quickly.

Application   If the opponent attacks you from the front, you can dodge a little to the left and move your body toward him. Then you can use your sword to attack his front hand or wrist from below (*fig. 9.2.3*). Here, the basic technique is beng, an explosive upward wrist flick, and dian, pointing with the tip.

10.1.1   10.1.2

10. PEI GONG CHOPS A SNAKE

Pei Gong's real name was Liu Bang, the first emperor of the Han Dynasty, who ruled China about 2200 years ago. The story is told that he killed a huge snake in the mountains and believed that he had been helped in this great feat by the gods. This inspired him to lead the people to destroy the old dynasty and build a new one. In this posture, you should think of the opponent as the snake and yourself as Pei Gong.

10.1 Block up with sword and make back insert step

Movements   Straighten your body. Move your right foot behind and to the left side of your left foot to form a back insert step. This will cause your body to turn slightly to the right. Keep your weight on your left leg, which should remain slightly bent. Let only the ball of your right foot touch the ground. At the same time, move both hands up until they are higher than your shoulders and then turn them inward. Point the tip of the sword and the jianjue to the same spot in front of and slightly above your head (*fig. 10.1.1*).

Internal Components   Look up and straight ahead. Focus your mind first on your right foot and then on the tip of the sword. Feel qi in both arms and extending to the tip of the sword and to the left jianjue.

Key Points   Keep your torso erect and feel as though your body wants to move forward (east). Both hands should feel powerful and ready to cut upwards.

Application   When the opponent attacks you from above, you can quickly move in close to him with a back insert step and use your sword to cut his arm from below (*fig. 10.1.2*). Here, the basic technique is shangjie, blocking up.

10.2.1   10.2.2

10.2 Step back and make a horizontal circle with sword

Movements   Step back with your right foot and shift your weight onto it. Raise the heel of your left foot so that only the ball of that foot touches the ground. Let your body lean back a little. Then, make a counterclockwise circle with your left arm and a clockwise circle with your right arm at the same time. This will cause the tip of the sword to move in a large horizontal circle in front of and above your head *(fig. 10.2.1)*.

Internal Components   Look up and put your mind on the baihui point, on top of the head. Feel qi go to the tip of the sword.

Key Points   The back step should be a little bit bigger than usual and your left knee should rise slightly. When your body moves back with the weight shift, you should feel that your whole body is relaxed and already starting to move forward.

Application   Continuing without interruption from the last movement, if you feel that the opponent's weapon is strong, you should follow the direction of his force and move your body back. At the same time, you can use your sword to make a circle that will change the direction of his force *(fig. 10.2.2)*. Here, the basic techniques are ge, blocking with the ridge of the sword, and dai, moving the sword straight back.

10.3.1   10.3.2

10.3 Step forward and cut attacker's waist

Movements Continuing without interruption from the previous movement, straighten your body. Step forward with your right foot putting only the ball of the foot on the ground. Shift eighty percent of your weight to your left leg to form a left insubstantial stance. At the same time, move both hands outward and then forward in a circular motion until they meet. Hold the sword in front of your body at waist level. The tip of the sword should be pointing forward and both palms should be facing up. Use your left hand in the jianfa position to hold the jiantan *(fig. 10.3.1)*.

Internal Components Look forward and focus your mind first on the baihui point, on top of the head, and then on your left hand. Feel qi on the tip of the sword and extending beyond it so that your arms feel as though they are stretching forward.

Key Points Use the top of your head to lead the movement of your body. Feel as though you can shift your weight forward quickly and that your hands are powerful.

Application Continuing without interruption from the previous movement, step forward quickly and use your sword to make a circle under the opponent's weapon in order to chop his waist horizontally *(fig. 10.3.2)*. Here, the basic technique is lan, blocking and breaking off in the middle.

10.4.1   10.4.2

10.4 Pull sword back while in insubstantial stance

Movements   Shift one hundred percent of your weight to the left leg, and move your right foot back a little to form a left insubstantial stance. At the same time, move your body back and put both hands together to pull the sword back horizontally *(fig. 10.4.1)*.

Internal Components   Keep looking forward and focus your mind on your left hand. Feel qi sink down to the dantian, in the lower abdomen.

Key points   When you pull the sword back, make sure that your body, the sword, and your right foot move back in unison. Your right knee should feel as though it is rising slightly. This will cause your body to be stable and your hands to be powerful.

Application   After chopping at the opponent's body in the last movement, you can continue by pulling your sword back to cut the opponent's midsection *(fig. 10.4.2)*. Here, the basic technique is chou, a pull-cut.

11.1.1   11.1.2

11. BRUSH DUST IN THE BREEZE

This relaxed and agile movement is based on a common mannerism of Daoist priests. You should think of the opponent's weapon as being like the dust and your sword as being like a brush that you are using very softly and lightly.

11.1 Make a closed circle with arms and assume insubstantial stance

Movements Turn your body to the right and raise your right knee slightly so that the ball of your right foot just touches the ground. This forms an insubstantial stance. At the same time, holding the sword with both hands, move your hands to the right side of your body at waist level. Point the sword straight up *(fig. 11.1.1)*.

Internal Components Look to the left and focus your mind on the jiantan. Feel qi extending in a circle through your arms.

Key Points Let your body sink down. Your hands, holding the sword, should drop down, too. This will cause your body to be very stable. Both arms should bend and form a circle. The sword should feel powerful on the right side but inside you should feel relaxed and comfortable, as if you were doing something easy like brushing dust.

Application When your opponent moves to attack your right side, turn your body to the right and use the jianji, the ridge of the sword, to block his weapon *(fig. 11.1.2)*. Here, the basic technique is ge, blocking with the ridge of the sword.

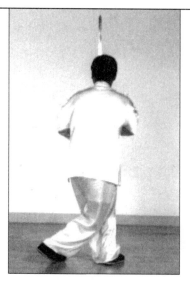

11.2.1   11.2.2

11.2 Hold sword vertically and assume rest stance

Movements   Take a half-step forward with your left foot, letting the heel touch the ground first. Then, turn to the left so that the toes of your left foot point to the north. While stepping, shift your weight forward until about eighty percent of your weight is on your left leg. Raise your right heel off the ground but keep the ball of the foot on the ground. This forms a rest stance. At the same time, turn your body to the left and sink down a bit. Use both hands to move the sword to the left side of your body while continuing to hold the sword vertically at waist level *(fig. 11.2.1)*.

Internal Components   Look around to the north and focus your mind on your right hand. Feel qi extending through both arms.

Key Points   Your step should be soft and agile. Keep your shoulders relaxed and let your elbows drop down. Feel as though you are using the sword to touch something lightly.

Application   When the opponent wants to attack your left side, just turn your body and use the jianji to block his weapon using a soft and sticking manner *(fig. 11.2.2)*. Here, as in the previous movement, the basic technique is ge, blocking with the ridge of the sword.

11.3.1   11.3.2

11.3 Raise sword and assume sitting stance

Movements   Turn your head to the right (east). Move the tip of the sword down in a clockwise arc until it is horizontal and pointing to the east at eye level on the left side of your head. At the same time, step forward with your right foot to make a left sitting stance *(fig. 11.3.1)*.

Internal Components   Look to the east. Focus your mind on your right hand. Feel qi sink down to the dantian, in the lower abdomen.

Key Points   Keep your body stable but your step nimble. Feel as though your body can move forward very quickly.

Application   Continuing without interruption from the previous movement, let your sword stick to the opponent's weapon and move the tip of your sword down to attack his front hand *(fig. 11.3.2)*. Here, the basic technique is dian, striking straight down with the tip.

11.4.1   11.4.2

11.4 Thrust straight ahead and assume bow stance

Movements Shift your weight forward to assume a bow stance. At the same time, hold the sword with both hands and move it forward in a thrusting motion *(fig. 11.4.1)*.

Internal Components Look forward and focus your mind on the mingmen point, in the center of the lower back. Feel qi reaching to the tip of the sword.

Key Points When your weight shifts forward, you can take a half-step forward with your right foot. This will cause your body to feel as though it can move forward very quickly. The step should be very agile, and your body should feel able to move quickly backward as well as forward.

Application Continuing from the last movement, after attacking the opponent's front hand, keep the sword going forward to prick his shoulder or chest *(fig. 11.4.2)*. Here, the basic technique is ci, thrusting.

11.5.1   11.5.2

11.5 Make a closed circle with arms and assume insubstantial stance

Movements Shift your weight back to your left leg. Turn your body to the left and raise your right knee slightly so that the ball of your right foot just touches the ground slightly, thereby forming a left insubstantial stance. At the same time, holding the sword with both hands and at waist level, move the sword back to the left side of your body. Form a circle with your arms and point the sword straight up *(fig. 11.5.1)*.

Internal Components Look to the left (north) and focus your mind on the jiantan. Feel qi extending through both arms.

Key Points During this movement, your body should sink down and your hands holding the sword should drop down, too. This will cause your body to be very stable. The sword, held on your left side, should feel very powerful, but your inner sensation should be of softness and comfort, as one would feel when doing something easy like brushing dust.

Application When the opponent wants to attack your left side, just turn your body to the left and use the jianji, the blade ridge, to block his weapon lightly *(fig. 11.5.2)*. Here, the basic technique is ge, blocking with the ridge of the sword.

11.6.1   11.6.2

11.6 Hold sword vertically and assume rest stance

Movements   Take a half-step forward with your right foot, letting the heel touch the ground first. Then turn to the right, so that the toes of your right foot point to the south. While stepping, shift your weight forward until about eighty percent of your weight is on your right leg. Let your left heel leave the ground but keep the ball of your left foot on the ground. This forms a rest stance. At the same time, turn your body to the right and sink down slightly. Move the sword to the right side of your body with both hands while continuing to hold the sword vertically at waist level *(fig. 11.6.1)*.

Internal Components   Look around to the south. Focus your mind on the left hand. Feel qi extending through both arms.

Key Points   Your step should continue to be soft and agile and your shoulders should remain relaxed. Keep your elbows down, as though using the sword to touch something lightly.

Application   When the opponent wants to attack your right side, turn your body and use the sword to block his weapon in a soft and sticking manner *(fig. 11.6.2)*. Here, the basic technique is ge, blocking with the ridge of the sword.

11.7.1 11.7.2

11.7 Raise sword and assume sitting stance

Movements Turn your head to the left and face east. Move the tip of the sword down in a counterclockwise arc until it is horizontal and pointing east at eye level at the right side of your head. At the same time, move your left foot forward to make a right sitting stance *(fig. 11.7.1)*.

Internal Components Look to the east and focus your mind on the left hand. Feel qi sink down to the dantian, in the lower abdomen.

Key Points Keep your body stable but your step nimble. Feel as though your body can move forward very quickly.

Application Continuing without interruption from the previous movement and keeping a sticking touch on the opponent's weapon, move the tip of the sword down to attack his front hand *(fig. 11.7.2)*. Here, the basic technique is dian, striking straight down with tip, or tiao, pricking in and cutting up.

11.8.1   11.8.2

11.8 Thrust straight ahead and assume bow stance

Movements Shift your weight forward into a left bow stance. At the same time, holding the sword with both hands, move it straight ahead (east) with a thrusting motion *(fig. 11.8.1)*.

Internal Components Look forward and focus your mind on the mingmen point, in the center of the lower back. Feel qi reach to the tip of the sword.

Key Points As your weight shifts forward, you can take a half-step forward with your left foot. This will create a feeling in your body of readiness to move forward or backward very quickly. Your step should be very agile.

Application After attacking the opponent's front hand, keep your sword going forward in a movement continuous with the previous one so that the tip of your sword will prick the shoulder or chest of your opponent *(fig. 11.8.2)*. Here, the basic technique is ci, thrusting.

| 12.1.1a | 12.1.1b | 12.1.2 |

12. DRAGONFLY SKIMS THE WATER

The movement of a dragonfly skimming the water is agile, brisk, lighthearted, and graceful. In this posture, the sword is like a dragonfly skimming over the water, the water representing the opponent.

12.1 Turn to the left and use sword to block back

Movements   Turn your body to the left and, holding the sword in your right hand, move it down to the left side of your body so that your right hand is beside your left hip and the tip of the sword points behind your body and down toward the ground. At the same time, release your left hand from the jiantan and make the left jianjue. Move the jianjue down to the front of your abdomen and under your right hand, so the jianjue points forward (east). At the same time, shift your weight backward and move your left foot back slightly with only the toes of the left foot touching the ground. This forms an insubstantial stance. Then shift your weight forward and turn your left foot to the left until the toes point north *(fig. 12.1.1a, b).*

Internal Components   Look down and forward. Focus your mind on the mingmen point, in the center of the lower back. Feel qi in the left jianjue.

Key Points   Move your body back slightly and with agility. Feel as though you are using your body to absorb something.

Application   If the opponent attacks you low on your left side, you can dodge back a little and use the sword to follow and block his weapon. If you are close to the opponent, you can use your left hand to help with the block *(fig. 12.1.2).* Here, the basic techniques are ge, blocking with the ridge of the sword, dai, moving the sword straight back, and xi, making sword circles diagonally around the body.

| 12.2.1 | 12.2.2 | 12.2.3 |

12.2 Point at the ankle

Movements Step forward with your right foot and let the toes of your right foot point left (north). Turn your body a little to the left so that it faces north. At the same time, cross your hands and move them up to the left side of your head *(fig. 12.2.1)*.

Let both hands continue to rise and then gradually separate them so that the left jianjue moves above your head and your right arm moves in a downward arc until the sword points to the ground. At the same time, raise your left knee up on the left side of your body so that the knee faces west. This is a one-legged stance *(fig. 12.2.2)*.

Internal Components Look forward and down. Focus your mind on your right hand. Feel qi reaching to the tip of the sword.

Key Points Your step should be nimble and quick. If there is any problem maintaining your position in the one-legged stance, think of the baihui point, at the top of the head, and imagine that it is suspended from above. Feel the internal force flow from your right wrist to the tip of the sword as you complete this movement in an agile and relaxed manner.

Application With this movement, you can use your sword to attack the lower part of the opponent's body, especially the jiexi acupoint, at the front of the ankle *(fig. 12.2.3)*. Here, the basic technique is dian, striking straight down with the tip.

| 13.1.1 | 13.1.2 | 13.1.3 |

13. WASP FLIES THROUGH A HOLE

This is a nimble and precise movement, in which the sword is likened to a wasp and the center of the opponent's chest is the hole.

13.1 Thrust to the Leg

Movements   Move the sword up with your right hand so that the tip circles up first, then left and down until it is under your left armpit. Keep the left jianjue near your right hand. Turn your body back counterclockwise, toward the west *(fig. 13.1.1)*.

Continue without interruption to turn your body counterclockwise by pivoting on your right heel until the toes of the right foot point to the southwest *(fig. 13.1.2)*. At the same time, straighten your left leg and put it down behind your pivoting right foot. This forms a back insert step. The toes of your left foot should point toward the northeast. At the same time, let both hands encircle your body, with the sword held close to your torso and the tip pointing toward your back. As the turn is completed, prick downward with the sword until the blade of your sword is under your left elbow and left jianjue is over the inside of your right elbow. The focus of your thrust should be your opponent's zhusanli acupoint, to the side and near the front of his leg. At the conclusion of the turn, your legs should be bent, forming a half-horse stance, and your right leg should bear about sixty percent of your weight. Your body should face the southeast and your head should be turned toward the northeast with your face tilted slightly down *(fig. 13.1.3)*.

Internal Components   Look back around your body as you turn. Focus your mind on baihui point, on the top of the head, and then on your left hand. Feel qi go to the baihui point and then sink down to the dantian, in the lower abdomen.

13.1.4   13.1.5

Key Points While your body turns from north to southeast, the sword under your left armpit must be moved quickly and accurately. While turning, your body should sink down. Your back should feel strong and expanded and your step should be quick and well-balanced.

Application Two basic techniques are used here. First, when the opponent is close to you and attacking from behind on your left side, you can turn your body and use your sword to thrust back at him *(fig. 13.1.4, 5)*. The second technique is used when the opponent is in front and close to you. In this case, you can use your left hand to block his weapon and the sword to thrust toward the lower part of his body. Here, the basic technique is ci, thrusting.

13.2.1   13.2.2   14.1.1

13.2 Hold sword vertically and assume insubstantial stance

Movements   Shift your weight to your left leg and bring your right foot forward until it is pointing to the east and is parallel with your left foot. Let your body sink down and turn slightly to the left. At the same time, move your right hand in an upward thrusting motion so that the sword points up and the ridge of the blade faces toward the northeast. The left jianjue should touch your right wrist *(fig. 13.2.1)*.

Internal Components   Let your gaze move upward and look toward the northeast. Focus your mind on your right hand and then on the left. Feel qi sink down to your right wrist.

Key Points   Relax your shoulders and drop your elbows down. This will cause your body to be heavy and stable. Use the internal force to prick the sword up and forward and then to push the sword down a little. Feel as though your whole body can shrink back and then spring forward quickly.

Application   With this movement, you can thrust the opponent from below, as though on a skewer *(fig. 13.2.2)*. Here, the basic techniques are ci, thrusting, and tiao, thrusting in and cutting up.

| 14.1.2 | 14.1.3 | 14.1.4 |

14. SCOOP THE MOON FROM THE OCEAN DEPTHS

This movement is composed of consecutive up and down motions, like waves. In this posture, you should imagine that you are big enough to scoop the moon up from the bottom of the ocean. Think of the sword as the scoop and the opponent as the moon.

14.1 Block up and take cover step

Movements   Turn your body slightly to the right and face east. Raise the sword with your right hand until it is higher than the top of your head. Keep the sword horizontal and point the tip to the north. Move your left hand up as your right hand is raised so that the left jianjue continues to touch your right wrist *(fig. 14.1.1)*. At the same time, kick your right foot forward heel first. The sole of your right foot should face forward. Keep your left leg bent *(fig. 14.1.2)*.

Internal Components   Look forward (east). Focus your mind on your left hand. Feel qi sink down to the dantian, in the lower abdomen, and then extend to your hands.

Key Points   Keep your body stable and well-balanced. The low kick should be quick and hard.

Application   If the opponent attacks your head from above, you should move in close to him and use your sword to block his attack *(fig. 14.1.3)*, and at the same time kick him *(fig. 14.1.4)*. Here, the technique is shangjie, blocking up.

14.2.1   14.2.2

14.2 Turn to the right and pull sword

Movements Put your right heel on the ground. Then, turn the toes of your right foot to the right (south), and shift your weight forward. Keep both legs bent with about eighty percent of your weight on the right leg. Raise your left heel off the ground but keep the ball of your left foot in touch with the ground. At the same time, turn your body to the right and look to the southwest. Pull the sword horizontally to the southwest so that the jiantan points in that direction. Let your left hand follow the right hand. Then move the left jianjue down to the side of your right elbow *(fig. 14.2.1)*.

Internal Components Look from east to southwest. Focus your mind on the left jianjue. Feel qi sink down to the dantian, in the lower abdomen.

Key Points Feel as though your body can move forward nimbly.

Application Continuing without interruption from the last movement, you can pull the sword back to cut the opponent as your body moves forward *(fig. 14.2.2)*. Here, the basic technique is chou, a pull-cut with the edge of the sword.

14.3.1   14.3.2

14.3 Raise a flag

Movements   Make your body erect and straighten your right leg. Then, raise your left knee straight up so that the kneecap points toward the east. At the same time, move your right hand down so that the sword is vertical and the tip points up *(fig. 14.3.1)*.

Internal Components   Continue to look toward the southwest. Focus your mind on your left knee and feel as though it is rising continuously. Feel qi reaching to the top of your head.

Key Points   Let your body rise up as one unit and be careful to stay well-balanced. Your right hand holding the sword should sink and feel stable as though it were holding a big flag in the wind. The top of your head should feel as though it were suspended from above.

Application   If the opponent attacks you from the right side, you can use your sword to touch his weapon or forearm and then push it outward using your left hand to help. Also you can use your left foot to kick him *(fig. 14.3.2)*. Here, the technique is cejie, blocking side to side with the edge of the sword.

14.4.1   14.4.2   14.4.3

14.4 Tree roots twine around each other

Movements Bend your right leg and let your body sink down. Move your left foot to the northeast and let your heel touch the ground, then shift your weight forward. At the same time, move the blade of the sword down and let the tip point southwest *(fig. 14.4.1)*.

Continuing without interruption, turn your head to face the northeast. Shift your weight to your left leg and turn your right foot on the ball of the foot so that both feet point to the east. This forms a left wide bow stance. At the same time, turn your body to the left and as it turns, move both hands to the left side of your body. The left jian-jue should be on the left side of your waist and your left palm should face up. Holding the sword in your right hand with yinba, palm facing up, move your right arm around in a cutting curve so that the sword arcs first down, then forward, and finally up until it is in front of your body and points to the east. Your right palm should face up and the sword should be parallel to the ground with the edges of the sword on a vertical axis *(fig. 14.4.2)*.

Internal Components Look down and then to the northeast. Focus your mind on your right hand. Feel qi in your right hand.

Key Points Bend your right leg and sink down before stepping forward with your left foot. Imagine that you are holding the handle of the sword with both hands and then sweeping it forward edge first in a smooth motion. Let your right wrist turn slightly clockwise at the end of the sweep so that the leading edge of the sword faces up.

Application You can use this movement to attack the opponent with an upward cutting motion *(fig. 14.4.3)*.

15.1.1   15.1.2

15. TURN AROUND AND HANG A GOLDEN BELL

This is a protective technique. Imagine that the tip of the sword is a bell and that the opponent is a hook. Hang the bell on the hook.

15.1 Turn around and block left and back

Movements   Turn your body slightly to the left and face the northwest. Move your right hand with the sword to the left side of your waist and incline the sword back toward the northwest with the tip pointing up. Then, turn the left jianjue over and place it beside your right wrist. At the same time, step forward with your right foot and make a left standard sitting stance *(fig. 15.1.1)*.

Internal Components   Look toward the tip of the sword and to a point in space just beyond the tip. Focus your mind on your left shoulder. Feel qi sink down to the dantian, in the lower abdomen.

Key Points   Keep your body stable when stepping forward with the right foot. Feel as though your left shoulder is dodging back.

Application   Use the sword to protect your left side, especially your left shoulder and elbow *(fig. 15.1.2)*. Here, the basic technique is fanjie, blocking back with the tip and top part of the sword, and gua, hanging.

15.2.1   15.2.2

15.2 Merge steps and block down

Movements   Turn your body slightly to the right. Step forward with your left foot so that it is beside your right foot. Let both feet feel as though they are merged together and let your body sink down. At the same time, holding the sword with your right hand, move it down to the left side of your left knee. Keep the left jianjue in touch with your right wrist. Point the tip of the sword to the west behind your body and hold the sword so that it is parallel to the ground *(fig. 15.2.1)*.

Internal Components   Keep looking just past the tip of the sword. Focus your mind on your left hand. Feel qi in the dantian, in the lower abdomen.

Key Points   Try to feel as though the sword remains still while your body moves forward and down.

Application   If the opponent attacks from the lower left side of your body, you can dodge to the right and use the sword to block down *(fig. 15.2.2)*. Here, the basic technique is xiajie, blocking down.

16.1.1   16.1.2

16. KUI XING RAISES HIS BRUSH

In Chinese mythology, Kui Xing is a god of hell who has a book in which are written the names of every living human being. If he uses his brush to check off a name in the book, that person must die. In this posture, the sword is the brush and it is already raised for writing.

16.1 Turn around and block side to side

Movements   Straighten both legs until they are only slightly bent and turn your body to the right until it faces east. Using your right arm, move the sword to the front of your body and raise it to head height. Your right hand should hold the sword in niba, the hand-turned-over grip. Let the tip of the sword point forward and down and keep the left jianjue in touch with your right wrist *(fig. 16.1.1)*.

Internal Components   Look forward (east), and focus your mind on your right hand. Feel qi move to your right hand and then to the tip of the sword. This causes a side-to-side force.

Key Points   When raising the sword, your body must be erect. Keep the sword in the centerline of your body and feel as though it can be pulled up and then made to prick down. Feel as though there is force on both sides of the sword and that it can be used to block both sides of your body.

Application   If the opponent directs an attack at your body, you can use the sword to touch, stick, and block his weapon from the right side, and you can also cut his hand in an upward motion *(fig. 16.1.2)*. Here, the basic techniques are ti, cutting up with the tip of the sword, and ge, blocking with the ridge of the sword.

| 16.2.1 | 16.2.2 | 16.2.3 |

16.2 Raise sword and assume single leg stance

Movements Continuing without interruption from the previous movement, raise your right arm up in front of and above your head so that the tip of the sword is at chest level and points diagonally down. At the same time, raise your body slightly and shift your weight to your left foot *(fig. 16.2.1)*. Move the left jianjue down and forward and let it point to the tip of the sword. At the same time, raise your right knee and let your right toes point up. This forms a solo stance. Keep your left leg slightly bent and your body erect throughout this movement *(fig. 16.2.2)*.

Internal Components Look forward and focus your mind on your left hand. Feel qi move up to your right hand and then out to the tip of the sword.

Key Points The force for raising the sword should come from your leg and body. Feel as though you are cutting up with the upper side edge of the sword.

Application With this movement, you can continue the cutting motion begun in the previous movement aimed at the opponent's front hand *(fig. 16.2.3)*. Here, the basic techniques are ti, cutting with the tip of the sword, and ge, blocking with the ridge of the sword.

17.1.1   17.1.2

17. THRUST SWORD DOWNWARD

This posture involves a thrusting movement that inclines downward.

17.1 Put foot and sword down

Movements   Put your right foot down with the toes touching the ground in front of your left foot. At the same time, use your right hand to move the sword down to chest level in a thrusting motion. Keep the left jianjue in touch with your right wrist *(fig. 17.1.1)*.

Internal Components   Look slightly down and focus your mind on your left hand. Feel qi reaching to the tip of the sword.

Key Points   Relax your shoulders, elbows, hips, and knees.

Application   Continuing without interruption from the previous movement, you can use your sword to prick down along the opponent's weapon *(fig. 17.1.2)*. Here, the basic techniques are ci, thrusting; ge, blocking with the ridge of the sword; and xi, making sword circles diagonally around the body.

17.2.1

17.2 Unicorn exploration

Movements   As the sword thrusts downward, let your body sink down. Stretch your right arm forward until your right hand is at abdomen level. Raise your right knee slightly and point the right toes to the ground. Bend your left leg and let your body sink slightly down to form a left insubstantial stance *(fig. 17.2.1)*.

Internal Components   Keep looking forward and down. Focus your mind on your right hand. Feel as though qi can extend to the tip of the sword.

Key Points   Your back should feel "full," meaning that qi is there and that internal force there is strong. Your abdomen should feel "empty," meaning that nothing there can be touched. Feel as though your arm is lengthening and that more force can be sent to the tip of the sword.

Application   Continuing without interruption from the previous movement, you can keep thrusting downward with your sword at the lower part of the opponent's body. Here, the basic technique is ci, thrusting.

18.1.1   18.1.2

18. STEP BACK WITH THREE REVERSE HITS

In all reverse hits, either your step or your body moves in a direction opposite to the one in which the sword is moving. This posture is also called "from failing to winning," which means that when the body goes forward as though to escape an attack from behind, the sword strikes back to counterattack.

18.1 Raise sword and turn it over while assuming bow stance

Movements   Turn over your right hand with the sword and raise the tip of the sword to face level, letting it point forward (east). Keep the left jianjue behind the jiantan. Turn your body to the left a little bit and lean slightly forward. At the same time, shift your weight forward and make a right standard bow stance *(fig. 18.1.1)*.

Internal Components   Look forward and focus your mind on your left hand. Feel qi extending both forward and backward in your right hand and left foot.

Key Points   Shift your weight forward. Your body can lean forward slightly and must sink down. Feel as though your right arm can reach far ahead and that your left foot is stretched back.

Application   As you turn the sword over, you can use the lower edge to cut the opponent's front hand or his front arm from below *(fig. 18.1.2)*. Here, the basic technique is shangjie, blocking and cutting up.

18.2.1   18.2.2   18.2.3

18.2 Turn and point sword back

Movements   Turn your body around counterclockwise by pivoting on your right heel and letting your right leg bear your full weight. Keep turning until your body faces to the southwest. Relax your right shoulder, drop your elbow and hold the sword behind your right shoulder with your right hand. The jiantan should point to the southwest and the tip of the sword should point diagonally down and toward the northeast. At the same time, relax your left hip and raise your left knee slightly, letting only the toes of your left foot touch the ground. This forms a right insubstantial stance. Point the left jianjue back to your right shoulder, then to the nose *(fig. 18.2.1)*, and finally sweep it forward until it points toward the southwest *(fig. 18.2.2)*.

Internal Components   Look from east to southwest and focus your mind on your left hand. Feel qi sink down to the dantian, in the lower abdomen.

Key Points   Relax your hips and keep your body stable while you turn. When the left jianjue points forward, feel as though your whole left arm is stretching forward and as though your body is pulling slightly back.

Application   When the opponent attacks from behind on your left side, you can turn your body back to prepare for fighting and use your left hand to block his long weapon *(fig. 18.2.3)*. Here, the basic technique is to block with the empty hand.

18.3.1

18.3.2

18.3 Chop forward and assume bow stance

Movements   Move the left jianjue clockwise in a circle that starts at about the two o'clock position and finishes slightly to the left of your body and in front of your head at about the eleven o'clock position. The jianjue should point diagonally up and toward the northwest. As the left jianjue completes its circle, relax your left knee and hip and step forward with your left foot, letting only the heel touch the ground. Then, shift your weight forward to make a left standard bow stance. At the same time, extend your right arm forward so that the sword chops over your right shoulder and then points to the southwest. Keep the tip of the sword level with the top of your head *(fig. 18.3.1)*.

Internal Components   Look forward and focus your mind first on your left hand and then on the tip of the sword. Feel qi move around with your left arm and then extend to the tip of the sword.

Key Points   Relax your left shoulder and elbow. Your left arm should feel nimble and quick and your body and right arm should move forward together with agility.

Application   If the opponent uses a long weapon (spear or staff) to attack you from the front, you can use your left hand to block his weapon and your sword to chop at him *(fig. 18.3.2)*. Here, the basic technique is pi, chopping down with the edge of the sword.

18.4.1a   18.4.1b   18.4.2a, b

18.4 Turn sword over and strike back while taking cover step

Movements Let both your right hand with the sword and your left hand drop directly down at the same time. Both hands should be in front of your body at chest level and the left jianjue should be beside your right wrist. At the same time, step forward with your right foot. When this foot crosses the left foot, turn the toes of your right foot to the right (northwest) and place the right foot fully on the ground to form a right cover step.

Continuing without interruption, shift your weight forward to your right leg. Straighten your left leg and raise your left heel off the ground. Move your body forward while shifting your weight to your right leg. Turn to the right and lean forward. At the same time, move both hands down so that the sword arcs downward and then up toward the northeast on the right side of your body, creating a strike back. Your right hand should be in niba position and the left jianjue should be under your right elbow. Turn your head to follow the movement of the sword through its downward arc to the northeast. At the end of the movement, the tip of the sword should point to northeast and the sword should be parallel to the ground. Your right arm and the sword should form one horizontal line *(fig. 18.4.1a, b)*.

Internal Components Look forward and then back to the tip of the sword as your body turns. Focus your mind on your left hand. Feel qi sink down to the dantian, in the lower abdomen, and then extend to the tip of the sword

Key Points Relax your right hip and knee. This will cause your right foot to be very nimble. The forward lean of your body and the backward strike of the sword must be coordinated. Your right forearm and wrist should feel agile and quick.

Application If the opponent attacks your upper body from behind, you can dodge to the left or forward and use your sword to attack back toward him from below *(fig. 18.4.2a, b)*. Here, the basic technique is fanji, a curving upward strike with the tip or upper part of sword.

| 18.5.1 | 18.5.2 | 18.5.3 |

18.5 Raise sword and assume insubstantial stance

Movements   Turn your body and head back to the front (southwest) and straighten up slightly. Move the left jianjue until it is in front of your face and opposite your nose. Relax your right hand. This will cause the sword to turn slightly *(fig. 18.5.1)*.

   Continue to straighten your body. Your right leg should be almost fully straightened as your body moves. Stretch your left arm forward and point the jianjue toward the southwest. At the same time, raise your right hand with the sword up to the top of your right shoulder. Point the jiantan forward and let the tip point down behind your back *(fig. 18.5.2)*.

Internal Components   Look from the back (northeast) to the front (southwest) and focus your mind on your left hand. Feel qi at the top of your head.

Key Points   Think of using the baihui point, on the top of the head, to lift your body into an upright position. Feel as though your body is flexible and agile.

Application   In this movement, your body turns to prepare for fighting and the left jianjue can be used to block the opponent's weapon *(fig. 18.5.3)*.

18.6.1   18.6.2

18.6 Chop forward and assume bow stance

Movements   Make a circle with the left jianjue, starting to the right and moving clockwise until the jianjue is slightly to the left and in front of and above your head. In this position, the jianjue should point diagonally up and toward the northwest. Relax your left knee and hip and step forward with your left foot, letting only the heel touch the ground. Then, shift your weight forward to make a left standard bow stance. At the same time, chop forward toward the southwest with the sword. Keep the tip of the sword level with the top of your head *(fig. 18.6.1)*.

Internal Components   Look forward, focusing your mind first on your left hand and then on the tip of the sword. Feel qi move around in the circle made by your left arm and then extend to the tip of the sword.

Key Points   Relax your left shoulder and elbow. Your left arm should feel nimble and your body and right arm should move forward simultaneously with agility.

Application   If the opponent uses a sword to attack you from the front, you can use your left hand to block his weapon-holding hand, and your sword to counterattack with a chop *(fig. 18.6.2)*. Here, the basic technique is pi, chopping down with edge of sword.

18.7.1   18.7.2

18.7 Turn sword over and strike back while taking cover step

Movements Let your right hand, holding the sword, and your left hand drop directly down at the same time. Both hands should be in front of your body and at chest level. Put the left jianjue beside your right wrist. At the same time, step forward with your right foot. When this foot crosses your left foot, turn the toes of your right foot to the right (northwest) and place your whole foot on the ground to form a right cover step.

Continuing without interruption, shift your weight forward to your right leg. Straighten your left leg and raise the left heel off the ground. As your weight shifts, move your body forward and turn to the right. Your body will lean forward. At the same time, move both hands down with your right hand, holding the sword, and the left jianjue beside your right wrist. Move the sword in an arc down and then up on the right side of your body as though to strike backward. Your right hand should be in neiba, the thumb-down grip. Put the left jianjue under your right elbow. Turn your head to follow the movement of the sword. Point the tip of the sword to the northeast and keep it parallel with the ground. Your right arm and the sword should be on a horizontal line *(fig. 18.7.1)*.

Internal Components Look forward and then backward toward and beyond the tip of the sword as your body turns. Focus your mind on your left hand. Feel qi sink down to the dantian, in the lower abdomen, and then extend to the tip of the sword.

Key Points Relax your right hip and knee to make your right foot very nimble. Let your body lean forward and the sword strike back in a coordinated motion. Your right forearm and wrist should feel agile.

Application If the opponent attacks the upper right side of your body from behind, you can dodge forward and left and use your sword to attack him from below *(fig. 18.7.2)*. Here, the basic technique is fanji, a curving upward strike with the tip or upper part of the sword.

| 18.8.1 | 18.8.2 | 18.8.3 |

18.8 Raise sword and assume insubstantial stance

Movements Turn your body and head back to the front (southwest) and straighten up slightly. Move the left jianjue in front of your face and opposite your nose. Relax your right hand. This will cause the sword to turn over slightly *(fig. 18.8.1)*.

Continue to straighten the body. As your body moves, let your right leg become almost straight. Stretch your left arm forward and point the jianjue to the southwest. At the same time, raise your right hand with the sword up to the top of your right shoulder. Point the jiantan forward and let the tip of the sword point down behind the back *(fig. 18.8.2)*.

Internal Components Look from back to front and focus your mind on your left hand. Feel qi at the top of your head.

Key Points Think of using the baihui point, on the top of the head, to lift your body into an upright position. Feel as though your body is flexible and agile.

Application In this movement, your body turns to prepare for fighting. You can also use the left jianjue to block the opponent's weapon *(fig. 18.8.3)*.

18.9.1   18.9.2

18.9 Chop forward and assume bow stance

Movements   Make a circle with the left jianjue, starting to the right and continuing clockwise until it is above and slightly to the left of and in front of your head. In this position, the jianjue should point diagonally up and to the northwest. Relax your left knee and hip and step forward with your left foot, letting only the heel touch the ground. Then, shift your weight forward to make a standard bow stance. At the same time, chop forward (toward the southwest) with your right hand holding the sword. Keep the tip of the sword level with the top of your head *(fig. 18.9.1)*.

Internal Components   Look forward and focus your mind first on your left hand and then on the tip of the sword. Feel qi move around in the circle made by your left arm and then extend to the tip of the sword.

Key Points   Relax your left shoulder and elbow. Your left arm should feel nimble and your body and right arm should move forward with agility.

Application   If the opponent uses a sword to attack you from the front, you can move slightly to the left to dodge his weapon and use your sword to counterattack with a chop *(fig. 18.9.2)*. Here, the basic technique is pi, chopping down with the edge of the sword.

18.10.1   18.10.2

18.10 Raise knee and push sword

Movements   Change the left jianjue to a jianfa and use it to hold the jiantan. Then, take the sword slightly back with both hands and let your body sink down and slightly back at the same time. Point the tip of the sword diagonally up toward the southwest. Straighten your left leg so that your body becomes erect and move your right foot forward. Raise your right knee in front of your abdomen until the knee touches the jiantan, forming a solo stance *(fig. 18.10.1)*.

Internal Components   Look forward (southwest) and focus your mind on your left hand. Feel qi on top of the sword.

Key Points   When your left hand just touches the jiantan, your body should stretch forward slightly, as though to pull the sword back slightly. When your right knee moves up and forward, your abdomen should pull slightly back.

Application   In this movement, the sword sinks down in order to block an attack to the lower part of your body *(fig. 18.10.2)*. Here, the basic technique is ya, pressing down.

18.11.1

18.11.2

18.11 Straighten body and thrust forward with sword

Movements   Straighten your body and at the same time take the sword in both hands to thrust forward and slightly up. The tip of the sword should be level with the top of your head *(fig. 18.11.1)*.

Internal Components   Keep looking forward and focus your mind on the mingmen point, in the center of lower back. Feel qi extend to the tip of the sword.

Key Points   The sword pricks forward but inside, your body should feel as though it is moving slightly back. It should also feel extended and stable.

Application   In this movement, you can keep pressing the opponent's weapon down and then thrust at him with the tip of your sword *(fig. 18.11.2)*. Here, the basic techniques are ya, pressing down, and ci, thrusting.

| 18.12.1 | 18.12.2 | 18.12.3 |

18.12 Turn sword over and strike back while in bow stance

Movements   Turn your head to look backward (northeast) and down. This will cause your body to turn back to the right. Turn your right foot to follow the turn of your body and step toward the northeast. This forms a right standard bow stance. Relax your shoulders and drop your elbows. Using both hands, move the sword downward and back along the front of your body *(fig. 18.12.1)*, so that it strikes up to the northeast at the end of the movement. Hold the sword in your right hand with niba. Change the left jianfa to jianjue and place it under your right wrist *(fig. 18.12.2)*.

Internal Components   Look from the southwest up to the northeast and then down. Focus your mind on the xuanguan point, between the eyebrows, and then on the tip of the sword. Feel qi extend to the tip of the sword.

Key Points   Your whole body must turn to the right in a smooth continuous movement in which your eyes move first, followed sequentially by your head, torso, foot, hand and sword. You should feel when you first look back as though the sword is already there. When the sword strikes forward, it should seem to be reaching far ahead and your left foot should feel as though it is stretching far back.

Application   If the opponent attacks you from the right or behind, you can turn your body and use the sword to block and strike simultaneously *(fig. 18.12.3)*. Here, the basic techniques are ge, blocking with the ridge of the sword, and fanliao, a small, smooth upward cut with the tip or front edge of the sword.

| 19.1.1 | 19.1.2 | 19.1.3, 4 |

19. CAPTURE A LEGENDARY TURTLE IN THE OCEAN DEPTHS

In traditional Chinese culture, the huge legendary turtle is an animal deity. It lives in the deep ocean and only a brave, smart, and dedicated person can capture it. In this movement, you should move up and down and turn over as though chasing a turtle at the bottom of the sea.

19.1 Block down while taking a back insert step

Movements   Turn the sword over so that the edge that was originally facing down turns to face up. Turn your body slightly to the left *(fig. 19.1.1)*.

Continue to turn your right hand, making the sword move in a counterclockwise circle down, right, up, left, then down again until the tip points to the ground and the sword is vertical. At the same time, place your right foot behind your left foot to form a back insert step and allow only the ball of your right foot to touch the ground in a twisting stance. Move your left hand back until your arm is parallel to the ground and the jianjue points down. Keep both arms on a northeast-to-southwest line *(fig. 19.1.2)*.

Internal Components   Look up and then down. Focus your mind on your left hand, and feel qi extend through both arms.

Key Points   The right step back should be nimble. When stepping back, keep your body stable and lean slightly forward. Feel as though your right foot can move forward and back very quickly.

Application   When the opponent's weapon is over your sword, you can turn your sword to cut up *(fig. 19.1.3)*. If he dodges and then attacks your front leg, you can move your leg back and use the sword to block down *(fig. 19.1.4)*. Here, basic techniques are jiao, stirring or making circles with the sword, and ge, blocking with the ridge of the sword.

19.2.1   19.2.2

19.2 Raise and straighten waist and move sword up

Movements   Turn your body to the left and face the northwest. Let your body sink down as you turn and let both hands drop down and then circle up in front of your abdomen. Let the left jianjue become a jianfa and touch the jiantan. Holding the sword with your right hand, let the tip of the sword point diagonally upward and toward the northwest. Then, raise your body up slightly *(fig. 19.2.1)*.

Internal Components   Shift your gaze from downward to the northwest. Focus your mind on your left hand. Feel qi sink down to the dantian, in the lower abdomen.

Key Points   Keep your body very stable as it sinks and turns. When your arms circle to the front, you should have a feeling of extension in them and of emptiness in the center of the arm-circle. Feel as though the top of your head is suspended from the bai-hui point, on the top of the head.

Application   You can use this movement to defend against an attack from the left or above *(fig. 19.2.2)*. Here, the basic techniques are xi, making a sword circle diagonally around the body, and lan, blocking and breaking off in middle.

19.3.1   19.3.2

19.3 Raise knee and push sword

Movements   Straighten your legs and torso. Using both hands, thrust the sword forward and up, keeping the tip level with the top of your head. At the same time, raise your right knee to the northwest until the knee is behind the jiantan, forming a solo stance *(fig. 19.3.1)*.

Internal Components   Continue to look forward and slightly up, focusing your mind on your left hand. Feel qi reach the tip of the sword.

Key Points   Feel as though your body is stable and the sword can prick very far.

Application   Use this movement to thrust up and forward at an attack from an oncoming opponent *(fig. 19.3.2)*. Here, the basic technique is ci, thrusting.

| 19.4.1 | 19.4.2 | 19.4.3, 4 |

19.4 Turn back and strike down

Movements Turn your body clockwise to face south. At the same time, bend your left leg and let it turn on the heel. Make a circle with the raised right leg toward the south so that it moves past your left leg. Let the toes of your left foot turn to face southeast and let your right foot pass the left before touching the ground, so that your legs are crossed at the end of the step. Shift your weight to your right leg and raise your left heel off the ground. Your left knee should be behind your right knee in a right low rest stance. Holding the sword in your right hand and with the left jianfa touching the jiantan, make a circle with both hands to the northwest and diagonally up. Continue without interruption to make a circle clockwise and on a diagonal downward slope until the tip of the sword points to the west and the sword is parallel to the ground. The blade of the sword should be horizontal. Your right hand should come to a stop in front of your right knee. Turn your head to the right and look at and beyond the tip of the sword *(fig. 19.4.1, 2)*.

Internal Components Shift your gaze from the upper northwest corner downward and to the west, just ahead of the tip of the sword as it makes its circuit. Then, look at the tip of the sword and beyond. Focus your mind on your left hand. Feel qi move in both arms and then extend through the sword to the tip.

Key Points The turn of your body must be quick and stable. Feel your left hand push the jiantan. This will cause your body to dodge slightly to the left.

Application If the opponent attacks you from the right or behind, you can use the sword to press down on his weapon. Letting your body sink and turn prevents his escape *(fig. 19.4.3, 4)*. Here, the basic techniques are xi, circling the sword diagonally around body, and ya, pressing down.

20.1.1

20.1.2

20. GODDESS SPREADS FLOWERS

In traditional Chinese culture, the "goddess spreads flowers" is suggestive of the most beautiful of movements. In this posture, your movements should be open and extended.

20.1 Hold sword horizontally and assume rest stance

Movements   Raise your head to look toward the west and move the sword upward in front of your body, which should be facing south. Keep the full weight on the right leg. The sword should be in front of the left side of your head, given that your head is turned toward the west. The sword should be pointing west and parallel to the ground *(fig. 20.1.1)*.

Internal Components   Look toward the west, focusing your mind on your right hand. Feel qi on top of your head.

Key Points   Keep your body erect. Feel as though the top of your head is suspended from above and that your right elbow and hand are pulling the sword to the left.

Application   From this low position, you can attack your opponent, using your sword to block from below *(fig. 20.1.2)*. Here, the basic technique is shangjie, blocking up.

20.2.1　　　　　　　　　　　　　　　20.2.2

20.2 Block arm and assume insubstantial stance

Movements　Step toward the west with your right foot, keeping your body at a constant level. Let your left foot just follow your right foot to the side without putting any weight on the left and with only the ball of your left foot touching the ground. This is called genbu or "following step." Keep your head facing west and turn your body slightly to the right. Using both hands, move the sword horizontally to the right until the tip points north and the jiantan points to the south. Then, without moving the sword, let your body sink slightly. Keep the sword level with the top of your head *(fig. 20.2.1)*.

Internal Components　Continue to look west and focus your mind on your right hand. Feel qi extend from the dantian, in the lower abdomen, to the hands.

Key Points　Your body should be nimble as it turns and the side step should be agile and stable. Feel as though the sword is pushing up as your body sinks down.

Application　When the opponent is in a position high above you, you can move close to him and use the sword to block from below *(fig. 20.2.2)*. Here, the basic technique is shangjie, blocking up.

20.3.1   20.3.2

20.3 Lower sword and assume side bow stance

Movements   Turn your body slightly to the right and then press the sword down in front of your right knee. Let your body lean forward and, at the same time, step with your left foot backwards toward the east to form a right, low bow stance *(fig. 20.3.1)*.

Internal Components   Shift your gaze down and forward. Focus your mind on your right hand. Feel qi in both hands making them become very heavy.

Key Points   When pressing the sword down, feel as though the sword is pushing slightly forward, your left foot is big and your right leg is simultaneously very heavy but springy.

Application   If the opponent attacks your leg, you can use the sword to stick his weapon and then press down. At the same time, your body should dodge back *(fig. 20.3.2)*. You can also push the sword forward to cut the opponent's arm. Here, the basic techniques are ya, pressing down, and hangjie, blocking and cutting forward.

20.4.1   20.4.2

20.4 Strike knee while taking a back insert step

Movements Change the sword to your left hand in yangba, the palm-down grip, and then move it back horizontally in a counterclockwise arc parallel to the ground until the tip points to the east at knee level. Make a jianjue with your right hand on the right side of your waist. At the same time, shift your weight to the left leg and take a back insert step with your right foot, letting the right foot cross behind the left leg and touch the ground with only the ball. This is a left rest stance. Turn your body to the left slightly and turn your head to face toward the east *(fig. 20.4.1)*.

Internal Components Look from west to east and focus your mind on your right hand. Feel qi reaching the tip of the sword.

Key Points When shifting your weight and stepping back, your body should maintain a constant level. Feel that your body can turn back quickly and with agility.

Application If the opponent is on your left or behind you, you can move close to him and use the sword to strike his knee from a low position *(fig. 20.4.2)*. Here, the basic techniques are ji, a curving strike with tip or upper part of sword, and jie, blocking with edge of the sword.

21.1.1   21.1.2

21. PICK UP STARS WITH AN UNERRING HAND

The name of this movement indicates that you must be quick, precise, and dexterous. Stars refer to your eyes. The movements of this posture are not big but they are nimble, accurate, and useful.

21.1 Turn hand over to pick up star

Movements   Turn your left hand with the sword so that the palm faces up. This involves changing from yangba, the palm-down grip, to yinba, the palm-up grip. At the same time, shift your weight to your right leg while your body rises up. Raise the heel of your left foot off the ground. Keeping your right knee in contact with the back of your left knee, let your hips face southwest, your torso face south, and your head face east. As your body rises, thrust the sword diagonally upward and to the east with the tip at eye level *(fig. 21.1.1)*.

Internal Components   Look upward and toward the east. Focus your mind on your left hand, and feel qi at the tip of the sword.

Key Points   When your body rises up, lean slightly toward the east. Feel as though your body is about to turn around.

Application   Use this move to attack the face of the opponent with a diagonal upward stroke *(fig. 21.1.2)*. Here, the basic technique is ci, thrusting.

21.2.1   21.2.2   21.2.3, 4

21.2 Step forward and thrust straight ahead with sword

Movements   Turn your body to the left but do not turn your hips. Move the right jian-jue across your body from right to left and let it point to the jiantan. At the same time, raise your left knee toward the west *(fig. 21.2.1).*

Continue without interruption to turn your body to the left. Let your left arm turn outward and extend toward the east. Although your left hand with the sword moves to the left, the tip of the sword should just turn without any movement occurring in the rest of the sword. The tip should remain pointing up and toward the east. At the same time, step back toward the east with your left leg and then shift your weight onto it to form a left standard bow stance. At the same time, push the right jianjue forward and to the right (southeast). It should point ahead and diagonally up *(fig. 21.2.2).*

Internal Components   Keep looking forward (east), and focus your mind on your right hand. Feel qi in the right jianjue and then feel it extend through your arms.

Key Points   When your left knee rises and the right jianjue points to the left, feel that your body is twisting and leaning to the east. Then, let your left foot unleash the power from this twist as it makes the step to the left. Feel as though your left wrist can make a small but quick, dexterous, and powerful turn and as though the right jianjue is another sword and points to the same spot as the real sword. The movement in the tip of the sword is small but must be quick and powerful.

Application   After beginning an attack to the opponent's face *(fig. 21.2.3)*, turn your body and continue to attack his face *(fig. 21.2.4)*. Here, the basic techniques are ji, a curving strike with the tip or upper part of the sword, and ci, thrusting.

22.1.1   22.1.2

22. RAISE WHIP AND ATTACK WRIST

Two techniques are combined in this posture. "Raise whip" refers to the sword and is a technique for counterattacking, while "attack wrist" changes the position of the sword from the back to the front of the body. These two techniques are done on both sides of the body.

22.1 Raise whip back and assume insubstantial stance

Movements   Turn your body to the right and turn your head back to face west. At the same time, shift your weight back to your right leg and raise your left heel off the ground to make a right insubstantial stance. At the same time, move both hands in front of your body and then across the body to the right and back toward the west. During this move, pass the sword from your left hand to your right hand, keeping the sword pointed vertically up. With your left hand form the jianjue. At the end of the movement, your right hand should hold the sword vertically and slightly behind the right side of your torso with the tip pointed up. Your left jianjue should be under your right elbow and should point to the west *(fig. 22.1.1)*.

Internal Components   Look back (west) and focus your mind on your left hand. Feel qi in your right hand and then on top of your head.

Key Points   Relax your shoulders and hips and keep the sword vertical. Although you are blocking backward, feel as though the body wants to move forward.

Application   If the opponent attacks from the right side or from behind, you can use the sword to block his weapon. Your body should move nimbly *(fig. 22.1.2)*. Here, the basic techniques are ge, blocking with the ridge of the sword, and lan, blocking and breaking off in middle.

22.2.1   22.2.2

22.2 Chop back while taking a pad step

Movements   Take a half-step forward (east) with your left foot and shift your weight forward to make a standard bow stance. Let your body lean slightly to the east. Face back toward the west and strike back toward the west with the sword which should, at the end of the movement, be parallel with the ground and pointing west *(fig. 22.2.1)*.

Internal Components   Continue looking back to the west and focus your mind on your right hand. Feel qi extend to the tip of the sword.

Key Points   The step forward, the leaning of the body in that direction, and the strike of the sword back should be done at the same time. Feel the internal force coming from your right wrist and moving very quickly.

Application   When the opponent attacks you at mid-level, you can dodge and use the tip of the sword to strike him quickly *(fig. 22.2.2)*. Here, the basic technique is ji, a curving strike with the tip or upper part of the sword.

22.3.1   22.3.2

22.3 Cut upward at attacker's wrist and assume bow stance

Movements   Step forward with your right foot to the east. Turn your head and body to the left and let your arms follow. Move the sword in a downward arc with your right hand. The tip should point toward the ground as the sword moves past your right thigh. Continue without interruption to sweep the sword forward and up toward the east until it extends in front of your body. Hold the sword with niba and keep the left jianjue behind the jiantan. At the end of the movement, the tip of the sword should point forward (east) at chest level and be parallel to the ground *(fig. 22.3.1)*.

Internal Components   Turn your head and look forward (east). Focus your mind on your right hand and feel qi extend to the tip of the sword.

Key Points   Make the change of step quick and nimble. As you move the sword forward, relax your right shoulder and raise your right elbow slightly to prevent the tip of the sword from touching the ground.

Application   Use your sword to touch your opponent's weapon on the inside or underside, and move it forward along his weapon to attack his front hand *(fig. 22.3.2)*. Here, the basic techniques are ti, cutting with the tip of the sword); ge, blocking with the ridge of the sword, and liao, a small upward cut with the tip or front edge of the sword.

22.4.1   22.4.2

22.4 Raise whip back and assume insubstantial stance

Movements   Turn your body to the left (north) and turn your head back toward the west, while shifting your weight back to your left leg and raising your right heel off the ground to form a left insubstantial stance. At the same time, holding the sword with your right hand, move it to the left and back toward the west. The left jianjue should touch your right wrist and move back as your right hand moves back. Keep the sword vertical as it moves. At the end of the movement, your right hand should hold the sword to the left of and behind your body. The tip of the sword should point up. Hold the left jianjue on the left side of your body at waist level between your right wrist and your body and continue to keep it in touch with your right wrist *(fig. 22.4.1)*.

Internal Components   Look back toward the west. Focus your mind on your left hand and feel qi extend through both arms, making them become heavy.

Key Points   Relax your shoulders and hips as the sword moves to the vertical position. Be ready to block backward but feel as though you want to move your body forward.

Application   If the opponent attacks you from the left side or from behind, you can use the sword to block his weapon. Your body should move nimbly *(fig. 22.4.2)*. Here, the basic technique is ge, blocking with the ridge of the sword.

22.5.1

22.5.2

22.5 Chop back while taking pad step

Movements   Take a half-step forward (east) with your right foot and shift your weight forward to make a right standard bow stance. Let your body lean slightly to the east. Continue to face back toward the west and use the sword to strike in that direction (west). At the end of the movement, the sword should be parallel to the ground and the tip of the sword should point to the west *(fig. 22.5.1)*.

Internal Components   Keep looking back to the west and focus your mind on your right hand. Feel qi extend to the tip of the sword.

Key Points   The step forward, the lean of your body and the strike of the sword to the west should all occur at the same time. Feel the internal force coming very quickly from your right wrist.

Application   When the opponent attacks you at mid-level, you can dodge away from the attack and use the jianfan, the tip of the sword, to strike him quickly *(fig. 22.5.2)*. Here, the basic technique is ji, a curving strike with tip or upper part of the sword.

22.6.1   22.6.2

22.6 Cut upward at attacker's wrist and assume bow stance

Movements Step forward toward the east with your left foot. Turn your head and body to the right and let your arms follow. With your right hand, move the sword in a downward arc. The tip of the sword should point toward the ground as the sword passes your left thigh. Continue without interruption to sweep the sword forward and up toward the east until it extends in front of your body. Your right hand should be in the niba position and the left jianjue should be held under your right wrist. At the end of the movement, the tip of the sword should point forward (east) at chest level and be parallel to the ground *(fig. 22.6.1)*.

Internal Components Turn your head and look forward (east). Focus your mind on your right hand and feel qi at the tip of the sword.

Key Points The change of step should be quick and nimble. As you move the sword forward, relax your right shoulder and raise your right elbow slightly to prevent the tip of the sword from touching the ground.

Application Use the sword to touch your opponent's weapon on the inside or underside and move it forward along the opponent's weapon to attack his front hand *(fig. 22.6.2)*. Here, the basic techniques are ge, blocking with the ridge of the sword, and liao, a small upward cut with tip or front edge of the sword.

23.1.1   23.1.2

23. BLACK DRAGON STIRS ITS TAIL

This is a very powerful movement. Think of yourself as a dragon and the sword as your tail. "Stirring the tail" requires that you use the force of your entire body.

23.1 Look back at the tail

Movements   Change the left jianjue to a jianfa and use it to hold the jiantan in order to help your right hand move the sword. Relax your shoulders and, using both hands, move the sword down and back along the left side of your body. During this motion, the tip of the sword should point diagonally back and down. At the same time, turn your body slightly to the left and turn your head back to look at the tip of the sword *(fig. 23.1.1)*.

Internal Components   Let your gaze move in a downward arc from the east to the tip of the sword and beyond. Focus your mind on your right hand and feel qi sink down to the dantian, in the lower abdomen.

Key Points   When moving the sword back, be careful not to shift your weight back. Instead, keep one hundred percent of your weight on your left leg. Feel as though your body will spring back as you twist from the waist.

Application   When the opponent's attack is low and from your left, you can use the sword to stick to his weapon and follow his force *(fig. 23.1.2)*. Here, the basic techniques are ge, blocking with the ridge of the sword, and dai, moving the sword straight back.

23.2.1   23.2.2

23.2 Step back and strike forward

Movements   Continue without interruption from the previous movement by moving the sword slightly further back and then up and forward so that it completes an almost vertical circle on the left side of your body. At the end of the movement, the tip of the sword should be level with the top of your head. As the sword moves forward to complete the circle, step backward with your left foot and shift your weight onto your right leg to form a right standard bow stance *(fig. 23.2.1)*.

Internal Components   Look from back (west) to front (east). Focus your mind on the weilü point, on the tailbone, and then on the mingmen point, in the center of the lower back. Feel qi extend in a spiraling movement from the dantian, in the lower abdomen, to the tip of the sword.

Key Points   The step backward and the weight shift should occur at the same time in a coordinated movement. Be careful to keep your body at the same level throughout this movement. When the sword moves up, feel as though it is going to stir something up. Use force from your waist and when the sword moves forward and down, feel as though it is going to chop something. Your hands and your left foot must move with force at the same time and in opposite directions. To create a powerful chop when the sword is higher than the top of your head, your left hand can be moved behind your right hand to hold the handle of the sword in heba, the two-handed grip. After the chop, change your left hand back to a jianfa to hold the jiantan.

Application   Keep your sword in continuous touch with the opponent's weapon. First stir up and then chop down at him *(fig. 23.2.2)*. Here, the basic techniques are dai, moving the sword straight back; jiao, making circles with the sword; and pi, chopping down with the edge of the sword, or zhan, a vertical cut.

23.3.1   23.3.2

23.3 Look back at the tail

Movements   Relax the shoulders and, using both hands, move the sword down and back in a downward arc along the right side of the body. Continue the arc to the back of the body until the tip of the sword points diagonally back and down. At the same time, turn the body slightly to the right, and turn the head back to look at the tip of the sword *(fig. 23.3.1)*.

Internal Components   Let your gaze shift from the east to the tip of the sword and beyond. Focus the mind on the right hand. Feel qi sink down to the dantian.

Key Points   When moving the sword back, be careful not to shift the weight back. Instead, keep one hundred percent of the weight on the right leg. Feel as though the body will spring back as you twist from the waist.

Application When the opponent's attack is low and on your right, you can use the sword to stick to his weapon and follow his force *(fig. 23.3.2)*. Here, the basic techniques are ge, blocking with the ridge of the sword, and dai, moving the sword straight back.

23.4.1   23.4.2

23.4 Step back and strike forward

Movements   Continue the previous movement without interruption by moving the sword slightly further back and then up and forward, so that it completes an almost vertical circle on the right side of the body. At the end of the movement, the tip of the sword should be level with the top of your head. As the sword moves forward to complete the circle, step back with your right foot and shift your weight onto your left leg. This forms a left standard bow stance *(fig. 23.4.1)*.

Internal Components   Look from back (west) to front (east). Focus your mind on the weilü point, on the tailbone, and then on the mingmen point, in the center of the lower back. Feel qi extend in a spiraling movement from the dantian, in the lower abdomen, to the tip of the sword.

Key Points   The step back and the weight shift should occur at the same time in a coordinated motion. Be careful to keep your body at the same level during the step and weight shift. When the sword moves up, feel as though it is going to stir something up. Use force from your waist and when the sword moves forward and down, feel as though it is going to chop something. Your hands and your left foot must move with force at the same time and in opposite directions. To create a powerful chop when the sword is higher than the top of your head, your left hand can be moved behind your right hand to hold the handle of the sword in heba, the two-handed grip. After the chop, your left hand can be changed back to a jianfa to hold the jiantan.

Application   Keep your sword in continuous touch with the opponent's weapon. First stir up and then chop down at him *(fig. 23.4.2)*. Here, the basic techniques are dai, moving the sword straight back; jiao, making circles with the sword; and pi, chopping down with the edge of the sword, or zhan, a vertical cut.

23.5.1   23.5.2

23.5 Look back at the tail

Movements   Relax your shoulders and using both hands, move the sword down and back in a downward arc along the left side of your body. Continue the arc to the back of your body until the tip of the sword points diagonally back and down. At the same time, turn your body slightly to the left and turn your head back to look at the tip of the sword *(fig. 23.5.1)*.

Internal Components   Let your gaze shift from east to the tip of the sword and beyond. Focus your mind on your right hand. Feel qi sink down to the dantian, in the lower abdomen.

Key Points   When moving the sword back, be careful not to shift your weight back. Instead, keep one hundred percent of your weight on your left leg. Feel as though your body will spring back as you twist from the waist.

Application   When the opponent's attack is low and on your left, you can use the sword to stick to his weapon and follow his force *(fig. 23.5.2)*. Here, the basic techniques are ge, blocking with the ridge of the sword, and dai, moving the sword straight back.

23.6.1   23.6.2

23.6 Step back and strike forward

Movements   Continue the previous movement without interruption by moving the sword slightly further back and then up and forward, so that the sword completes an almost vertical circle on the right side of your body. At the end of the movement, the tip of the sword should be level with the top of your head. As the sword moves forward to complete the circle, step backward with your left foot and shift your weight onto your right leg. This forms a right standard bow stance *(fig. 23.6.1)*.

Internal Components   Look from back (west) to front (east). Focus your mind on the weilü point, on the tailbone, and then on the mingmen point, in the center of the lower back. Feel qi extend in a spiraling movement from the dantian, in the lower abdomen, to the tip of the sword.

Key Points   The step back and the weight shift should occur at the same time in a coordinated motion. Be careful to keep your body at the same level during the step and weight shift. When the sword moves up, feel as though it is going to stir something. Use force from your waist and when the sword moves forward and down, feel as though it is going to chop something. Your hands and your left foot must move with force at the same time and in opposite directions. To create a powerful chop when the sword is higher than your head, your left hand can be moved behind your right hand to hold the handle of the sword in heba, the two-handed grip. After the chop, change your left hand to a jianfa to hold the jiantan.

Application   Keep your sword in continuous touch with the opponent's weapon. First stir up and then chop down at him *(fig. 23.6.2)*. Here, the basic techniques are dai, moving the sword straight back; jiao, making circles with the sword; and pi, chopping down with the edge of the sword, or zhan, a vertical cut.

23.7.1   23.7.2

23.7 Look back at the tail

Movements   Relax your shoulders and using both hands, move the sword down and back in a downward arc along the right side of your body. Continue the arc to the back of your body until the tip of the sword points diagonally back and down. At the same time, turn your body slightly to the right and turn your head back to look at the tip of the sword *(fig. 23.7.1)*.

Internal Components   Let your gaze shift from east to the tip of the sword and beyond. Focus your mind on the right hand. Feel qi sink down to the dantian, in the lower abdomen.

Key Points   When moving the sword back, be careful not to shift your weight back. Instead, keep one hundred percent of your weight on your right leg. Feel as though your body will spring back as you twist from your waist.

Application   When the opponent's attack is low and on your right, you can use the sword to stick to his weapon and follow his force *(fig. 23.7.2)*. Here, the basic techniques are ge, blocking with the ridge of the sword, and dai, moving the sword straight back.

23.8.1

23.8.2

23.8 Step back and strike forward

Movements Continue the previous movement without interruption by moving the sword slightly further back and then up and forward so that it completes an almost vertical circle on the right side of your body. At the end of the movement, the tip of the sword should be level with the top of your head. As the sword moves forward to complete the circle, step back with your right foot and shift your weight onto your left leg. This forms a left standard bow stance *(fig. 23.8.1)*.

Internal Components Look from back (west) to front (east). Focus your mind on the weilü point, on the tailbone, and then on the mingmen point, in the center of the lower back. Feel qi extend in a spiraling movement from the dantian, in the lower abdomen, to the tip of the sword.

Key Points The step back and the weight shift should occur at the same time in a coordinated motion. Be careful to keep your body at the same level throughout the step and weight shift. When the sword moves up, feel as though it is going to stir something. Use force from your waist and when the sword moves forward and down, feel as though it is going to chop something. Your hands and your left foot must move with force at the same time and in opposite directions. To create a powerful chop when the sword is higher than your head, your left hand can be moved behind your right hand to hold the handle of the sword in heba, the two-handed grip. After the chop, change your left hand to a jianfa to hold the jiantan.

Application Keep your sword in continuous touch with the opponent's weapon. First stir up and then chop down at him *(fig. 23.8.2)*. Here, the basic techniques are dai, moving the sword straight back; jiao, making circles with the sword; and pi, chopping down with the edge of the sword, or zhan, a vertical cut.

24.1.1   24.1.2

24. JUMP OVER A RAVINE TO BLOCK AND INTERCEPT

In this posture, your movements should be continuous, agile, and quick, like a tiger jumping over a ravine.

24.1 Turn back and block down

Movements   Turn your body back in a clockwise direction, letting your left foot turn on the heel. Relax your right hip and raise your right knee slightly so that only the toes of your right foot touch the ground. At the same time, move your hands apart toward the sides of your body. Change the left jianfa to a jianjue and keep it pointing down and to the east. Move your right hand with the sword toward the west. Hold the sword vertically with the tip pointing down *(fig. 24.1.1)*.

Internal Components   Look from east to west and down. Focus your mind on your left hand. Feel qi at the center part of the sword.

Key Points   Your body should turn nimbly to the right side and this side should feel "empty," as though nothing on this side can be touched.

Application   When the opponent attacks you from the right or from behind, you can turn your body and use the sword to block his weapon from one side to the other *(fig. 24.1.2)*. Here, the basic techniques are lan, blocking and breaking off in middle, and ge, blocking with the ridge of the sword.

24.2.1   24.2.2

24.2 Raise knee and block outside

Movements   Raise your right knee toward the south. Keep your body facing the south-west but your head facing west. At the same time, turn your right hand over and move the sword to your left hand and in front of your head. This is neiba, the palm-inward grip. Let the left jianjue touch the jiantan. Point the tip of the sword slightly down and toward the northwest at shoulder level *(fig. 24.2.1)*.

Internal Components   Look slightly up and focus your mind on your right hand. Feel qi in your hands.

Key Points   Raising your right knee will cause your body to be nimble. Feel as though your body can move forward and slightly to the left with agility. Inside, there should be a feeling of readiness to jump.

Application   When the opponent attacks you from straight ahead or from above, you can dodge to the left, move close to him, and use your sword to block his front wrist *(fig. 24.2.2)*. Here, the basic technique is jie, blocking with the edge of the sword, and fanti, raising with palm-inward grip.

| 24.3.1 | 24.3.2 | 24.3.3 | 24.3.4, 5 |

24.3 Chop and block with jump step

Movements   Step toward the west with your right foot and put it down with the toes pointing to the west. Turn your to the right slightly *(fig. 24.3.1)*. Shift your weight on to your right foot when it touches the ground, make a half-step forward with the left foot and raise the left heel up as soon as possible *(fig. 24.3.2)*. At the same time, move the sword down, right, and up, making a half circle. This should bring the sword to the center of your body. Point the tip up and forward (west). The jiantan should be in front of your left knee *(fig. 24.3.3)*.

Internal Components   Keep looking forward (west) and focus your mind on your right hand. Feel qi on top of your head.

Key Points   The weight shift must be quick, like a little jump. Your body should feel stable and as though it is sinking down.

Application   Continuing without interruption from the previous movement, you can use your sword to circle the opponent's weapon as though to stir it and then to press straight down on it, or down and slightly to the left *(fig. 24.3.4)* and *(fig. 24.3.5)*. Here, the basic techniques are xi, making a sword circle diagonally around the body, and ya, pressing down.

24.4.1   24.4.2

24.4 Block down and reverse hit using cover step

Movements Take a step forward with your left foot and turn the toes of this foot to the left when your foot touches the ground to form a cover step. Shift about eighty percent of your weight to your left leg and keep your right leg slightly bent with only the ball of your right foot touching the ground. At the same time, stretch your right arm toward the west so that the sword can thrust at a distant target and turn your right hand over, forming niba, the thumb-down grip. The tip of the sword should point slightly up and toward the west. Put the left jianjue under your right elbow and let your body lean forward slightly *(fig. 24.4.1)*.

Internal Components Keep looking forward (west) and focus your mind on your right hand. Feel qi extend to the tip of the sword.

Key Points The step forward and the sword prick forward should be done at the same time. The movement should be quick and extended. Keep your body low and leaning forward.

Application When the opponent attacks the upper or middle part of your body, you should keep your body low, move close to him and then use your sword to pierce him under his arm *(fig. 24.4.2)*. Here, the basic techniques are fanji, a curving upward strike with the tip or upper part of the sword, and ci, thrusting.

25.1.1

25.1.2

25. FISH LYING AT THE BOTTOM OF A POND

In this posture, the sword remains low like a fish on the bottom of a pond.

25.1 Raise the body and block up

Movements Step forward with your right foot and turn your body to the left. Keep your weight on your left leg and your body erect to form a left side bow stance. At the same time, move the sword to the left and back (southeast) with the tip pointing down and the left jianjue under the right wrist. Both hands should be on the left side of your left shoulder and a little bit higher than your shoulder. Turn your head to face toward the southeast *(fig. 25.1.1)*.

Internal Components Look from west to southeast and focus your mind on your left hand. Feel qi extend through your arms.

Key Points The step forward and the turn of your body must be coordinated and nimble. Feel your body dodging to the right and pushing the sword to the left.

Application If the opponent attacks your left shoulder, you can dodge slightly to the right and use the sword to block his arm *(fig. 25.1.2)*. Here, the basic technique is jie, blocking with the edge of the sword.

| 25.2.1 | 25.2.2 | 25.2.3 |

25.2 Wave whip and take a back insert step

Movements   Raise both hands and then separate them and bring them down alongside your torso. Straighten your body. At the same time, cross your left foot behind your right foot to form a back insert step with only the ball of your left foot touching the ground *(fig. 25.2.1)*. Then, let your body sink down to form a right rest stance. Let your left knee touch the back of your right knee. Move your hands so that they meet in front of your right knee. Keep your right palm facing outward (south) and hold the sword parallel to the ground with the tip pointing to the west. Hold the left jianjue beside your right wrist and turn your head to the right and look toward the tip of the sword *(fig. 25.2.2)*.

Internal Components   Look from southeast to west and then down, letting your gaze follow the tip of the sword. Focus your mind on your left hand. Feel qi sink down to the dantian, in the lower abdomen.

Key Points   First extend your body as though to fly. Then sink down, feeling stable and agile.

Application   If the opponent is on your right, you can use a back insert step to move your body close to him and your sword to strike him *(fig. 25.2.3)*. Here, the basic techniques are pi, chopping down with the edge of the sword, and jie, blocking with the edge of the sword.

25.3.1   25.3.2

25.3 White crane spread wings

Movements   Turn to the left on the balls of both feet and circle counterclockwise to face north. At the same time, straighten and raise your body and separate your hands, moving your arms alongside your torso. Let both palms face toward the north. Both the left jianjue and the tip of the sword should point down *(fig. 25.3.1)*.

Internal Components   Look to the north while your body turns. Focus your mind on the baihui point, at the top of the head. Feel qi on top of your head.

Key Points   Straighten your body and rise up at the same time. Feel stable and nimble throughout the movement.

Application   Turning your body to the left, you can use your sword to block lightly *(fig. 25.3.2)*. Here, the basic technique is dai, moving the sword straight back.

| 25.4.1 | 25.4.2a, b | 25.4.3 |

25.4 Swallow settles down on duckweed

Movements   Move both hands up in an arc to meet in front of and above your head and then move them down together *(fig. 25.4.1)*. Then, touching the left jianjue with your right wrist and holding the sword with your right hand, move the sword down until it is parallel to the ground and the tip points to the west. Point the left jianjue to the east and place it beside your right wrist. At the same time, cross your right foot behind your left foot to make a back insert step. Let your body sink down to form a left rest stance. Your right knee should touch the back of your left knee. Turn your head to the left and look toward the tip of the sword *(fig. 25.4.2a, b)*.

Internal Components   Look from north to west and then let your gaze move down to follow the movement of the tip of the sword. Focus your mind on the left jianjue. Feel qi sink down to the dantian, in the lower abdomen.

Key Points   The movement of your body to the left and down should be nimble. Feel as though the sword and your body are pressing down powerfully together.

Application   If the opponent is on the left, you can use a back insert step to move close to him and use your sword to block his arm *(fig. 25.4.3)*. Here, the basic techniques are jie, blocking with the edge of the sword, and ya, pressing down.

26.1.1   26.1.2

26. TURN AROUND AND CHOP THE FACE

"Turn around" here means that you pretend to be running away, but actually you are preparing to fight back. This posture is sometimes called "changing a loss to a win." This technique will be done twice, once on the left side and once on the right.

26.1 Turn sword over and cut up while assuming bow stance

Movements   Step to the right (east) with your right foot and shift your weight to it. Let your left leg stretch out until it is straight. This forms a right standard bow stance. At the same time, hold the sword with your right hand in niba, the thumb-down grip, and move the sword forward with the tip pointing to the east at knee level. Place the left jianjue under your right wrist *(fig. 26.1.1)*.

Internal Components   Look from west to east and focus your mind on your right hand. Feel qi extend to the tip of the sword.

Key Points   The step to the right should be nimble. Feel relaxed and ready to move quickly and lightly. Also feel as though the sword can hit a target far away.

Application   Using this movement, you can strike the opponent's forearm from below *(fig. 26.1.2)*. Here, the basic technique is fanjie, a curving downward strike with the tip or upper part of the sword.

26.2.1   26.2.2

26.2 Feign escape and pull sword back

Movements   Shift your weight back to your left leg and turn your body to the left to form a left side bow stance. At the same time, pull the sword back (west) with both hands in heba, a two-handed grip, until the sword is in the front of your abdomen. Keep the sword parallel to the ground and the tip pointing to the east *(fig. 26.2.1)*.

Internal Components   Keep looking at the tip of the sword. Focus your mind on your right hand. Feel qi sink down to the dantian, in the lower abdomen.

Key Points   When pulling the sword back, you should also push or press down on it. Feel nimble and agile, ready to take a quick step back. Before pulling the sword back, you should feel inside as though you are feigning an attack forward. Outside, this movement relies on shen to capture the attention of the opponent.

Application   With this movement, you can use your sword to press down on and block the opponent's weapon. Relax your whole body and feel as though the sword is heavy. When the opponent comes at you with speed and power, do not meet him directly. Instead, just follow his momentum and then fight back. Sometimes, for a quick movement, you can also step forward *(fig. 26.2.2)*. Here, the basic techniques are ya, pressing down, and dai, moving the sword straight back.

26.3.1   26.3.2   26.3.3

26.3 Turn around and raise knee

Movements Continuing without interruption from the previous movement, turn your body to the left to face west. Bring your right foot forward and across your left foot and turn it so that it points to the southwest, what is called the the kaobu step. As your foot turns, your body should face south and your head should face east *(fig. 26.3.1)*. Then, relax your left hip and raise your left knee toward the west. Your body should also lean slightly toward the west. Hold the sword in front of your right shoulder with both hands in heba, a two-handed grip *(fig. 26.3.2)*.

Internal Components Let your gaze move in a counterclockwise circle that starts and ends in the east. Focus your mind on your left knee. Feel qi originate from the dantian, in the lower abdomen, and extend throughout your body.

Key Points The step must be quick and nimble. Your body should turn quickly and remain stable. Feel as though your raised left knee can touch your chest. This will cause your body to feel compressed. There should be a feeling of excitement in this movement.

Application In this movement, you should turn your body away from the opponent and then strike back skillfully. Also, you can raise your leg for dodging a lower attack *(fig. 26.3.3)*. Here, the basic technique is dai, moving the sword straight back.

26.4.1   26.4.2

26.4 Assume bow stance and chop at face

Movements Continuing without interruption from the previous movement, step forward toward the east with your left foot to form a left standard bow stance. With both hands holding the sword, chop forward (east). As the movement ends, the tip of the sword should be level with the top of your head (*fig. 26.4.1*).

Internal Components Keep looking toward the east. Focus your mind on your right hand. Feel qi extend to the tip of the sword.

Key Points The left step can be big and should be quick. Feel a powerful force coming from your waist and your right leg.

Application In this movement, you can use your sword to chop back at the opponent's face or head (*fig. 26.4.2*). Here, the basic technique is pi, chopping down with the edge of the sword.

| 26.5.1 | 26.5.2 | 26.5.3 |

26.5 Feign loss and take sword back

Movements Turn your body to the right and back so that it faces to the south. At the same time, shift your weight to your right leg to form a right side bow stance. Holding the sword with both hands and keeping it in front of your abdomen, pull it back toward the west and push down on it. Keep the sword parallel to the ground and the tip pointing to the east *(fig. 26.5.1)*.

Continuing without interruption, step forward with your left foot so that it moves in front of your right foot. As your left foot touches the ground, turn it on the heel to the northwest, the kaobu step *(fig. 26.5.2)*.

Internal Components Look down and let your gaze follow the tip of the sword. Focus your mind on your left hand. Feel qi in the dantian, in the lower abdomen.

Key Points As your weight shifts back, your body can lean back and slightly to the right. Both hands should simultaneously pull back and press down on the sword. Your body should feel agile and heavy. The weight shift and the step forward should be continuous and smooth.

Application When the opponent attacks you, you can dodge back and use the sword to block along the line of his attack and follow the direction of his force *(fig. 26.5.3)*. Here, the basic techniques are ya, pressing down, and dai, moving the sword straight back.

26.6.1   26.6.2   26.6.3, 4

26.6 Turn around and chop at face

Movements Continuing without interruption from the previous movement, turn your head back to face east. Raise your right knee toward your left shoulder. Using both hands in heba, hold the sword in front of your left shoulder *(fig. 26.6.1)*.

Step forward with your right foot to make a right standard bow stance. Using both hands, move the sword forward in a chopping motion. The tip of the sword should be level with the top of your head and the tip should point toward the east *(fig. 26.6.2)*.

Internal Components Keep looking toward the east and focus your mind on your right hand. Feel qi extend from the tip of the sword to the dantian, in the lower abdomen.

Key Points Do not pause between raising your knee and stepping forward. These two parts of the movement must be nimble and smoothly integrated into one motion.

Application   In this movement, you can dodge forward slightly and then chop back quickly at the opponent *(fig. 26.6.3, 4)*. Here, the basic technique is pi, chopping down with the edge of the sword.

27.1.1   27.1.2

27. WHITE SNAKE FLICKS ITS TONGUE

This is a very fast attack skill. Here, the body is like the snake's mouth with the head as the upper lip and the feet as the lower lip. The sword is like the tongue.

27.1 Take sword back and assume sitting stance

Movements   Relax your shoulders and let your right hand holding the sword drop down. Change your left hand to a jianfa, and use it to hold the jiantan. Hold the jiantan opposite your right knee and point the tip of the sword diagonally up and toward the east. Then, relax your left hip and knee and step forward with your left foot to make a right standard sitting stance *(fig. 27.1.1)*.

Internal Components   Keep looking forward and focus your mind on your right hand. Feel qi sink down to the dantian, in the lower abdomen. This will cause your abdomen to pull back slightly.

Key Points   The sword should drop straight down but the tip should remain pointing upward. All your weight should be on your right leg. This will make your right leg feel very stable and your left leg feel very agile.

Application   In this movement, you can use the sword for defense by pressing it down on the opponent's weapon and at the same time prepare for an attack by stepping forward *(fig. 27.1.2)*. Here, the basic technique is ya, pressing down.

27.2.1   27.2.2

27.2 Thrust sword upward

Movements   Take a half-step forward (east) with your left foot and then immediately shift your weight forward. Let your right foot follow with a half-step to form genbu, the left following stance. Straighten your body and move slightly up. Using both hands, thrust directly up with the sword. The tip of the sword should be level with the top of your head *(fig. 27.2.1)*.

Internal Components   Keep looking forward and focus your mind on your left hand. Feel qi extend from the dantian, in the lower abdomen, to the tip of the sword.

Key Points   Use force from your arms to strengthen the upward thrust of the sword. This is a ji and ci skill and must be done with a feeling of great agility.

Application   In this movement, you can use your sword to attack the opponent's face directly *(fig. 27.2.2)*. Here, the basic technique is ji, a curving strike with the tip or upper part of the sword, and ci, thrusting.

27.3.1   27.3.2

27.3 Take sword back and assume sitting stance

Movements   Relax your left hip and knee. Relax your shoulders and using both hands, drop the sword down so that the jiantan is opposite your left knee and the tip of the sword is pointing up and forward (east). Then, relax your right hip and knee and step forward with your right foot to make a left standard stance *(fig. 27.3.1)*.

Internal Components   Keep looking forward and focus your mind on your left hand. Feel qi sink down to the dantian, in the lower abdomen. This will cause your abdomen to pull back slightly.

Key Points   Drop the sword straight down. Keep all your weight on your left leg. This will make your left leg feel very stable and your right leg feel very agile.

Application   In this movement, you can use the sword for defense by pressing it down on the opponent's weapon and at the same time prepare an attack by stepping forward *(fig. 27.3.2)*. Here, the basic technique is ya, pressing down.

27.4.1   27.4.2

27.4 Thrust sword forward

Movements   Take a half-step forward with your right foot and then immediately shift your weight forward. Let your left foot follow with a half-step to form genbu, the right following stance. Straighten your body and move forward slightly. Using both hands, move the sword directly forward in a thrusting motion. The tip of the sword should be level with your chest *(fig. 27.4.1)*.

Internal Components   Keep looking forward and focus your mind on your left hand. Feel qi extend to the tip of the sword.

Key Points   The sword should thrust forward directly, using force from your waist. This is a ci skill and must be done with a feeling of great power.

Application   In this movement, you can use your sword to attack the opponent's chest directly *(fig. 27.4.2)*. Here, the basic technique is ci, thrusting.

226 • THE THIRTY-TWO POSTURE FORM

27.5.1   27.5.2

27.5 Take sword back and assume sitting stance

Movements   Relax your right hip and knee. Relax your shoulders and, using both hands, drop the sword straight down so that the jiantan is opposite your right knee and the tip of the sword is pointing up and forward (east). Then, relax your left hip and knee and step forward with your left foot to make a right standard sitting stance *(fig. 27.5.1)*.

Internal Components   Keep looking forward and focus your mind on your left hand. Feel qi sink down to the dantian, in the lower abdomen. This will cause your abdomen to pull back slightly.

Key Points   Drop the sword straight down. Keep all your weight on your right leg. This will make your right leg feel very stable and your left leg feel very agile.

Application   In this movement, you can use your sword for defense by pressing it down on the opponent's weapon and at the same time prepare an attack by stepping forward *(fig. 27.5.2)*. Here, the basic technique is ya, pressing down.

27.6.1   27.6.2

27.6 Thrust sword down

Movements   Take a half-step forward (east) with your left foot and then immediately shift your weight forward. Let your right foot follow with a half-step to form genbu, the left following stance. Straighten your body and lean forward slightly. Using both hands, move the sword directly down in a thrusting motion. The tip of the sword should be level with your ankle *(fig. 27.6.1)*.

Internal Components   Keep looking forward and focus your mind on your left hand. Feel qi extend to the tip of the sword.

Key Points   The sword should thrust down toward the jiexi point, at the front of the opponent's ankle. Use force from your wrists to thrust powerfully down with the sword. This is a dian skill and must be done with a feeling of great agility.

Application   In this movement, you can use your sword to attack the opponent's leg or foot directly *(fig. 27.6.2)*. Here, the basic techniques are dian, striking straight down with the tip of the sword, and ci, thrusting.

28.1.1   28.1.2

28. LI GUANG SHOOTS A STONE

Li Guang was a famous general who lived about two thousand years ago. He was a great archer and this posture is based on one of his famous feats. According to the story, Li Guang had too much to drink one night, and on his way back to camp, he saw a tiger, took out his bow and arrow, and shot at it. He then went to bed. The next morning, he went to see if the tiger had died. When he arrived, however, he saw no tiger, but rather a stone, which his arrow had pierced. A very powerful shot, indeed! In this posture, think of your sword as Li's arrow.

28.1 Make a back insert step and lower sword

Movements   Step back with your right foot and turn your body to the right so that the toes of your right foot point to the south. At the same time, with your right hand holding the sword and your left hand changed to a jianjue and placed beside your right wrist, use both hands to move the sword back to the side of your right hip. As soon as possible, move your left foot across and behind your right foot, letting only the ball of your left foot touch the ground. This forms a back insert step *(fig. 28.1.1)*.

Internal Components   Look down and back to the left jianjue. Focus your mind on your right hand. Feel qi in the dantian, in the lower abdomen, and extending to both arms. This will cause the sword to become heavy.

Key Points   Make sure that the two steps are continuous and smooth. Feel as though your whole body is very nimble and excited.

Application   You can use this movement to dodge an attack and use the sword to press down on the opponent's weapon. Here, the basic techniques are ya, pressing down, and xiajie, blocking and cutting down *(fig. 28.1.2)*.

28.2.1   28.2.2

28.2 Turn around and strike back

Movements Bend your right leg and drop your whole body down into a right rest stance. Then turn your body to the right and back toward the southwest. At the same time, separate your arms so that your left hand moves to the left and the left jianjue points to the east at shoulder level. Move your right hand to the right so that the sword points to the west at knee level. Turn your head back to face west and look at the tip of the sword *(fig. 28.2.1)*.

Internal Components Look back at the tip of the sword and focus your mind on your left hand. Feel qi reach both the left jianjue and the tip of the sword.

Key Points Your legs should be stable and your waist very nimble. Your body should be erect. Feel as though you can quickly move in any direction.

Application If the opponent is at your back or right side and attacks you from above, you can squat down and use the sword to attack his leg *(fig. 28.2.2)*. Here, the basic techniques are ji, a curving strike with the tip or upper part of the sword, and zhan, cutting off.

| 28.3.1 | 28.3.2 | 28.3.3, 4 |

28.3 Raise knee and hide tip of sword

Movements　Move your body up and at the same time, shift your weight back to your left leg. Keep both knees touching and your right leg almost straight. At the same time, turn both arms over so that both palms face up. Keep the left jianjue pointing diagonally up and toward the east and the tip of the sword pointing diagonally up and toward the west *(fig. 28.3.1)*.

Continuing without interruption, raise your right knee toward your chest and drop both elbows diagonally in toward the centerline of your body so that they both point to your right knee. Be sure that your right knee is directly opposite the two elbows *(fig. 28.3.2)*.

Internal Components　Look up and focus your mind on your left hand. Feel qi in the dantian, in the lower abdomen. This will cause a feeling of compression throughout your body.

Key Points　When your body moves up and your weight shifts to your left leg, keep your balance and maintain stability. Your body can lean slightly to the west. Feel as though you are rising up to mount a powerful attack.

Application　After you have attacked the opponent's leg, you can turn your sword up to attack his chest or face *(fig. 28.3.3, 4)*. Here, the basic technique is ci, thrusting.

| 28.4.1 | 28.4.2 | 28.4.3 |

28.4 Hold bow and arrow

Movements   Use your right hand to move the sword in a small counterclockwise circle and then pull the sword to the northwest. Let the tip of the sword point to the south and the jiantan point to the north, put the left jianjue beside your right wrist *(fig. 28.4.1)*. Move your left hand back to your right hand and then forward along the ridge of the sword until the left jianjue points to the south. Turn your body to the right as your hands move and let your right leg follow your body's momentum by stepping forward and to the right to form a right wide bow stance. Both feet should point to the southwest *(fig. 28.4.2)*.

Internal Components   Look to the south and focus your mind on your right hand. Feel qi in the dantian, in the lower abdomen, and extending to the arms.

Key Points   Your body can lean to the west as your right foot steps forward. Feel a powerful force through your arms and body as though you were pulling a stiff bow.

Application   In this movement, you can dodge to the right and use the ridge of the sword to block the opponent's sword *(fig. 28.4.3)*, or you can put the sword under the opponent's arm as you make the small circle with your right hand and then pull the sword back to cut him. Here, the basic techniques are jiao, blocking by making a circle with the sword, and chou, pulling to cut with the edge of the sword.

29.1.1   29.1.2

29. HOLD THE MOON IN YOUR ARMS

The name of this posture indicates that it is essentially making a big circle.

29.1 Move sword around and thrust forward while in bow stance

Movements   Move the sword forward (south) with your right hand in a thrusting motion and then move it toward the southeast. This movement is called quanci, thrusting around. Put the left jianjue beside your right wrist. At the same time, turn your body slightly to the left *(fig. 29.1.1)*.

Internal Components   Move your gaze from the south to the southeast. Focus your mind on your right hand. Feel qi from the left jianjue extend through your body to your right arm and then to the tip of the sword.

Key Points   After pricking forward with the sword to the south, move the sword in an arc to the southeast but feel as though your body is moving toward the southwest.

Application   If the opponent attacks the center or left side of your body, you can dodge to the right and use your sword to thrust him in his left side *(fig. 29.1.2)*. Here, the basic technique is ci, thrusting.

29.2.1   29.2.2a   29.2.2b

29.2 Turn and make a horizontal circle

Movements Shift your weight to the left. At the same time, turn your body to the left and let the sword move with a pricking motion in a horizontal arc toward the east *(fig. 29.2.1)*.

Continue without interruption to move the sword through an arc so that the tip points to the north and then to the west *(fig. 29.2.2a, b)*. At the end of this movement, your right hand should be in yinba, the palm-up grip, and the left jianjue should point to the east. As the sword moves through the arc, shift your weight to your right leg *(fig.29.2.3)*.

29.2.3 29.2.4 29.2.5, 6

Internal Components   Move your gaze from east to west. Focus your mind on your left hand. Feel qi extend through the arms and the whole body.

Key Points   Use force from your waist to make the horizontal circle above your head. When the sword moves in front of your body, let your body lean back slightly.

Application   If the opponent attacks you from the front, you can dodge slightly and thrust his chest with your sword *(fig. 29.2.4)*. If the opponent attacks you from above, you can use this as a defensive skill *(fig. 29.2.5, 6)*. Here, the basic techniques are lan, blocking and breaking off in the middle); dai, moving the sword straight back; jiao, making a circle with the sword; and ya, pressing down.

29.3.1   29.3.2

29.3 Block side to side while taking a step forward

Movements Continuing without interruption from the previous movement, shift your weight to the left, and move your right foot to the front of your body, letting only the toes of your right foot touch the ground. At the same time, move both arms in front of your abdomen. This will cause the sword to create a horizontal chop. The tip of the sword should point to the south and both palms should face up. Change the left hand to a jianfa and use it to hold the jiantan as the movement ends *(fig. 29.3.1)*.

Internal Components   Look ahead to the south. Focus your mind on your left hand. Feel qi in the dantian, in the lower abdomen.

Key Points The right step forward and the horizontal cut should be made at the same time. This will cause a powerful, relaxed, and vigorous movement.

Application   You can continue from the previous movement by using your sword to press down on the opponent's weapon and then cutting his arm or waist *(fig. 29.3.2)*. Here, the basic techniques are xiao, cutting along a gap, and zhan, cutting off.

29.4.1   29.4.2

29.4 Circle block and cut to waist

Movements   Take a half-step back with your right foot, letting only the ball of the foot touch the ground This forms a left insubstantial stance. Pull your abdomen back a little and at the same time, pull the sword back *(fig. 29.4.1)*.

Internal Components   Keep looking straight ahead (south). Focus your mind on your left hand. Feel qi sink down to the dantian, in the lower abdomen.

Key Points   While pulling the sword back, let your body sink down to maintain stability.

Application   If your sword already touches the opponent's body, just pull the sword back to cut him *(fig. 29.4.2)*. Here, the basic technique is chou, pulling to cut with the edge of the sword.

30.1.1   30.1.2

30. SINGLE WHIP

In this posture, the sword is waved like a whip.

30.1 Step back and sweep sword to the left

Movements Turn your body to the left and face east. Use both hands to hold the sword with the blade parallel to the ground and then chop toward the east by moving the sword in a horizontal arc. The tip of the sword should point to the east. At the same time, move your right foot back to the side of your left foot and then use it to step toward the west to form a left side bow stance *(fig. 30.1.1)*.

Internal Components Look from south to east. Focus your mind on the left jiaji point, in the center of the back. Feel qi in the dantian, in the lower abdomen, and extending to the tip of the sword.

Key points Keep your weight on your left leg and sink down. Turn your waist but not your hips. Your left leg should feel stable and your right leg nimble.

Application If the opponent is on your left, you can turn to the left, dodge with your left shoulder, and use your sword to chop at him horizontally *(fig. 30.1.2)*. Here, the basic technique is xiao, cutting along a gap.

30.2.1   30.2.2

30.2 Turn around and sweep sword back

Movements   Turn your body to the right and face west. Use your right hand with the sword to chop back horizontally until the tip of the sword points to the west. Hold the sword with yinba, the palm-up grip. Keep the left jianjue to the left of your body and continue to point it to the east. Both palms should face up. At the same time, shift your weight to your right leg to form a right side bow stance *(fig. 30.2.1)*.

Internal Components   Look from east to west. Focus your mind on your right hand. Feel qi reach to the tip of the sword.

Key Points   Your right leg should feel stable and your left leg, nimble.

Application   If the opponent is on your right and behind you, turn your body toward him and chop back horizontally with your sword *(fig. 30.2.2)*. Here, the basic technique is xiao, cutting along a gap.

31.1.1   31.1.2

31. GOLDEN COMPASS POINTS SOUTH

The function of a compass is to provide the correct direction. This posture points the way to the correct completion of the form, and is, therefore, a very important part of your practice.

31.1 Encircle arms

Movements   Bend both elbows so that your arms turn in to the center of your body and your hands are in front of your chest. At the same time, turn both arms inward so that your palms face down. Hold the sword under your left forearm and point it toward the east. This part of the movement is called "encircle arms." Put the left jianjue over your right hand. Turn your head to the east. At the same time, relax your left hip and take a half-step back with your left foot, letting only the ball of the left foot touch the ground. Your left knee should point to the east to form a right side insubstantial stance *(fig. 31.1.1)*.

Internal Components   Look from west to east. Focus your mind on the yuzhen point, at the back of the head. Feel qi extend through your encircling arms.

Key Points   Keep your body erect and raise your left knee slightly to increase both the stability of your right leg and the agility of your left leg as it steps back. Feel as though your head is suspended from above so that your whole body will be relaxed, comfortable and light.

Application   If the opponent is on your left and attacks you with great force, you can dodge back. The feeling inside, however, should be that you want to attack forward. In the attack, you can use your sword to pierce the opponent under his left arm *(fig. 31.1.2)*. Here, the basic technique is ci, thrusting.

31.2.1

31.2 Change hand that holds sword

Movements   Grasp the handle of the sword with your left hand in fanwo, the reversed holding position. Release the sword with your right hand and then make the right jianjue and put it in front of the handle. The right jianjue should be opposite your left index finger. Turn the palm of your left hand over so that it faces outward (south) and hold the sword in front of, and in touch with, your left forearm *(fig. 31.2.1)*.

Internal Components   Continue looking to the east. Focus your mind on your right hand. Feel qi on top of your head.

Key Points   When your left hand takes the handle of the sword, your left elbow should stay in touch with the blade. Feel as though both elbows are extending out to your sides.

Application   Switching the sword to the left hand has many uses.

31.3.1   31.3.2

31.3 Turn left and point to the sky

Movements Turn your body to the left and sink slightly down on your right leg. At the same time, separate both hands and move your left hand with the sword to the left and upward so that the jiantan points up. Move the right jianjue a little bit back so that it is in front of your right shoulder. Turn your head to look up *(fig. 31.3.1)*.

Internal Components Look up and to the east. Focus your mind on the right quchi point, on the right elbow. Feel qi extend to the jiantan and to your right elbow.

Key Points At the same time your body turns to the left, it should sink down to the right. This will cause your left leg to feel agile. Feel as though your right elbow is pulling back. This will cause your left arm to feel powerful.

Application If the opponent attacks you from above and on the left, you can use the handle of your sword to block the attack *(fig. 31.3.2)*.

31.4.1   31.4.2

31.4 Hold sword and block horizontally

Movements Turn your body to the right and move your left hand with the sword back toward your body in front of your left shoulder and then in front of your chest *(fig. 31.4.1)*.

Internal Components Look down and then forward. Focus your mind on your left elbow. Feel qi sink down to the dantian, in the lower abdomen, and let your chest become empty.

Key Points Keep the sword vertical and in touch with your left arm. Feel as though the body is moving very nimbly.

Application If the opponent attacks your torso, you can move your body slightly to the right and use your sword to block the attack *(fig. 31.4.2)*.

31.5.1   31.5.2

31.5 Block down as if to draw a line on the earth

Movements   Turn your body to the left and sink down slightly. At the same time, sweep your left hand with the sword down and then to the left. The sword should be held along the outside of your left arm and the tip should point up. Move the right jianjue up to the side of your right ear *(fig. 31.5.1)*.

Internal Components   Look to the left and then down. Focus your mind on your right hand. Feel qi extend to the jiantan and the right jianjue.

Key Points   Feel as though your left leg can be moved back quickly and that your left hand is extended downward. Move your body slightly to the right.

Application   If the opponent attacks your lower torso or leg from the left side, you can block down with the handle of your sword *(fig. 31.5.2)*.

31.6.1   31.6.2

31.6 Stretch arm and point forward while in bow stance

Movements Step to the left (northeast) with your left foot, letting the left heel touch the ground first. Then shift your weight to your left leg. Turn your right foot on the ball of the foot so that both feet point to the east. This forms a standard left bow stance. At the same time, stretch the right jianjue out in front of your body and point it to the east. Your left hand with the sword should be on the left side of your body and the tip of the sword should point up *(fig. 31.6.1)*.

Internal Components Look forward and focus your mind on your left hand. Feel qi reach the right jianjue.

Key Points Be careful to adjust your right foot. This will coordinate the external move-ment with the internal force. Pushing your left hand down so that the jiantan points to the ground will increase the feeling of power in your right hand.

Application Continuing without interruption from the previous movement, keep the handle of your sword in contact with the opponent's weapon and use the right jianjue to attack him *(fig. 31.6.2)*.

| 31.7.1 | 31.7.2 | 31.7.3 | 31.7.4 |

31.7 Turn around and poke from side to side

Movements Move your left forearm up until the jiantan is in front of and to the left of the head. Move the right jianjue so that it points diagonally down toward the ground and then sweeps to the right side of your body and extends toward the south *(fig. 31.7.1)*. At the same time, turn your body to the right and turn your left foot on its heel so that the toes of the left foot point to the south *(fig. 31.7.2)*. Relax your right hip and knee and step to the south with your right foot. Your right heel should touch the ground and the toes of your right foot should point up. This forms the left sitting stance *(fig. 31.7.3)*.

Internal Components Look down and then to the right, up, and forward (south). Focus your mind on your right hand. Feel qi extend to the jiantan and to the right jianjue.

Key Points When your body turns to the right, keep your left leg stable. Your left elbow should bend and drop down. Your right leg should feel very agile and able to step in any direction.

Application If the opponent attacks you from the lower right side, you can dodge to the left and use the right hand to block the attack *(fig. 31.7.4)*.

31.8.1   31.8.2

31.8 Strike with handle while in bow stance

Movements   Shift your weight forward to your right leg. Turn on the ball of your left foot to adjust the foot so that it points to the south. This forms a standard right bow stance. At the same time, strike forward with your left hand holding the sword, letting the jiantan point to the south. Hold right jianjue beside your right thigh *(fig. 31.8.1)*.

Internal Components   Keep looking forward (south). Focus your mind on your right hand. Feel qi reach the jiantan.

Key Points   Make the jiantan strike straight ahead but keep your mind focused on your right hand. This will help your internal force move to the left quickly and smoothly.

Application   Continuing from the previous movement, you can use your right hand to block the opponent's attack and the jiantan to strike at him *(fig. 31.8.2)*.

32.1.1

32. MERGE STEPS AND CLOSE THE FORM

This is the closing posture of the form. It must be relaxed, smooth, and slow. Adjust the internal components of shen, yi, and qi, and let your whole body cool down.

32.1 Merge hands and feet

Movements Move the jiantan and right jianjue down together so that they point to the big toe of your right foot. At the same time, step forward with your left foot and place it beside your right foot (*fig. 32.1.1*).

Internal Components Look down and focus your mind on the right jianjue. Feel qi moving down to the dantian, in the lower abdomen.

Key Points Keep all of your weight on your right leg and crouch down.

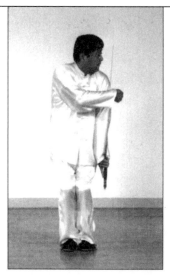

| 32.2.1 | 32.2.2 | 32.2.3 |

32.2 Push up with jianjue finger

Movements   Turn your head to face east. Move the right jianjue to the left side of the sword and then move it up along the blade of the sword until it is higher than the top of your head *(fig. 32.2.1, 2)*. Then, turn your right hand over so that the palm faces up and the jianjue points to the east. At the same time, pull the jianjue slightly to the right until it is above your head and stand straight up. Keep the sword on the left side of your body with the tip pointing up *(fig. 32.2.3)*.

Internal Components   Look to the east and focus your mind on your left hand, then on right jianjue. Feel qi moving up along the dumei, the centerline on back of torso, to the baihui point, at the top of the head.

Key Points   In this movement, the right jianjue moves up and the jiantan points down.

| 32.3.1 | 32.3.2 | 32.3.3 |

32.3 Right hand stretches to the right

Movements   Turn your head to the right (west) and move the right jianjue down to point to the right. Your right palm should be facing forward *(fig. 32.3.1)*.

Internal Components   Look to the west and focus your mind on your left hand. Feel qi moving down from the baihui point, at the top of the head, to the renzhong point, in the center of the face between the nose and upper lip, thereby connecting the dumei, the centerline on the back of the torso, with the renmei, the centerline on the front of the torso.

Key Points   Extend your left arm down and your right arm to the right side of your body. Feel your body relaxing.

32.4 Lower the right jianjue

Movements   Relax your right shoulder and drop your right elbow so that your right hand drops down beside your right thigh. Point the right jianjue to the south with your palm facing down. At the same time, turn your head to face south *(fig. 32.3.2)*. Adjust your breath and relax your whole body. Then point the jianjue to the ground with your right palm facing your right leg *(fig. 32.3.3)*.

Internal Components   Keep looking forward (south). Focus your mind on your right hand. Then, forget everything. Feel qi moving down to the dantian, in the lower abdomen, along the renmei, the centerline on the front of the torso, and then down to your feet.

Key Points   Adjust your breath so that it is smooth, slow, and deep. Inside you should feel quiet and comfortable. This is the end of the form.

1   2

RETURN TO ORIGINAL POSITION

Stand at ease. Carry the sword in the standard way.

Hold sword in left hand

Movements   Relax both shoulders and drop your elbows. Move both forearms up in front of your chest. The sword should be under your left arm and the tip should point down. Use you right hand to help your left hand adjust the sword to the regular carrying position *(fig. 1, 2)*.

Internal Components   Forget everything.

Key Points   Carry your sword in this way when you are not practicing the form. If you do not carry the sword in the proper manner, people will assume that you are a beginning practitioner or that you have never received serious traditional training.

Adjust breath and relax whole body

Movements   When all the joints of your body are relaxed and you are breathing comfortably, you are finished practicing.

Key Points   You are not finished until you feel completely comfortable.

SUMMARY OF MOVEMENT DIRECTIONS

When you practice this form, you must pay attention to the direction of the movements. This will help you remember the movements in sequence. Here is a summary of the movements and the directions in which they are practiced. Whatever direction you are facing when you begin your practice with the Preparation posture will be considered south for the remainder of the form. This direction does not have to be true south.

The first posture in the form (Commencing Form) and the second posture (Spread-eagled Sword Passes By Seven Stars) are practiced toward the west. Posture three (Step Forward and Shelter Knee) through posture eight (Thrust Sword in the Opposite Direction) are practiced toward the northwest. Posture nine (Turn Back While Pricking Lightly Up) though posture seventeen (Thrust Sword Downward) are practiced to the east. Posture eighteen (Step Back with Three Reverse Hits) through posture nineteen (Capture a Legendary Turtle in the Ocean Depths) are practiced toward the southwest. Posture twenty (Goddess Spreads Flowers) through posture twenty-two (Raise Whip and Attack Wrist) are practiced toward the east. Posture twenty-three (Black Dragon Stirs its Tail) through posture twenty-six (Turn Around and Chop the Face) are practiced toward the west. Posture twenty-seven (White Snake Flicks Its Tongue) is practiced toward the east and posture twenty-eight (Li Guang Shoots a Stone) is practiced back toward the west. The remaining postures are practiced from the same spot at which posture twenty-eight concludes, and if your steps throughout the form have been correct, you will end your practice in the same spot at which you began. If you are a beginner, you need not be overly concerned about this requirement, and when you are able to do everything well, you will do it correctly without thinking about it.

7

HOW TO PRACTICE TAIJI JIAN

I f you already have some experience with Taiji Quan, you will be familiar with many of the guidelines that apply to the practice of Taiji Jian. Nevertheless, you will need to pay attention to the unique qualities of Taiji Jian. Every aspect of jian practice must come from your heart. Taiji Jian is not just a set of postures and movements. It is a form of expression like art and music, and it draws at least as much on your emotions as on your intellect and your physical being.

STAGES OF PRACTICE

It is helpful when beginning the study of any new discipline to have some understanding of the phases that comprise the undertaking. Your ability to acquire each skill or technique will be enhanced by an awareness of the context from which that skill or technique derives. With such an awareness, you will be less likely to view any detail as irrelevant or dispensable. If you work hard and progress through each stage of the learning sequence, your training will be successful. This section describes the basic phases of Taiji Jian practice.

Understand Taiji Quan as the Foundation of Taiji Jian

It is said that "the empty-handed form is the mother of all other skills." Before you begin your study of Taiji Jian, you should study the empty-handed Taiji Quan form. All the basic movements and principles of Taiji Jian are similar to those of Taiji Quan. Taiji Jian, however, is more difficult than Taiji Quan simply because in Taiji Jian you must hold and manipulate a weapon. Traditionally, students were expected to practice the empty-handed form for at least one year (usually three years) before they could touch a sword.

The practice of Taiji Quan provides a strong foundation for the study of Taiji Jian and will increase your proficiency in the jian form. The more thoroughly you have

| 1 Holding seven stars | 2 Brush knee and twist step |

mastered Taiji Quan, the more easily you will learn Taiji Jian. All the benefits of Taiji Quan practice are naturally and directly transferable to your Taiji Jian training. If you know how to relax your arms and hands when they hold nothing, for example, you will more readily learn how to relax them when they hold a sword.

Once your Taiji Jian footwork and body movements are well integrated and reliably executed with accuracy and ease, you should begin to attend carefully to your internal feelings and to each of the internal components. Here, again, your Taiji Quan knowledge will inform and enhance your training in Taiji Jian. If your mind, for example, can lead qi to any part of your body, you can begin to learn how to send your qi to the tip of the jian. Only if you know how to release jin, internal force, from your body, can you learn how to release jin from your sword. In general, the deeper and stronger your foundation in Taiji Quan, the more highly skilled you can become in Taiji Jian.

Although a detailed discussion of Taiji Quan form is beyond the scope of this book, illustrations of several of the most important Taiji Quan postures from the Wu style empty-handed form are presented here (fig. 1–4). They are meant to remind you that the Taiji Quan form is of central importance to your practice of Taiji Jian and that it must never be overlooked.

Practice Basic Skills
It is very important to practice basic Taiji Jian movements and techniques so that you can hold the jian comfortably and flexibly and can move it as though it were an extension of your body. When, as has traditionally been advised, "the sword becomes part of your body," you will be able to perfect sword movements and let them be led by and integrated with the internal components and your feelings.

Each of the grips, stances, steps, and techniques described in previous chapters should be thoroughly studied and practiced, apart from your Taiji Jian form training. When you have separately mastered each movement in detail, you will be able to perform each one almost without conscious effort. It is often said that one must study the

| 3 Part the wild horse's mane | 4 Single whip |

basic skills in great detail so that they can vanish as separate elements and become an integral part of the whole form.

Study Each Movement Separately

The movements of the Taiji Jian form should be studied individually and carefully so that each one is correct before you turn your attention to the next. Separate attention to each will increase your ability to concentrate and will help you master its details; gradually, you will develop a clearer feeling for how each movement should be performed. Then, in your form training, you will be ready to pay more attention to the internal components and your acquisition of skill will accelerate. Separate attention to each movement will increase your chances for success in the art of Taiji Jian.

Understand Each Movement and Skill

As your understanding of each movement and skill increases, your awareness of the internal and external components of the form will also increase. Every movement of the Taiji Jian form has been designed for a particular purpose: either fighting, internal practice, or performance. An understanding of the purpose of each movement and skill will help you develop your ability to use the internal components of shen, yi, and qi. For example, if you fully understand a posture that involves turning your body around to attack your opponent from behind, your shen will move behind you, leading yi and qi in this direction even before your body actually turns. The involvement of these internal components will create movements that are agile, energetic, and intense. If you do not understand the purpose of a posture, it will be difficult to execute the movements clearly and precisely. Your actions will be tentative and your spirits will be low.

Feel the Internal Components and Use Them to Lead External Movements

Developing an awareness of the internal components of shen, yi, and qi will improve your ability to move with grace and ease. Students of Taiji Jian are always admonished to "do everything from the heart." If you can do this, your Taiji Jian form will be effective and beautiful and will feel like a natural expression of your character. In the beginning, this is difficult to accomplish, but as you become more advanced, your movements will seem naturally to become more fully imbued with your feelings. At the beginning of your training, your feelings will emerge unpredictably and only occasionally. When you become aware of an internal feeling, you should seek guidance from your master to insure that it is correct and appropriate. If it is, you should try to follow it by remaining aware of it and letting it influence the timing and shape of your movements. Do not try to force the appearance of such feelings and do not try to construct them consciously. They must develop and express themselves naturally and should be gently led by your mind rather than created by it. Do not strive for feelings. Just practice the form attentively and your feelings will eventually make themselves known.

Study Principles

To achieve high-level skill and knowledge, the study of principles is the most important part of your training. These principles include the fundamental concepts of both Taiji Quan and Daoism, and the many traditional attitudes and values that have shaped Chinese culture for centuries. One of these traditional principles is that "without principles, there can be no high-level practice." Taiji Quan is often said to be one of the most highly developed of the Chinese martial arts precisely because it embodies a complete, detailed, systematic, and profound set of principles. Taiji Jian incorporates not only the principles of Taiji Quan but also high-level principles of its own. This fundamental precept will be discussed in more detail below and in the next chapter.

TWO STYLES OF PRACTICE

There are two styles of practice in Taiji Jian. The most common, called the "regular style," looks like the empty-handed Taiji Quan form. When you use this style in your practice, your movements should be slow, relaxed, smooth, and nimble, and you should maintain a steady tempo. You should pay attention in as much detail as possible to all the external movements first. Then, shift your attention to the details of the internal components and the flow of their movements. Once you are sure that every movement is correct, imagine using each movement as a fighting technique and then feel qi and jin. Finally, practice focusing yi and shen. This sequence of learning is very important for your practice at any stage, but never more important than at the beginning of your training.

The second style of practice for Taiji Jian is called "freestyle." It is meant for people who have already mastered the whole form and want to increase their internal awareness. It is not commonly used and cannot be substituted for practice using the regular style. Although it can be very helpful, you will not have many occasions to use it, even when your practice is advanced. In freestyle practice, all movements are executed according to the immediate internal feelings of the practitioner. Speed and detail are secondary and do not need to follow the generally prescribed conventions. Whatever feeling you have, just follow it.

It is equally important, as has been mentioned earlier, that you not contrive a feeling just for the sake of practicing at a given time or of doing what others around you are doing. If you begin to practice and find that you are not feeling anything inside that seems to direct your movements, stop and wait for another time to practice. With freestyle practice, you should do the form only if you have discernible feelings for the movements as you do them. If your feelings are not good or discernible, forget practicing for the moment and try again later. When you practice freestyle, the speed and exact appearance of your movements may differ markedly from one day to the next because your feelings are different on different days. Nevertheless, your practice will always be correct as long as your movements express your feelings.

Customarily, it is advisable to use only the regular style of Taiji Jian practice for at least one year. This advice is based on the assumption that you have already practiced Taiji Quan for several years. When you can execute all the movements correctly and at a consistent speed, when the jian can be manipulated as though it were a part of your body, when qi can move smoothly and immediately to the tip of the jian, and when you can perform all sword movements easily and adeptly, you are ready to begin practicing freestyle. You will know when you have reached this point from the quality of your feelings as you practice the Taiji Jian form. It will happen very naturally and comfortably.

HIGH-LEVEL PRINCIPLES

Taiji Jian principles are derived from two sources and have developed into a single system. One source is derived from Taiji Quan principles, which in turn are drawn from Daoist philosophy. The second source is composed of traditional views and values, some recorded more than two thousand years ago, relating to the jian. Some of the basic principles from the first source have been discussed earlier and are described in many other books. In this chapter, principles from the second source are presented as well as some principles relating specifically to Taiji Jian.

Understanding Taiji Jian principles at a high level and appreciating the traditional Chinese culture from which Taiji Jian derives can significantly improve your skills. The jian is a unique and special weapon. You must practice it with diligence and devotion and understand the context in which it was developed. It is often said that the practitioner of Taiji Jian should invest time and energy in many pursuits, especially cultural activities such as art, literature, music, and dance. All of these will deepen your practice of Taiji Jian and allow your growing skill to reflect an appreciation for the broader culture. If your cultural knowledge is narrowly limited, it will not be possible for you to reach the highest level of jian mastery. Clearly, it is way beyond the

5   6   7

scope of this, or any book to explicate exactly how one should go about achieving knowledge of this kind. Be assured, however, that such knowledge will enrich your practice of Taiji Jian as it enriches your life.

There are two fundamental high-level principles in Taiji Jian practice. The first is called *renjian heyi*, meaning "unite body and jian," and referring to the goal of coordinating the movements of the jian so closely with the gestures of the individual that sword and practitioner come to function as one entity. The second high-level principle is called *wujian*, or "jian dance," and refers to the goal of performing the Taiji Jian form so beautifully that it becomes like dance.

The real meaning of uniting the practitioner and the jian is that everything must come from the heart, that is, from the emotions. Your skill level depends not just on the appearance of your movements and other objective qualities, but also on your ability to use your feelings to approximate the ideal of perfect union of movement and personal expression. This is often a difficult point to understand, especially for beginning students and it is also a difficult one to explain. You must practice long and hard and then you will begin to grasp this principle more by intuition than by intellect. Practice alone, no matter how disciplined and intense, will never bring you to high-level mastery. Such mastery results only from committed practice combined with a deep awareness of and appreciation for the principles of unity and beauty.

A serious but prevalent misunderstanding is that because the martial arts are not primarily for show, the beauty of the movements is not important and need not be a goal of practice. In fact, one of the central purposes of traditional Chinese martial arts is to train practitioners to make elegant movements. When martial arts were developed, it was found that the ability to perform the movements in an aesthetically pleasing way contributed to the attainment of high-level skill. Beautiful movements help develop shen, yi, and qi, and increase your internal awareness. For example, large movements, generally considered to be beautiful, are thought to make one's shen reach farther,

8   9   10

one's mind more expansive, and one's qi move more smoothly throughout the body. All the great masters demonstrate not only superior fighting skills, but also beautiful movements. Practitioners who do not pay attention to internal training or who do not enjoy beautiful movements will have difficulty attaining great fighting skills.

The importance of aesthetically pleasing jian movement was recognized more than two thousand years ago. At that time, jian practice was referred to as wujian, or "jian dance," meaning that the jian form was executed as though it were a dance. The beauty of jian movements was extolled in a variety of poetic phrases: "Up like a phoenix flying to the sky and down like a dragon swimming in the ocean," "Sometimes like a big river, sometimes like a small stream," "Appearing and disappearing in turn," "A flash of lightning," and "Interior scenery and exterior landscape." Some jian postures which illustrate these ideals are shown here *(fig. 5–10)*.

Only through beautiful movements can one gain a real understanding of the internal components of all Taiji forms and only through beautiful movements can one develop the light and agile techniques that make it possible to reach a high level of expertise. Beauty is even more central to the practice of Taiji Jian than to the practice of other weapons forms. You must always bear this in mind when you practice Taiji Jian and combine it with your practice of techniques and fighting skills. It is difficult to explain this principle clearly; it can only be felt from your practice.

Martial arts like Taiji Jian are sometimes practiced solely for show, by those with no interest in developing fighting skills. These practitioners may have very good basic Kungfu and often modify aspects of the form in clever and imaginative ways so that the movements can be choreographed as dance performances. Much hard work and creativity go into these performances and such efforts can be artistic and very worthwhile. They can also, however, foster the false impression that the beauty of movements is unrelated to the application of the movements in combat or competitive situations. Occasionally, practitioners whose main interest is in the application of Taiji

Jian movements show a disdain of any concern for the beauty of those movements. In fact, if one really understands the principles that underlie the martial arts, one will recognize that beauty of movement is as essential to successful fighting as it is to dance. Movements that are beautiful just for their own sake and do not reflect a true knowledge of martial arts skills and principles have no place in serious training. The two kinds of movement may appear superficially similar but they differ significantly in terms of the feelings and experiences they generate within the practitioner. In your practice, please pay careful attention to this distinction.

8

BASIC FIGHTING PRINCIPLES

Taiji Jian employs a special weapon and the principles which guide its use for fighting are highly refined. An understanding of these principles will be very helpful as you work toward mastery of jian skills. While previous chapters have made reference to the many fighting applications of Taiji Jian, this chapter presents a more detailed account of the principles that apply to Taiji Jian combat.

INTERNAL AND EXTERNAL TECHNIQUES

The basic techniques of Taiji Jian are directly related to the features of the jian itself. First, that the jian is double-edged and that its edges are very sharp along the top third of the blade as well as at the tip means that the jian can be used in very subtle ways. Although the movements of jian can be large and vigorous, the sharpness of the two edges allows for movements that are effective without necessarily being large or powerful. In fighting, the movements of the jian should, for the most part, be small and precise but "the mind should be big." When fighting, in other words, use your mind rather than your physical strength. You should also understand and practice the thirteen key techniques described in Chapter 5, especially the first four: ji, ci, ge and xi. An important goal of your training should be to become so comfortable holding the sword that its movements follow your mind as though it were a natural part of your body.

Regarding internal practice, you should develop shen so that it becomes concentrated, alert, quiet, and not outwardly visible but always leading the way for the mind to follow. You should practice yi so that it can be focused on any part of your body or sword, in order to lead the movement of qi smoothly throughout your whole body. You should train qi so that it can move fully and freely through your body, so that it becomes ever stronger, and so that it invests your external movements with power. You should also work attentively to increase your internal force so that it can follow qi and become more integrated with your movements.

1 Focus the mind and wait
for the attack

2 Step forward and use the
jian ridge to touch the spear

3 Lean back and raise the jian

4 Make a horizontal circle with the
jian and block spear to right

5 Step forward and a make
side-to-side chop

It is important that external movements be combined and coordinated with Taiji Jian techniques. The movements of the jian should be a natural extension of the movements of your body, and the movements of different parts of your body should be integrated with each other. Arm movements, for example, should be coordinated with those of your legs, and hand techniques should be coordinated with footwork. Internal force should always come from your feet and flow through your body directly to the tip of the jian. Integration among all external components of movement and the internal components of shen, yi, qi, and internal force, should be as complete as possible. Finally, you should feel that everything you do comes from your heart.

SEVEN KEY PRINCIPLES

The basic principles that guide the development of jian fighting skills are easy to describe but difficult to follow. Most importantly, you must be able to feel shen, yi, and qi. It is also important that your movements be relaxed, nimble, smooth, and concentrated before you begin to direct your study to basic fighting principles.

In general, the principles that apply to Taiji Jian are the same as those that apply to Taiji Quan. These include the concepts of yin and yang, open and closed, substantial and insubstantial (full and empty), and of sticking, connecting, and following. The principles that are unique to Taiji Jian are less widely known and are the focus of this chapter. As the seven principles that apply uniquely to jian combat are presented, remember that the jian is considered the "general of all weapons." This means that

6 Focus the mind and wait
for the attack

7 Step forward and use the
jian ridge to touch the spear

8 Step forward and make the jian
stick the spear

9 Step forward and chop

jian skills depend on cleverness and resourcefulness rather than on sheer power or ferocity. The jian is a "gentle weapon," used to convince people by reasoning rather than by brute force. The seven principles are described in detail below.

Use a Short Weapon as a Long Weapon

A general principle of weapons practice is that long weapons should be used like short weapons and short weapons should be used like long weapons. When you have a short weapon, such as the jian, and your opponent has a long weapon, it is very difficult to mount an effective attack because your opponent's weapon can reach you more easily than yours can reach him. You must be able, therefore, to move close to him so that your weapon will be useful and his weapon will be rendered ineffective.

To accomplish this, the important external components are footwork and the smooth, fluid movement of your waist. Regarding the internal components, it is important not to pay attention to the tip of the long weapon but rather to focus on and defend against the middle part of the weapon. Your goal should be to bypass your opponent's attack and move in close to him. If your opponent attacks with a spear, for example, he can change the movements of the tip very quickly, making it difficult to defend against directly. Instead, you must wait for an opportunity, when the spear tip passes over your body. You can then move in and counterattack.

Figures 1–5 show the use of the dai, or bringing back, technique, with a horizontal circle to defend and then a counterattack if your opponent directs a spear attack at your face. *Figures 6–9* show the use of ge, blocking with the ridge, with its quick foot-

10 Focus the mind and wait for the attack

11 Step forward and use the jian to touch the spear

12 Make a front circle and block the spear

13 Tuck in stomach and continue front circle

14 Step forward and stick the spear with the jian

15 Move close to the opponent and attack

work to defend and counterattack when your opponent thrusts his spear at your chest, a very common spear attack. *Figures 10–15* show the use of the jiao, or stirring, technique with a front circle. Here, your body should be pulled back in defense and then you should counterattack when your opponent strikes at your stomach.

Attack the Opponent's Front Wrist

Attacking the opponent's front wrist with the jian is a special fighting tactic. If your opponent attacks you with a long weapon that he holds in both hands, his front wrist is considered to be the one closer to your side. If he attacks with a short weapon that he holds in just one hand, the front wrist is the one belonging to the hand that wields the weapon. Because the top six inches of the jian blade are very sharp, it is not necessary to use great force when attacking your opponent. Instead, attack with subtlety, surprise, and quickness, and always aim the tip of the jian at the opponent's front wrist. Your goal is to make your opponent drop his weapon and this can be done only if you keep your attention focused on his hand rather than on his weapon. This is difficult to learn but it can bring you much success. *Figures 16* and *17* show the use of ti, raising up, to attack the opponent's front wrist when he uses a spear. *Figures 18–20* show the use of dian, pointing, to attack the opponent's front wrist when he uses a short weapon like the broadsword.

16 Focus the mind and wait for spear attack

17 Use tip of the jian to attack opponent's front wrist

18 Focus the mind and wait for sword attack

19 Use tip of the jian to attack opponent's front wrist

20 Dodge left and use tip of the jian to attack opponent's front wrist

Avoid Hard Blocks with the Jian

When your opponent mounts a strong attack, try to dodge it. Under no conditions use the jian to block hard. When you find a weakness in your opponent, then you can attack quickly and hard; however, the jian must never be used in a crude or rash manner. Regardless of the kind of weapon used by your opponent, you must never use the jian, especially not the jianren, the edge of the sword, to block forcefully. You may use jianji, the ridge of the sword, to block, but never with force or a noisy clashing of weapons. Rather, you should touch your opponent's weapon lightly with the jian and then use the jian to stick, connect, and follow the movements of the opponent's weapon. Blocking hard with the jian reveals a lack of understanding of the jian techniques and the special qualities the weapon possesses.

The injunction against hard blocks applies also to blocks by your opponent. If your opponent, for example, starts to use a hard block to defend against one of your attacks, you must change your attack so that you do not cause forceful contact between the weapons. According to Taiji tenets, strong contact by both weapons creates double-weightedness, a condition that is always to be avoided. It violates the yin and yang of Taiji because both weapons are exerting yang force simultaneously. *Figures 21* and *22* show a double-weighted hard attack and *Figures 23* and *24* show a double-weighted hard block. Both are incorrect applications of jian skills.

To avoid hard blocks, do not allow your jian to hit the opponent's weapon directly. You should instead defend from the side or back of his weapon. The movements of the jian should always be circular and carefully timed. This will preserve energy and improve your techniques. When it is necessary to dodge an opponent's attack, use as small and subtle a movement as possible. *Figures 25–27* show some movements that illustrate this.

Move Like the Dragon and Phoenix

"Rise like a dragon, fall like a phoenix" is a well-known phrase in the martial arts. According to Chinese legend, a dragon rising to the sky is thought to do so in a quickly rotating spiral that heads straight upward. A phoenix flying back to its nest is thought to descend in circles. The dragon embodies yang; the phoenix, yin.

The fourth principle of the jian refers to these two basic yang and yin movements, the straight and the circular. Most jian attacks are made in a straight line and all are quick. Jian defensive moves follow a circular pattern and must be smoothly executed. This principle incorporates the Taiji tenet that circles must be included in straight lines and straight lines must be included in circles. If your practice of Taiji Jian is guided by this principle, the beauty of your movements will be enhanced.

Be careful to shape all your movements by the activities of your mind. "Rise like a dragon," for example, does not refer literally to all upward movements of the jian, nor "fall like a phoenix" to all downward movements. Rather, these concepts should be in your mind when you move the jian in whatever direction is required by a particular movement. The correctness and effectiveness of the movement will depend more on the activity of your mind than on your body.

Be Still While in Motion; Move While Remaining Still

The relationship between the qualities of motion and stillness was expressed in a classic response attributed to the famous female jian master Yue Nü to a question asked by King Yue regarding the central principle of the jian. Yue Nü's answer was as follows. "The Dao (Way) of this skill is detailed and changeable, serene and deep. There are yin and yang, which are always being exchanged as if opening and closing a door. When fighting, you must concentrate *jingshen* (the mind and spirit combined) inside and make qi ready. On the outside, you must maintain good posture and position and show only calmness and agreeableness. You must behave outwardly like a fair lady but be ferocious as a tiger inside. Remain as vague as the mist and as alert and quick as a fleeing hare. Let the body and the shadow chase each other and let your sword be bright and dazzling like lightning. Adjust your breath and set aside the rules so that you can move about freely and quickly in all directions, and so that nothing can interfere with you. A person who understands this principle can defend against ten others, and if there are one hundred soldiers who follow this precept, it will be as though there are ten thousand. If you want to test this, I can show you right now."

21 Raise the jian in a two-handed grip to chop forcefully

22 Defend against opponent's chop

23 Remain steady when opponent makes hard block

24 Make a hard, direct block

25 Prepare a defense

26 Raise the jian to touch opponent's sword from right

27 Turn jian over and block opponent's sword down

The most celebrated and often repeated directives from Yue Nü's reply, as apt today for martial arts practitioners as they were in her own time, are to "behave outwardly like a fair lady but be like a ferocious tiger inside" and "to be as alert and quick as a fleeing hare." The contrast between fair ladies and tigers and the invocation of the agility of hares illustrate the relationship between moving and remaining still, the fifth principle of the jian.

When you practice the jian, you should pay attention to the state of stillness or motion of both the inside and outside of your body. Sometimes, as Yue Nü described, your external movements will be characterized by a sense of calm, while inside you should be experiencing a sense of heightened activity and excitement. This kind of balance is referred to as "finding motion within stillness." At other times, your external movements will be energetic and intense while your inner state should be characterized by steadiness and stillness. This configuration is described as "creating stillness within motion." The combination of stillness and motion in either configuration expresses the Taiji concepts of yin, associated with stillness and yang, associated with the quality of motion. It is important to maintain both of these forces throughout your practice and in all applications.

Launch Late but Arrive First

"The jian practitioner should assume a non-threatening posture to lead the opponent into thinking that he can gain some benefit from initiating an attack. You should launch your techniques later than the opponent does but reach him earlier than he can reach you." This principle was put forth in *Theory of Jian* by Zhuangzi, one of the founders of Daoism. Zhuangzi suggests that you lure your opponent into an attack, which you have anticipated and for which you are prepared. Your best opportunity to attack will be after your opponent has committed himself to an offensive move. Having tricked your opponent into thinking that you are vulnerable, you should then launch your attack. Wait patiently for an opportunity and never take action without having a clear objective. Be ready with a quick and efficient technique to attack the opponent as soon as the opportunity arises.

Unite the Body and the Jian

"The body follows the jian in movement and the jian covers the body in movement" is a famous dictum that describes the feeling you should have when you practice the jian. In the first part of the sentence "follow" means support, and indicates that you should brandish the jian with your whole body rather than only with your hand or arm. Your waist should function as the controller of your body and your feet and legs should act as the sources of internal force. Using control provided by your waist and internal force from your feet and legs, your body's movements should be seamlessly integrated with the movements of the jian.

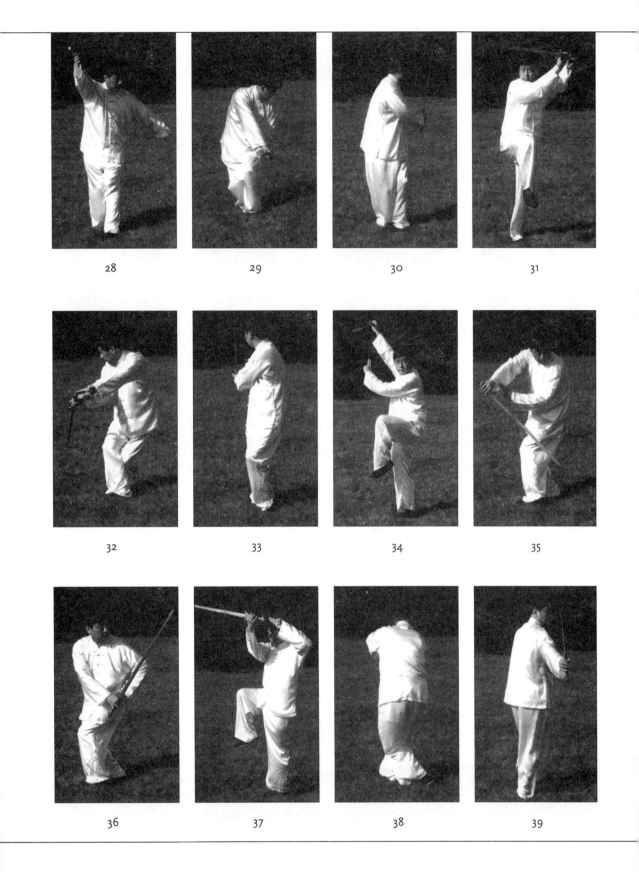

28   29   30   31

32   32   34   35

36   37   38   39

40 A and B stand face to face
three steps apart

41 When A steps forward and thrusts,
B makes left block with no step

42 When A thrusts, B steps forward with
back foot and makes right block

43 When A thrusts, B steps forward with
front foot and makes left block

The second part of the sentence implies that your steps should be nimble and that your body should be hidden behind the jian. Here, "cover" means to conceal what you want to do and where you want to go. You should use the jian to confuse or mislead your opponent about your intentions. Whether you are moving forward or backward, left or right, up or down, the movements of your body must be agile, flexible, quick, and variable behind the jian.

The most important aspect of the seventh principle is that the body and the jian act as a unit. The overall feeling of the practitioner should be that the jian is part of his body and that his body is part of the jian.

The movement that embodies this principle in practice is called xijian, or washing the sword. In this movement you should imagine that you are standing in a river and turning your body side to side as you insert your jian repeatedly into the water. The upswings and downswings of your body as it turns from side to side should follow the swooping arcs of your jian. The jian, as it arcs, should cover the area of your body. *Figures 28–39* show these movements.

HOW TO PRACTICE FIGHTING SKILLS

It is often mistakenly thought that the training of real fighting skills must include a two-person fighting form. Although such forms are interesting in their own right, they are, in fact, only modestly useful in the training of fighting skills and techniques. You do, however, need a partner with whom to practice fighting techniques according to your needs and skill level. You and your partner should practice the techniques one

44 A and B stand face to face
three steps apart

45 When A makes thrust as he steps
forward, B defends with left block

46 B sticks A's sword as he steps forward
with his back foot to move in

47 B attacks A

48 A and B stand face to face
three steps apart

49 When A makes thrust as he steps
forward, B defends with right block

50 B sticks A's sword as he steps forward
with his back foot to move in

51 B attacks A

52 A and B stand face to face
three steps apart

53 A chops as he steps forward
while B blocks upward

54 B pulls his sword to left

55 B makes side-to-side hit

56 A and B stand face to face
three steps apart

57 A thrusts as he steps forward
while B dodges to left and makes
explosive attack to A's front wrist

58 B continues to dodge and
prepares attack by pointing
sword at A's forearm

59 B steps forward holding sword
with two-handed grip

60 B makes a powerful thrust

by one and with much repetition. In this way, you can help each other increase internal and external feelings and sensitivity.

For safety reasons, it is best not to use metal jian in partnered practice. Although a wood or bamboo sword may not feel as comfortable in your hand, it is a wiser choice when you are training fighting skills with another person. When you want to experience the heft and feel of a metal sword while practicing fighting techniques, you should use a dummy as your opponent. Partnered practice should proceed in stages. First, one partner should practice attacking techniques, while the other practices defensive techniques. The attacking partner should focus on learning to use internal force, to move his body into correct positions and to execute the techniques properly. The defending partner should focus on learning about timing, correct positions, attack points, and defensive techniques. The partners should choose one technique and practice it over and over again until both feel that they understand the technique and its applications and until both are comfortable in their movements. This kind of practice may seem tedious at first, but you will eventually appreciate its considerable usefulness. *Figures 40–43* show one partner (A, swordsman on the right, in black) thrusting and the other (B, swordsman on the left, in white) blocking in a three-step movement.

In the second stage of partnered practice, the partners should take turns practicing attacking and defensive techniques in a freely alternating pattern. Each person should try to make the transition between attack and defense movements smoothly and naturally. Timing and position require special attention in this phase of practice. The movements of swordsman B in *figures 44–51* illustrate the proper way to make the transition between defense and attack techniques.

In the third stage of practice, each partner should combine two or three techniques to form his favorite skills and partners should help each other repeatedly practice each of these skills. At this stage, special attention should be paid to increasing internal and external integration. *Figures 52–55* show a two-technique combination, using first shangjie, an upward intercept block, and then ceji, a side-to-side hammer hit. *Figures 56–60* show a three-technique combination of beng (explode), dian (point), and ci (thrust).

After completing the three stages of partnered practice, you should practice together freely as Taiji Quan partners do in push hands. Little by little, try to feel the techniques becoming part of your nature. Let everything come naturally and without detailed mental effort. Reflect on Taiji ideas and jian principles. Be guided by the adage that "When you practice, there is a process that should be followed; when you fight, there is no one path that must be followed." In the final analysis, the only important measure of everything you do in practice and in fighting is how fully your actions express the ideals of Taiji.

APPENDIXES

LINEAGE CHARTS

The origins of Taiji Quan are not clear. It has been surmised that one thousand years ago there were already five different Taiji Quan styles in existence. One of them, the Zhang Sanfeng style, also called the Thirteen Postures and named after its founding master, was more widespread than the others. Today when people talk about Taiji Quan, they are usually referring to the Zhang Sanfeng style. For the most part, knowledge of the other four styles has been lost.

The reliable history of Taiji Quan begins with Chen Changxing, who taught Taiji Quan in the Chen Village (Chen Jia Gou) of Wen County, in the Henan province of China around 1800. It was Chen's student Yang Luchan who brought this skill to Beijing and whose teachings made it popular and widely respected.

But who taught Taiji Quan to Chen Changxing? Who was his master and who was his grandmaster? There are two opposing schools of thought on this question. The first asserts that Taiji Quan was passed from Zhang Sanfeng to several generations of practitioners and that at some point it was taught to Wang Zongyue, who wrote the most famous of the Taiji Quan classics. Wang Zongyue, in turn, taught the skill to his student Jiang Fa, who taught it to Chen Changxing. In this first view, Jiang Fa would be considered Chen Changxing's master, and Wang Zongyue, a previous master in his lineage.

Because martial arts history is largely an oral history, however, no completely convincing evidence exists to support this assumed lineage. It has, nevertheless, been the predominant view of Taiji Quan groups for about two hundred years and has been accepted as valid by most people.

Starting in the 1930s, a second hypothesis regarding the lineage of Taiji Quan was developed. In this view, a ninth-generation member of the Chen Village named Chen Wangting, rather than Zhang Sanfeng, is said to be the originator of Taiji Quan. Over the years, this assertion has caused intense controversy. The dispute has been especially intense since the 1950s when, for complicated reasons, the second view became the more widely promulgated and apparently more popular one. Readers interested in the lineage issue should examine this period closely, bearing in mind that the popularity of the second view may have more to do with the contemporary social and political factors in China than with genuine historical evidence.

Although it is impossible to prove that Zhang Sanfeng invented Taiji Quan and passed it on to Wang Zongyue, the historical record does suggest strongly that Wang Zongyue was the greatest Taiji Quan master of his time and that he taught Taiji Quan to Jiang Fa and others. After a careful study of the evidence, it is my strong opinion that Wang Zongyue was, indeed, the founder of Taiji Quan. I do not believe the more recently promulgated view that Chen Wangting invented Taiji Quan because it does not seem to me to be consistent with historical details. These details are presented in an article which I hope shortly to translate into English and to present for publication. For the time being, I will adhere to the older and more traditional view that Zhang Sanfeng is the founder of Taiji Quan, but the reader should bear in mind that the matter is still the subject of much debate.

Because Taiji Quan has become so widespread, I cannot include the names of masters from all generations. I have listed only the most important masters of my lineage in Chart 1 and the partial lineage of my own group in Chart 2. Martial arts groups are very traditional, and in the past, many people held to the conservative notion that if you were not a disciple of a master from one of the older generations, you could never achieve authentic and high level skill. Today, although some people still believe this, the idea is no longer widely accepted and need not be an important consideration in your study of Taiji Quan.

Zhang Sanfeng Style Taiji Quan, Northern Branch Lineage

Chart 1 begins with Zhang Sanfeng, the most famous master of Taiji Quan lineage. It is said that Zhang Sanfeng invented Taiji Quan in the Wudang mountains. The discipline was then spread along two separate routes, one to the south and one to the north. Today, the details of the southern style of Taiji Quan have been lost. The northern style was differentiated into several styles and has now spread in a variety of forms throughout the world.

Once Taiji Quan became well known and widely practiced, several famous masters developed and taught their own modifications. When these modifications were first differentiated, only about fifty years ago, they were called the five styles or the six sub-branches. The five styles became known as the Yang, Wu (tone 2), Wu (tone 3), Chen, and Sun styles of Taiji Quan. Later, a sixth style called Li was added. A second system of classification organized the modifications into six sub-branches of Taiji Quan, called Yang, Wu (tone 2), Wu (tone 3), Chen, Sun, and Hao. Taiji Quan variations and the founders of each style are indicated where appropriate in many books. There may be differences of opinion about some of these attributions, but I hope that more research will ultimately lead to consensus.

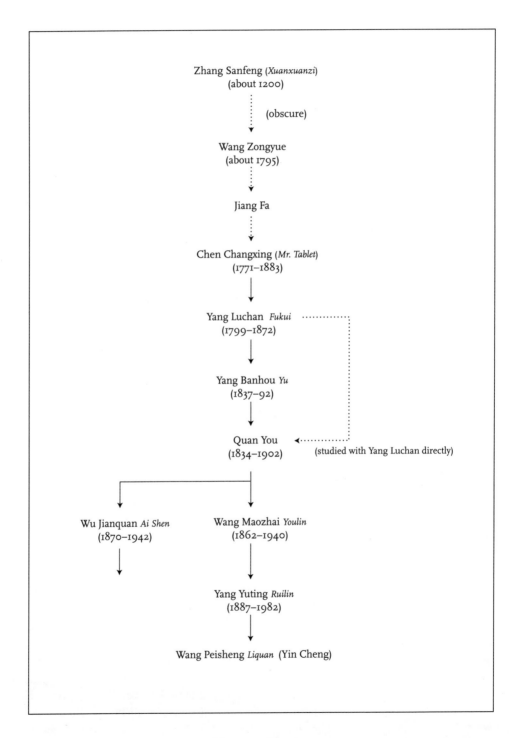

Zhang Sanfeng (*Xuanxuanzi*)
(about 1200)

(obscure)

Wang Zongyue
(about 1795)

Jiang Fa

Chen Changxing (*Mr. Tablet*)
(1771–1883)

Yang Luchan *Fukui*
(1799–1872)

Yang Banhou *Yu*
(1837–92)

Quan You
(1834–1902)
(studied with Yang Luchan directly)

Wu Jianquan *Ai Shen*
(1870–1942)

Wang Maozhai *Youlin*
(1862–1940)

Yang Yuting *Ruilin*
(1887–1982)

Wang Peisheng *Liquan* (Yin Cheng)

Lineage Chart 1

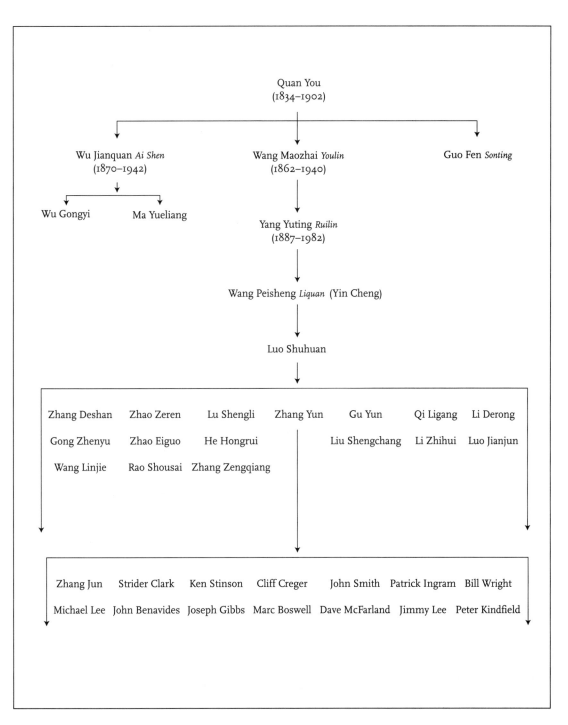

Lineage Chart 2

Over the years, styles of Taiji Quan have continued to proliferate. Although the movements of different styles vary noticeably, each variation follows the same basic set of principles. Individual masters began developing stylistic variations based on their personal feelings and experience with the form. While individual masters taught these variations to their students, most of the stylistic modifications were not passed down in any consistent way and so today are not particularly important. It should be noted that even within a given style or group, skill levels can vary widely, and these differences are far greater than the contrasts between different styles. Genuine Kungfu can be assessed only from one's skill level, not from the group or style to which one bears allegiance.

Wu Style Taiji Quan, Beijing Branch Lineage

One of Master Chen Changxing's students, Master Yang Luchan, taught Taiji Quan in Shen Ji Ying (the Emperor's security camp) in the mid-nineteenth century. He had three excellent students, all of whom were Manchurian: Wan Chun, Ling Shan, and Quan You. King Duan was also one of Master Yang's students and a classmate of the three. Because it was forbidden for commoners to become Kungfu brothers to a ruler, however, Master Yang arranged for Wan Chun, Ling Shan, and Quan You to become disciples of his second son, Yang Banhou. This meant that the three accomplished students could be viewed as members of a lower generation than that of the ruler. Although Wan Chun, Ling Shan, and Quan You became nominal disciples of Yang Banhou, they nevertheless continued to study directly with Master Yang Luchan.

Of these three outstanding students, only Quan You passed his skills on to subsequent generations and as a result, only he was responsible for the development of a new and distinctive style. Because Quan You's family changed its Manchurian name to the Chinese name of Wu (tone 2) after the Republican Revolution of 1911, the style that Quan You developed became known as Wu style. In time, Quan You was recognized and respected as the founder and first master of Wu style Taiji Quan.

Quan You had many disciples in Beijing. The most famous were Wang Maozhai and Quan You's son Ai Shen, who is more commonly known as Wu Jianquan. In 1928, Wu Jianquan moved to Shanghai, in southern China, while Wang Maozhai remained in Beijing. These two great Taiji Quan masters came to be known respectively as Nan Wu and Bei Wang (South Wu and North Wang), and Wu style was differentiated into two main groups, one in Beijing and one in Shanghai. Today Master Ma Yueliang, who is Wu Jianquan's disciple and son-in-law, is the leader of the Shanghai group. Later Wu Jianquan's son, Wu Gongyi, organized a third group in Hong Kong. Today, therefore, there are three distinct groups of Wu style practitioners.

After Wu Jianquan moved to Shanghai, Master Wang Maozhai continued to lead the Wu style Beijing group and this group became the biggest Taiji Quan group of its time. Master Wang Maozhai also founded the Beijing Tai Miao Taiji Quan Association and had thousands of students, from the Mayor of Beijing to army generals and from business people to martial arts experts. His high level of skill earned him a justifiably excellent reputation.

Of Master Wang Maozhai's one hundred disciples, Yang Yuting was the best. When he was only twenty years old, Yang Yuting started to teach Taiji Quan, and during his more than seventy years of teaching, he trained several thousand people. After Wang Maozhai passed away, Yang Yuting became the leader of the Wu style Beijing group.

Today, Master Wang Peisheng, one of Master Yang Yuting's first seven disciples, is President of the Beijing Wu Style Taiji Quan Association and leader of the Wu style Beijing group. Master Wang also received many years of intensive training from Master Wang Maozhai. This combination of teachers brought his mastery to a level even higher than that of his most accomplished classmates. He has now taught Taiji Quan for more than sixty years and still works hard and travels far to bring his knowledge of the martial arts and his great wisdom of traditional Chinese culture to people all over the world. Master Wang has several hundred disciples, and most of them have disciples of their own. I regret that because there are so many high level practitioners in these generations, I cannot list them all. Chart 2 delineates only a small part of the Wu style Beijing group.

Master Luo Shuhuan is Master Wang's earliest disciple. He was thirteen years old when he began his study of Taiji, Bagua, and Xingyi with Master Wang. He remained unswervingly loyal and obedient to Master Wang and to the traditional principles and values of Taiji Quan through many difficult and terrible times. As a result, Master Wang trusted Luo Shuhuan more than any of his other students or disciples.

I began martial arts practice in 1973, and in 1975 I had the good fortune to begin my study of Taiji Quan with Master Luo, later becoming one of his disciples. The names of all of Master Luo's disciples are shown in Chart 2. In 1976, Master Luo sent me to Master Wang's home for intensive training. Most of my knowledge and skill derive directly from the teachings of Master Wang and I have endeavored to pass this tradition on to my students. At the bottom of Chart 2, I have listed the names of my disciples.

KEY ACUPOINTS OF THE HUMAN BODY

A practitioner of traditional Chinese medicine must be able to identify and understand the function of about five hundred acupuncture points (acupoints). A practitioner of Qigong or the martial arts, however, must be familiar with only about fourteen key acupoints for the study of basic Kungfu and about fifty to one hundred acupoints for advanced study. In this section, fourteen key acupoints useful in the study of Taiji Jian practice will be described, with another fifty-six indicated on charts.

In any Qigong or martial arts practice, the acupoints are important as mental focal points. The practitioner must "think" an acupoint, that is, focus the mind on that acupoint. When this is done repeatedly, the acupoint gradually gains influence over the flow of energy inside the body. Because activity at each acupoint causes responses in internal organs as energy flows along the meridians (channels), the practice of external movements eventually creates internal effects. A detailed discussion of the vast and complex acupoint system goes well beyond the scope of this book but some of the basic concepts and definitions are included here. Readers who seek to achieve the highest level of Taiji skill should undertake a careful study of the acupoint system and incorporate this knowledge into their practice.

When people talk about acupoint locations, the most common unit of measure is the *cun*. One cun equals the width of the interphalangeal joint of the thumb. Three cun equal the width of the four remaining fingers (the index, middle, ring, and pinkie fingers) held next to each other and measured at the level of the proximal interphalangeal creases. These measurements are illustrated below *(fig. 1)*. The cun is a useful means of measurement because each practitioner has access to the necessary measurement tools, namely his or her own fingers.

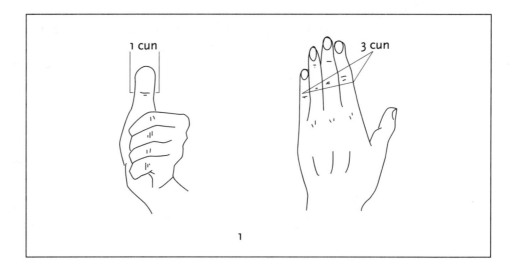

1

The following charts show the locations of the fourteen key acupoints and fifty-six additional acupoints that are important to the development of basic Kungfu skills. These fourteen key acupoints are the most important and are always used in the practice of any of the martial arts and in Qigong. You should become familiar with their names, locations, and functions. They are listed here according to their locations, from head to toe and from front to back.

Baihui

LOCATION: On top of the head, five cun directly above the midpoint of the anterior hairline, at the midpoint of the line connecting the apexes of both ears.

FUNCTION: The baihui, also known as the "head star," is a key point for the control of the whole body. It can help you relax so that qi can move smoothly throughout your body. It is also important in maintaining balance. In fact, it is considered to be a *dingpanxing* of the body, a key point for maintaining balance. Consequently, if you cannot keep it properly aligned, you will lose your balance. Keeping the baihui acupoint in mind will also increase the nimbleness and agility of your movements.

Xuanguan

LOCATION: At the center of the face along the midline, as it extends vertically downward from a point midway between the two eyebrows.

FUNCTION: The xuanguan is a key point for control of shen and of the direction of your movements. It can help you focus shen and adjust your direction.

Yuzhen

LOCATION: On the occiput (the back part of the skull), 2.5 cun directly above the midpoint of the posterior hairline. Although the yuzhen acupoint is usually spoken of as one point, it is actually two points, each of which lies 1.3 cun lateral to the midline of the occiput in the depression along the upper border of the external occipital protuberance.

FUNCTION: The yuzhen acupoint is a key point for controlling the alignment of the neck. Think of the neck as being suspended from this point. This will insure that your larynx does not protrude.

Tanzhong

LOCATION: On the anterior midline of the chest, at the level of the fourth intercostal space and on the midpoint of the line connecting the nipples.

FUNCTION: Tanzhong is a key point for creating an empty chest, for increasing the nimbleness of your movements, and for relaxing your body so that qi can sink down to the dantian.

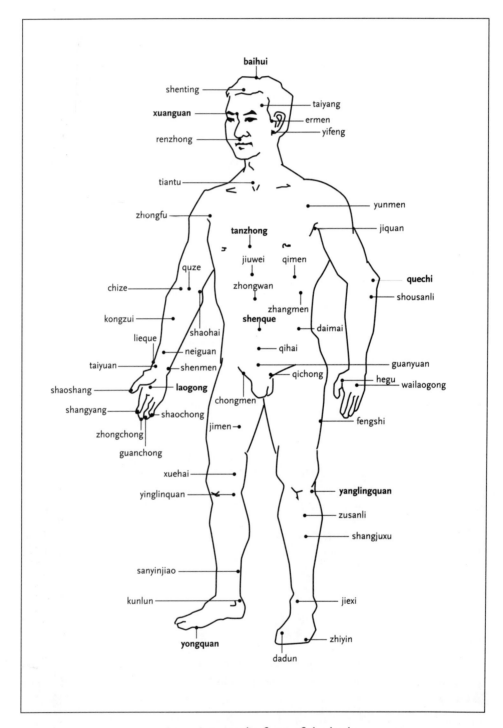

2 *Acupoints on the front of the body*

Jiaji

LOCATION: On the lower back, covering a vertical span of seventeen points on each side of the spine from just below the spinal processes of the first thoracic vertebra to the spinal processes of the fifth lumbar vertebra, and 0.5 cun lateral to the posterior midline. Although jiaji is actually a series of thirty-four points, in Qigong practice and the martial arts it usually refers to the general area at the center of the back.

FUNCTION: The jiaji is very important for controlling qi as it moves up along the dumai, the meridian on the centerline of the back of the torso. It is one of the three back passes, or gateways, for Qigong practice. Focusing your mind on the jiaji will help you keep your back straight.

Shenque

LOCATION: On the middle of the abdomen at the center of the umbilicus.

FUNCTION: The shenque is very important for adjusting the breath and for controlling the flow of qi so that it can sink down to the dantian at the center of the abdominal cavity.

Mingmen

LOCATION: On the lower back along the posterior midline, in the depression below the spinal process of the second lumbar vertebra.

FUNCTION: The mingmen is considered to be a "door of life." It is a key point for control of the waist, the arms, and the legs. It is always referred to as the "master of the body." Focusing your mind on the mingmen will help you relax your waist so that qi can pass through the waist and move freely up or down to the hands and feet. The mingmen, considered the center of the body, is also important for maintaining zhongding, which is the body's alignment and stability.

Huiyin

LOCATION: On the perineum, at the midpoint between the sexual organs and the anus.

FUNCTION: The huiyin, located at the lower dantian, connects the dumai, the meridian on the centerline of the back of the torso, with the renmai, the meridian on the centerline of the front of the torso. It is a key point for insuring the smooth flow of qi through the body along the xiaozhoutian, which is the microcosmic orbit, and the dazhoutian, the macrocosmic orbit. The huiyin is also important for maintaining the stability of the body.

Jianjing

LOCATION: On the shoulder, directly above the nipple, at the midpoint of the line connecting the dazhui (on the posterior midline, in the depression below the seventh cervical vertebra) and the acromion (the outer edge of the scapula).

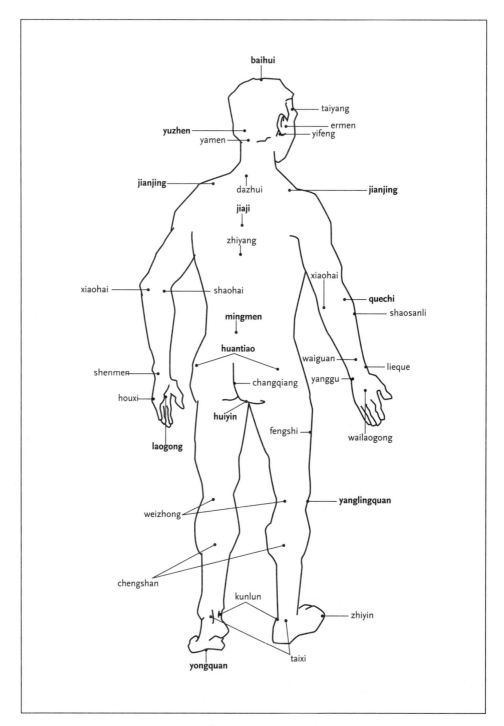

3 *Acupoints on the back of the body*

FUNCTION: The jianjing, also called the "shoulder star," is a key point for controlling the arms. Focusing your mind on the jianjing can help relax the shoulders so that qi can move smoothly from the shoulders to the elbows.

Qiuchi
LOCATION: When the elbow is flexed, the qiuchi is located at the lateral end of the cubital crease, at the midpoint of the line connecting the chize acupoint with the external humeral epicondyle, the bony protuberance at the elbow joint.

FUNCTION: The qiuchi, also called the "elbow star," is a key point for controlling the forearms. Focusing on it can help relax the elbows so that qi can move smoothly from the elbows to the hands.

Laogong
LOCATION: At the center of the palm, between the second and third metacarpal bones, but close to the latter, and in the part that touches the tip of the middle finger when a fist is made.

FUNCTION: The laogong, also called the "hand star," is a key point for controlling the hands. Focusing on it can help relax the wrists so that qi can move smoothly past the hands to the fingers.

Huantiao
LOCATION: On the lateral side of the thigh, at the junction of the middle third and lateral third of the line connecting the major trochanter, the larger of the two jutting processes at the upper end of the femur or upper leg bone, and the sacral hiatus when the body is in a lateral recumbent position with the thigh flexed.

FUNCTION: The huantiao, also called the "hip star," is a key point for controlling the legs. Focusing on it can help relax the hips so that qi can move smoothly past the hips to the knees.

Yanglingquan
LOCATION: On the lateral side of the leg, in the depression in front of and just below the head of the fibula, the long, thin bone of the lower leg.

FUNCTION: The yanglingquan, also called the "knee star," is a key point for controlling the legs. Focusing on it helps relax the knees so that qi can move smoothly past the knees to the feet.

Yongquan
LOCATION: On the sole of the foot, in the depression that appears on the anterior part of the sole when the sole is flexed. It is approximately at the junction of the anterior

third and posterior two-thirds of the line connecting the base of the second and third toes to the heel.

FUNCTION: The yongquan, also called the "foot star," is a key point for controlling the feet. Focusing on it helps relax the ankles so qi can move smoothly past the feet to the toes.

Advanced students of Qigong and the martial arts should know an additional fifty-six key acupoints. These are indicated in *Figures 2* and *3*. For additional information a book on the subject should be consulted.

ABOUT THE AUTHOR

ZHANG YUN began studying martial arts in 1973 in his native China. He studied both Taiji Quan and its weapons forms with Master Luo Shuhuan and then with the renowned Master Wang Peisheng, president of the Beijing Wu Style Taiji Quan Association, and went on to study Bagua, Xingyi, and Qigong. He began teaching in Beijing in 1983, and now teaches in Princeton, New Jersey.

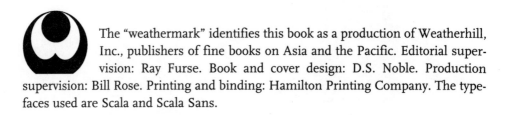 The "weathermark" identifies this book as a production of Weatherhill, Inc., publishers of fine books on Asia and the Pacific. Editorial supervision: Ray Furse. Book and cover design: D.S. Noble. Production supervision: Bill Rose. Printing and binding: Hamilton Printing Company. The typefaces used are Scala and Scala Sans.